ENVIRONMENTAL ANARCHY?

Security in the 21st Century

Mark Beeson

I0222858

BRISTOL
UNIVERSITY
PRESS

First published in Great Britain in 2021 by

Bristol University Press
University of Bristol
1-9 Old Park Hill
Bristol
BS2 8BB
UK
t: +44 (0)117 954 5940
e: bup-info@bristol.ac.uk

Details of international sales and distribution partners are available at
bristoluniversitypress.co.uk

© Bristol University Press 2021

British Library Cataloguing in Publication Data
A catalogue record for this book is available from the British Library

ISBN 978-1-5292-0938-9 hardcover
ISBN 978-1-5292-0939-6 paperback
ISBN 978-1-5292-0941-9 ePub
ISBN 978-1-5292-0940-2 ePdf

The right of Mark Beeson to be identified as author of this work has been asserted by him in
accordance with the Copyright, Designs and Patents Act 1988.

Cover design: blu inc, Bristol
Front cover image: iStock/snb2087

To Joni and Bob, for the soundtrack of
my life

Contents

List of Abbreviations

AIIB	Asian Infrastructure Investment Bank
ASEAN	Association of Southeast Asian Nations
BRI	Belt and Road Initiative
BWIs	Bretton Woods institutions
CCP	Chinese Communist Party
CO_2	Carbon dioxide
EU	European Union
IFIs	international financial institutions
IMF	International Monetary Fund
IOs	international organizations
IPCC	Intergovernmental Panel on Climate Change
IR	International Relations
NATO	North Atlantic Treaty Organization
PRC	People's Republic of China
UK	United Kingdom
UN	United Nations
US	United States

Acknowledgements

Many thanks to Bruce Campbell, Ann Firth and Chengxin Pan for reading and/or commenting on parts of the book. Needless to say they are absolved of all responsibility for any remaining shortcomings. Thanks also to Isabella Karelis for research assistance, and to Stephen Wenham and Bristol University Press for helping to bring this to fruition.

As this will likely be my last academic book, let me also acknowledge the help, encouragement, influence, assistance and even inspiration of various friends, colleagues and a (rather large) collection of co-authors. My alphabetically ordered appreciation goes to Amitav Acharya, Alice Ba, Steve Bell, Alex Bellamy, Mark Berger, Sven Biscop, Nick Bisley, Roland Bleiker, Alan Bloomfield, Sue Boyd, Shaun Breslin, Paul Brooks, Andre Broome, Lou Cabrera, David Camroux, Ann Capling, Bill Case, Phil Cerny, Priya Chako, Jie Chen, Andrew Chubb, Mark Cloney, Thomas Diez, Claire Dupont, Robyn Eckersley, Farida Fozdar, Julie Gilson, Vedi Hadiz, Shahar Hameiri, Baogang He, Kai He, Richard Higgott, Emma Hutchison, Yan Islam, Kanishka Jayasuriya, Steven Kennedy, Will Lee, Troy Lee-Brown, Fujian Li, Leong Liew, Alexander Lukin, Greg McCarthy, Matt McDonald, Lukas Müller, Philo Murray, Ted Newman, Ronen Palan, T.J. Pempel, Hung Pham, Ben Reilly, Dick Robison, Garry Rodan, Andrew Rosser, Jürgen Rüland, David Schak, Krishna Sen, Richard Shapcott, Mills Soko, Xianlin Song, Diane Stone, Gerry Strange, Richard Stubbs, Jeannette Taylor, Hang Thuy, Bill Tow, Dave van Mill, Yong Wang, Nathan Watson, Heloise and Martin Weber, Alex Wendt, Wahyu Wicaksana, Jeff Wilson, Shaomin Xu, Hidetaka Yoshimatsu, Ben Zala, and Jinghan Zeng. Apologies to any friends and collaborators I may have inadvertently overlooked.

Introduction

Books inevitably reflect the ideas, prejudices, background and the obsessions of their author. As I have no wish to put off prospective readers by indulging in a tangential autobiographical digression, let me just say that I didn't mean to become a 'security expert'. Hitherto my principal interests were 'international political economy' and, more recently, the politics of climate change. I should confess that I cannot claim specialist knowledge in the underlying science of global warming, but that has not stopped me from thinking about the political and security implications of climate change and the impact it is having on the natural environment upon which we all ultimately depend. It shouldn't stop anyone else either. On the contrary, one of the animating ideas that run through this book is that many of the policymakers and strategic thinkers who shape security policy have a remarkably impoverished and limited view of the nature of security in what we now call the Anthropocene. Such views were arguably always problematic; now they are indefensible.

It is the recognition that our collective impact on the natural environment presents the greatest security threat we have ever faced as a species that has encouraged me to think about its increasingly obvious security implications. To be fair, the potentially catastrophic consequences of climate change have not escaped the notice of mainstream strategic thinkers, or the policymakers they advise. Their responses are often depressingly familiar, however, and reflect *their* intellectual assumptions and prejudices, even if they are often unrecognized. Indeed, the 'strategic cultures' within which ideas about, and even psychological dispositions toward, security are formed play a profoundly important and limiting role in what sorts of policy are deemed appropriate, 'rational' or feasible by the people who dominate the debates in this area. More importantly, they have got us to where we are today: unhappy, insecure, facing the – still unlikely, but real – possibility of great-powers' war and a natural environment that may not be capable of supporting human life in the foreseeable future; or, at the very least, not in the numbers and style to which we are accustomed.

Some will say it was ever thus, and that it is entirely appropriate that 'serious' thinkers, steeped in the mysteries of grand strategy and familiar with the machinations and military capabilities of their counterparts in other countries, should continue to oversee our collective security. Even if that was once a plausible and uncontested argument, it is plainly no longer the case. A continuing focus on the sorts of 'traditional' security threats that have preoccupied hard-headed realists for hundreds if not thousands of years is quite simply no longer appropriate or capable of producing feasible and sustainable responses to *collective* challenges such as climate change.

The point to emphasize at the outset is that there can be no 'real' security that is not based on policies that transcend national borders. This claim is fundamentally at odds with the most basic of assumptions that shape strategic thinking around the world: the first responsibility of policymakers is to secure the safety of the nation, which usually means 'the state' itself. It is not necessary to indulge in Dr Strangelove-style conspiracy theories to recognize that there might be a fundamental disconnect in the way that policy elites might view security priorities, and the way those of us who inhabit less rarefied strategic circles do. This is not a trivial point.

One of the reasons, I shall suggest, why there is currently such a widespread loss of confidence in policymakers and their capacity to actually deliver on some of the most basic parts of their notional job descriptions – that is, the security of the people who make up the nation they claim to represent – is because few of us actually *feel* secure anymore. While those of us fortunate to live in some of the wealthier, comparatively well-functioning parts of the 'developed world' may not lie awake at night fretting about the fear of invasion, many people really do lose sleep over their possible fate and that of their offspring. It's possible to ignore the scientific evidence and policy debates about climate change, but not the evidence of one's own eyes. If policy cannot produce a degree of psychological security there is a good case for saying it's failed.

Although some limited attention has been paid in the scholarly literature to the actions of individual political leaders and decision making under conditions of extreme psychological pressure, it remains a relatively unexplored field. This is rather surprising, given some of the larger-than-life political figures that currently dominate the political landscape. The unpredictable, impulsive and unfathomable decisions that were routinely made by Donald Trump, for example, look like a potentially fertile field of study. But the failure to consider the psychological dimension of security is even more remarkable, given the apparent epidemic of unhappiness, anxiety and even fear that currently grips so many people, especially in the still comfortable and relatively orderly Western world. Achieving something resembling 'human security' is quite clearly a work in progress, even in the affluent parts of the world. It is still a distant dream, and one that looks increasingly unlikely to be achieved in many impoverished parts of the world where even the most rudimentary forms of security remain elusive.

No doubt this will strike some prospective readers as an excessively pessimistic tone to adopt at the outset of a book, especially one that the author hopes they will take the trouble to read. My sincerest wish is that my fears are unfounded and the current crop of world leaders will prove more capable, informed and far-sighted than they seem. Perhaps international cooperation will prove effective, after all. Perhaps some technological fix or other will come along and prove to be the proverbial game changer, bringing peace and prosperity to all. In the absence of any evidence that this is actually happening, though, it seems advisable to assume the worst; this is, after all, precisely what the security specialists who are charged with keeping us safe do. Unfortunately, many of them remain preoccupied with the prospect of foreign forces coming over the horizon or – more 'realistically', perhaps – challenges to our general strategic environment or that of our allies.

There is some justification for this: some countries do behave badly; some leaders are mad and unpredictable – and not all of them are in 'rogue states', either. But given that all countries must make choices and calculations about the possible threats they face, the question is about priorities: which threats should be prioritized and why? Given that it is impossible to imagine the circumstances in which China's leaders might decide to invade Australia, for example, does it really make sense for the government to spend so much of the country's limited resources in preparing for a highly improbable threat? The 'opportunity costs' of this strategic calculation have been thrown into sharp relief by the bushfires of 2019–20, which consumed vast tracts of agricultural land and forests, not to mention a billion or so native animals. Would a larger investment in water-bombing aircraft have been a wiser use of limited taxpayer dollars than the traditional variety, especially as the lives and properties of Australians were actually being lost? Some of the more traditionally minded security specialists might counter by saying that this is a separate public policy issue and really not the concern of those whose primary responsibility is the safety of the nation. But if the security of individual members of the national population isn't the principal concern of those charged with keeping us safe, what is? It is for this reason that many scholars working in the area of broadly conceived security studies have adopted the idea of 'human security' as the principal focus of their attention.

Outline of the book

I consider some of most influential and/or illuminating theoretical approaches in the formal study of International Relations (IR) in Chapters 1 and 2. Some of this material may already be familiar to other students and scholars, but it merits re-examination because some strands of IR have, explicitly or implicitly, exercised a powerful influence. Liberalism and, especially, realism are by far the most important in this regard, and their ideas and claims about the way the world works, or should work, have exercised a powerful hold over the minds of policymakers, especially in the United States (US). I also explore the ideas of constructivists and – some readers will no doubt be astounded to learn – Marxists. While the latter have plainly had an influence on policymakers from time to time, my principal interest is in their ideas about ecology, capitalism and the evident limits to endless growth and consumerism. If we are to get out of the mess we find ourselves in and approach something resembling a secure future, these are ideas and arguments we need to take seriously. One possibly unlikely but potentially important recent addition to IR's conceptual universe has been the incorporation of quantum theory, originally developed by physicists to explain the subatomic world. Its significance for and impact on the social sciences remains contentious and limited thus far, but it may yet help us to unravel some of the more challenging conceptual and practical challenges we collectively face.

Chapter 3 spells out the nature of the environmental challenges we collectively face, and explains why we have come to call our era the Anthropocene. The fact is that we have already had such an impact on the natural environment that we are enmeshed in a complex interactive process with biophysical processes upon which our lives ultimately depend. If the COVID-19 pandemic that continues to ravage the world at the time of writing did nothing else, it ought to have alerted policymakers and strategic thinkers to the interconnection between us and the environment: we abuse and destroy it at our collective peril. One might think in such circumstances that the necessity for, and benefits of, international cooperation would be so blindingly self-evident that policymakers everywhere would make climate change their principal priority. Alas, not. I detail some of the efforts that have been made to foster international cooperation and explain the factors that are seemingly making it more difficult just when we need it most.

Given the rather doom-laden content of Chapter 3, it may not surprise the reader to learn that Chapter 4 considers the psychological dimensions of security. Although there is also ample evidence of the fact that many people – even the privileged denizens of the Western world – feel increasingly *in*secure, this is generally not a reality that security experts engage with. And yet, even if we put to one side the fact that 'national security' is supposedly dedicated to protecting people and actually making them *feel* more secure, there are plenty of reasons to take the insights of psychologists, cultural theorists, sociologists and even quantum physicists seriously. As noted, there has been some work on the psychology of decision making, but ideas about policy are products of a wider social, intellectual and even cultural milieu. Indeed, as I suggest, the strategic culture of nations can differ in important ways, influencing the way individual states behave and imparting a degree of institutionalized path dependence to ideas about security.

The possible significance of this sort of thinking about security and the ideas that appeal to policymakers in different circumstances becomes more apparent in Chapter 4, which considers the nature and impact of 'grand strategy'. Grand strategies are perhaps the quintessential expression of realist thinking and power politics. Consequently, much of the discussion in this chapter focuses on the actions of the US and the current challenger to American dominance, the People's Republic of China (PRC). There aren't many people alive today who can remember anything other than a world that was shaped by the grand strategic ambitions of the US. For better or worse, that order is seemingly unravelling before our eyes, not least because of the actions of the Trump administration. At the very least, leadership, identity and the ideas that countries have about themselves and their possible historical roles help to explain why grand strategies can vary, despite emanating from the same 'structural' foundations.

If there is one area in which both the US and the PRC could claim some success, it is economic development. The period of American hegemony coincided with one of the longest periods of economic expansion and development the world has even known. Even China was and arguably still is a beneficiary of the economic order the US helped to create. And yet, as Chapter 5 explains, despite some remarkable progress, the world remains a strikingly unequal place in which the idea of basic economic security remains a pipe-dream for millions of people around the world. Not only does this mean that any notion of meaningful security is absent from much of the world, but this inevitably exacerbates both domestic and international security, not least because of the migration that such highly visible inequalities generate. At the level of traditional interstate competition, the 'low politics' of economics has consequently come to assume a more prominent place as China's model of development attracts increased interest and admirers and the neoliberal, divisive policies promoted under the banner of the 'Washington consensus' look increasingly threadbare. More importantly, there are fundamental questions about the sustainability of any sort of capitalism based on endless expansion and growth.

The Conclusion pulls together the main threads of the discussion and offers a few observations. I would like to be able to assure the reader that the final discussion is full of brilliant insights about what needs to be done and provides an optimism-inducing and uplifting finale. Unfortunately, it doesn't. Plenty of other people have made very sensible and even plausible suggestions about how to restructure economic activity along more sustainable lines. The Green New Deal has much to recommend it and could actually make a real difference, not least as a model of radically different priorities for the world we actually inhabit. But it is difficult to see generations of strategic thinkers and 'realistic' policymakers whole-heartedly embracing such a strategy, especially if it meant diverting resources from traditional defence measures and continued spending on military hardware.

The unpalatable reality is that, despite the urgency of the environmental challenge we collectively face as a species, international cooperation of the sort we desperately need seems a bit too difficult. Even getting domestic agreement on what needs to be done is well-nigh impossible in a world of competing interests and ideas. Thinking about why that might be the case may be a small step in the right direction, though.

1

Getting Real: The Way
the World Works?

What does it mean to be secure? One might be forgiven for thinking that security ought to be relatively easy to define, even if there's less agreement about how best to actually achieve it. One of the problems is deciding quite what the 'referent object' might be when deciding whether someone, or more commonly some*thing*, is secure or not. At the outset, therefore, it is important to recognize that not only are some of the issues to be discussed often theoretically contested and reflective of the normative preferences of the observer, but they are also inherently political and anything but objective. At one level, this is a manifestation of the nature of material reality and our interaction with it, especially at the most infinitesimally small scale. At another comparatively mundane and familiar level, what we consider to be causally significant is – in part, at least – a judgement about what matters, in every sense of the word. As Colin Wight puts it, 'politics is the terrain of competing ontologies'.[1] Despite the not unreasonable expectation that theory is supposed to help us understand something, in the academy theory frequently contributes to the confusion, not least because different people think that security should be defined in relation to different things.[2]

While this may sound like an unpromising prelude to the sort of arcane discussion academics are often accused of indulging in, the debate is important and surprisingly interesting. It even has major consequences in the much-invoked 'real world'. The scare quotes – of which there are a lot in what follows, I'm afraid – are merited in this case because some observers think there is no such thing.[3] Or, to put it slightly less provocatively, perhaps, it is increasingly common to suggest that the way we individually and collectively think about the world has consequences for the way that we act in the world. If you think the world is still a Darwinian struggle for survival, for example, in which no one can be trusted and everyone else is as mean spirited, conniving and untrustworthy as you are, then that might reasonably be expected to influence the way you behave. Whether such a response is reasonable, 'realistic' or likely to add to your sense of security is another matter. Either way, this is the first of two very different chapters about IR theory, and this one begins by considering some of the most innovative approaches to theory, which draw their inspiration not from the social sciences but from the natural variety. Not only do some of these ideas enjoy considerably more prestige but – with some important caveats –their claims to veracity are also more 'robust'. As such, I think they merit examination as a way of contextualizing a discussion of the human condition, especially at a time when the natural environment is likely to have a much more immediate impact on our actions, options and sensibilities than ever before.

This chapter focuses on various forms of 'realist' thinking, including not only some of the more traditional varieties found in conventional IR scholarship but also the contribution of analysts who draw their principal influence from Marxism. Engaging with Marxist scholarship at all will no doubt strike some readers as anachronistic and/or somewhat eccentric, but I shall suggest that some of its main claims about the way the world works and the 'contradictions' that shape it look alarmingly plausible, not least in connection with growing inequality and environmental degradation. They also have more in common with realist thinkers than either camp might care to admit, and their preoccupation with material reality's impact on the course of human history also chimes with some of the claims by natural scientists about the forces that shape the environment on which human beings depend.

The (very) big picture

Many of us working in the social sciences suffer from a form of 'physics envy': a sense that the conclusions we come to about the nature of reality are partial at best, hopelessly subjective at worst, and generally lacking the 'rigour', credibility and falsifiability of our counterparts in the 'hard' sciences. Let me confess at the outset that I suffer from this affliction more than most, and consequently have a possibly naive enthusiasm about the sorts of genuine discoveries that have come about as a result of scientific methods. At one level, I think my admiration for science is understandable and really ought to be universal: the *fact* that we know that the Earth orbits the sun rather than vice versa, for example, is an unambiguous, easily verifiable empirical reality that we collectively benefit from understanding. We can still come to different conclusions about what scientific knowledge might mean for us as individuals and our place in a universe that is rule governed in ways that social life is not, but we cannot dispute the links between gravity and momentum, to take another consequential example. There are no such facts in the social sciences. 'Social facts' and 'structures', by contrast, are human creations, even if they help to shape our actions and the way we think about ourselves, each other and the physical world we collectively inhabit. They are subject to change and contestation at a theoretical and practical level in ways that at least *some* scientific knowledge and universal physical explanations are not.

As I shall (try to) explain, at the cutting edge of contemporary physics even science becomes complex and – in the words of no less a figure than Albert Einstein – rather 'spooky'. Indeed, quantum physics, which seeks to understand the nature of reality at the most microscopic, subatomic level, is characterized by uncertainty, unpredictability and indeterminacy. Physical reality behaves in startling and rather shocking ways that are still not fully understood, and the associated physics seems to raise as many questions as it answers. However, before any of my social science colleagues start feeling smug, it is worth making two very important points: while there still may be the most profound and possibly unanswerable questions about quite what quantum physics *means* or actually explains in the most fundamental sense, there is less disagreement about the underlying science and the sorts of problems that remain to be solved. Equally importantly, the associated mathematical explanations appear to work brilliantly.

I say 'appear' for two reasons. First, any existing explanation is always capable of being refuted or replaced by a better one that more adequately fits or explains the facts. The quintessential example of this possibility was the appearance of quantum theory itself, which had the effect of overturning the hitherto dominant Newtonian paradigm of classical physics. While many of the ideas and principles of Newtonian physics still provide a working explanation of phenomena such as the sun's daily appearance in the sky, it became increasingly apparent in the first part of the twentieth century that there were things that the classical model could not explain or even conceptualize. New mathematical approaches and models provided explanations of the otherwise baffling behaviour of the subatomic universe. The second reason for saying 'appear' to explain physical conundrums is that the explanations were (and are) written in a language I do not speak and am unlikely to learn.

Why, then, you may be wondering, bother to engage with a theoretical model that I am incapable of fully understanding? Excellent question. My answer is also twofold, even if some may find both parts unpersuasive. First, even those who can speak the language of mathematics are still flummoxed when it comes to thinking about, much less explaining, what the ultimate significance of underlying physical reality might be. As John Polkinghorne points out, 'despite the physicists' ability to do the calculations, they still do not understand the theory'.[4] Given that nobody has yet come up with a 'theory of everything' that accounts for reality at macro and micro levels and the forces that determine their interactions – or the role that reflective consciousness might play in such processes – then physicists are plainly no better qualified to think about the social or philosophical implications of the world they have discovered than are their counterparts in the social sciences. The second reason for engaging with quantum theory, therefore, is precisely because some of the less mathematically able among us are also trying to think about the implications of what the new(ish) science may mean. For anyone even remotely interested in what's happening to the visible parts of the natural environment it seems remiss not to do so.

The quantum mind

Alexander Wendt has been at the forefront of attempts to grapple with the implications of quantum theory for the social sciences generally and IR in particular. Given that his book *Quantum Mind and Social Science* is a marked departure from his earlier, highly influential and well-regarded volume, *Social Theory of International Politics*,[5] this is a noteworthy development in itself, given Wendt's prominence in debates about IR theory. Indeed, the *Quantum Mind* is a fairly explicit repudiation of his earlier position on the construction of social reality and its implications for theory. As Wendt puts it, 'if human beings really are quantum, then classical social science is founded on a mistake, and social life will therefore require a quantum framework for its proper understanding'.[6]

To substantiate this claim, Wendt embarks on a detailed survey of the literature that has emerged around both the development of quantum physics and its possible implications for the way we think about human consciousness, its role and its interaction with physical reality. Given that the detail of these highly complex arguments is not central to the concerns of this book, the reader may be relieved to know that I shall make no attempt to replicate, much less unpick, Wendt's arguments in their entirety. However, it is necessary to say something about some of the foundational assumptions of quantum theory to understand why some observers find them both so potentially important and even revolutionary. They certainly were for the extant Newtonian scientific orthodoxy that experienced a Kuhnian-style paradigmatic shift as a new consensus emerged about the most accurate way of understanding reality. It is important to emphasize that no such wholesale paradigmatic transformations occur in the social sciences,[7] which is another reason, perhaps, for some intellectual modesty on the part of social scientists.

But even if natural scientists know what they don't know with greater confidence than do their counterparts in the social sciences, and collectively recognize the limits of the existing knowledge in a particular area, this doesn't make what they do know any easier to understand. There is something deeply mysterious, not to say unsettling – or possibly even liberating – about the fundamental uncertainty and unpredictability of reality at the most microscopic level. Given that we – and the cosmos, of course – are made of such mysterious matter, this makes our individual and collective futures even more unknowable and open ended than we might have imagined, and a striking contrast with the era of the clockwork, predictable world of Newtonian physics. Even more startlingly, the very act of trying to understand how the world 'really' works at the subatomic level seems to involve human consciousness in ways that potentially overturn any notion of an objective, 'external' world that we dispassionately observe, much less act upon in a 'rational' manner.

The story of the emergence of the 'new physics' has been frequently told and there is no intention to try to reproduce – much less add to – that story here.[8] A few simple points about, and aspects of, this process are relevant here, however. First, and most famously, perhaps, sub-atomic particles such as electrons or photons (particles of light) can also behave as waves. In fact, left to its own devices, wave-like states seem to the 'natural' condition of light, for example; or they are until human beings try to measure them, at least. This act of consciously intervening in the physical world seems to cause the wave-like function to 'collapse', revealing the location and behaviour of the packets of energy from which light is ultimately composed. Put differently, whether something is a wave or a particle depends on the environment in which it is embedded, not the least of which is the experimental apparatus used to detect it.

While this may seem a long way from the usual concerns of IR theory, the implications of our enhanced and more accurate collective understanding of reality are potentially profound. Capra and Luisi argue that what this means is that subatomic particles

> are not 'things' but are interconnections among things, and these in turn, are interconnections among other things, and so on. In quantum theory we never end up with 'things'; we always deal with interconnections. This is how the new physics reveals the oneness of the universe. It shows that we cannot decompose the world into independently existing smallest units. As we penetrate into matter we do not perceive isolated building blocks, but rather a complex web of relations between the various parts of the whole.[9]

It is not necessary to believe that this is indicative of some sort of divinely inspired purposive order to recognize that the possible importance of wholeness, interconnection and interaction suggests a very different set of underlying dynamics between human beings and the natural environment they inhabit than we are accustomed to considering. Such possibilities – and the consequences of inadvertently destabilizing or unravelling them – seem especially germane when contemplating the finite biosphere upon which we ultimately depend. Again, it's not necessary to believe in the 'Gaia hypothesis',[10] or the idea that planet is a self-regulating, profoundly interconnected and interdependent entity, to recognize that this might actually be a useful way to think about the biosphere, whether it's 'true' or not: the links between pandemics and our destruction of the natural environment are but one reason to take the environmental consequences of our actions more seriously.[11] It's also clear that such ideas do not feature in mainstream IR, much of which, as we shall see, remains deeply embedded in a Newtonian view of reality and envious of a form of scientific understanding that has actually been abandoned by the scientific community.

To be fair, there has been a good deal of interest in 'network theory' across the social sciences,[12] and some leading IR theorists have long been alert to the possible non-linearity and significance of 'system effects' in international politics.[13] However, it is noteworthy that theorists from the natural sciences have thought about the broader implications of the new physics more seriously than many of us have in the social sciences. Although there is still a good deal of debate and disagreement about the implications of quantum reality for human development, they are potentially vital parts of any explanation of structure and agency that form such prominent parts of social science debates. Karen Barad argues that 'agency is not an attribute but the ongoing reconfigurings of the world. The universe is agential intra-activity in its becoming'.[14] The fundamental 'entanglement' of the constituent parts of the physical universe at the most minute scale may mean, Barad suggests, that 'changes do not follow in continuous fashion from a given prior state or origin, nor do they follow some teleological trajectory – there are no trajectories'.[15]

This is clearly a major claim and, if accurate, poses a profound challenge for ideas about path-dependency, the importance of institutions, intentionality, the structure–agency debate, not to mention 'grand narratives' such as Marxism and liberalism regarding the possible direction of human history. And yet it is also important to recognize that mathematically literate scholars have come to very different conclusions about the possible implications of the new physics, which place much greater emphasis on the importance of human consciousness and the recognition of 'reality'. Indeed, the apparently intimate connection and interaction between physical reality and the human observer leads Wendt to suggest that 'we are walking wave functions. I intend the argument not as an analogy or metaphor, but as a realist claim about what people really are'.[16] In such a schema, nation-states – the foundational ontological units of conventional realist understandings of social reality – are ultimately manifestations of shared mental states in which the individuals who populate and ultimately constitute social structures 'are expressing its teleological purpose'.[17] The implication is that 'society itself is an organism, with subjectivity and consciousness'.[18]

Despite some of the criticisms that have been levelled at quantum theory's failure to actually explain the basis of reflective human consciousness,[19] it is hard to overstate what a departure from 'normal' social science and IR this potentially is. Significantly, however, as this discussion suggests, Wendt's status as one of the leading IR scholars of the era means that his ideas are taken seriously, even if there is some condescension at times about his apparently inability to 'do the math'.[20] What we can say is that there have already been some imaginative attempts to apply concepts such as the 'holographic state' to rethink the nature of interstate relations, foreign policy and even human consciousness and its part in shaping 'international' reality.[21] In this context, such efforts resonate with and build on the ideas of prominent physicists such as David Bohm, who argues that 'the attempt to live according to the notion that the fragments [of reality] are really separate is, in essence, what has led to the growing series of extremely urgent crises that is confronting us today'. To escape from this misconception, Bohm suggests, 'we need to recognize life itself has to be regarded as belonging in some sense to a totality, including plant and the environment'.[22]

The potential relevance of quantum theory for thinking about physical reality, of which human beings and the biosphere upon which they ultimately depend is a noteworthy example, is still highly contested. Despite the inherent uncertainty of the quantum world and the difficulty of understanding it, even for those who *can* do the maths, it is potentially so consequential that it would be remiss not to at least try to understand its implications; not least because they bear directly upon our collective, deeply entangled relationship with the natural environment. As Stapp points out, 'the magnitude of difference between the quantum and classical conceptions of the connections between mind and brain can scarcely be exaggerated';[23] and yet, it is one that is studiously ignored by the world's security establishments, despite the fact that their collective consciousness and the actions it encourages may actually help to instantiate a particular version of social 'reality'. As we shall see, paradoxically enough, some of the assumptions about strategic reality, which are seemingly based on an inaccurate and potentially misleading understanding of the social world of which we are a part, are leading us to collectively prioritize the wrong problems and act in ways that imperil rather than enhance our collective security.

As Der Derian and Wendt point out, however, 'the absence of laboratory proofs or sufficient measurement tools should not impede an inquiry into the most perplexing questions of the human condition for which quantum science might provide the best possible answers'. No problem is more perplexing or important than the nature of nature and what it says about us and our possible future – if we actually have one, of course. And yet, much of social science remains surprisingly immune to such unsettling, increasingly evident realities. Ironically, this is especially true of realism itself.

Realism

It has become increasingly clear that the biggest security challenge we have ever faced stems from climate change. For reasons that are well understood and evident, 'this changes everything', as the redoubtable Naomi Klein might say.[24] Part of the reason why it is proving so difficult to address climate change is not simply because of the unprecedented nature and extent of the problems it is generating, but that any effort to address it will also mean thinking seriously about 'structural' inequality and the sorts of very immediate challenges that presents to at least some people's individual security. Any theoretical perspective that is self-consciously grounded in material reality, and which claims an unrivalled insight into the human condition as a consequence, ought to be taken seriously, therefore. I should point out that I am not terribly optimistic about our prospects for collectively addressing the problems that unmitigated climate change will undoubtedly bring; or at least not in the forbidding time frames available to us and without unprecedented levels of international cooperation. No doubt this influences the way I think about the world and why I consider some explanations more plausible than others. It gives me no pleasure to say that I fear that realists may have some good arguments to make about the implications of climate change, not least because those steeped in realist assumptions are likely to be calling the literal and metaphorical shots in dealing with some of its more alarming effects.

Taking realism seriously

For a theory that claims to have been around for several thousand years and which is concerned with the supposedly timeless and universal forces that create conflict and which make peace – at least the permanent variety – such an elusive goal, realism has become a surprisingly broad church. In addition to the 'classical' variety, there are neo-realism, defensive and offensive 'structural' realism, as well as a neoclassical variety.[25] There is also a very different sort of 'critical realism' that provides another important perspective, but which is not usually considered part of the realist tradition in IR, but arguably should be. All of them have their admirers and their relative strengths and weaknesses. Some are explicitly and intentionally more policy oriented and 'relevant' than others, but all make some broadly similar basic assumptions that provide underlying unity to the approach as a whole.

Whatever we may think about the validity, impact or assumptions of mainstream realism, when the formal study of IR is transferred to the lower-case world of international relations practice, it is realists and their assumptions that tend to have the most influence. If for no other reason, then, it is worth understanding what realists think precisely because they exercise so much influence over policymakers, whether the latter are aware of it or not.[26] The other point to make about realists at the outset is that some of them are very smart, persuasive and mount powerful, depressingly persuasive arguments. You may not care for their ideas, but that's not a compelling reason to ignore them, especially when they continue to have much more practical impact than any of the other paradigms we shall consider.

One tried and tested way of illustrating the major claims and ideas of a school of IR, of course, is to look at some of its most prominent and influential exponents. Realism has more than its fair share to choose from, some of whom – Henry Kissinger and Zbigniew Brzezinski in recent American history, for example[27] – are widely known among at least some of the general public. True, they may be more famous as practitioners than theorists, as were the likes of Otto von Bismarck in the 19th century or Vladimir Putin today, but they share some common assumptions about the importance of power and the potential effectiveness of coercive force. One of the widely recognized founders of what we describe as realism now – Thucydides – was both an Athenian general and a dispassionate observer of empirical evidence; his description of the war between Sparta and Athens in the fifth-century BCE remains one of the landmarks in both the analysis of conflict and its causes and a 'scientific' approach to scholarship more generally.[28] Some of his conclusions have echoed down the years: 'the strong do what they can and the weak suffer what they must', being one famously bleak example.

Other stars in the realist firmament were observers and thinkers first and foremost. Many contemporary realists claim that precisely the same forces apply to our own time, all of the remarkable changes in economic, political and even strategic life that have occurred in the intervening two and half thousand years notwithstanding. Critics from what used to be known as the Third World and is now more fashionably called 'the South', argue that in some ways the realists may be right. Mohammed Ayoob, for example, suggests that 'the rhetoric of globalization and of the global society is employed to provide a veneer for the operation of a very realist paradigm by the powerful states of the global North in their relationship with the states of the global South'.[29]

These claims will be explored in subsequent chapters, but they reflect a particular view of the nature of power politics and 'human nature' that has its roots in the ideas of realism's founding fathers – and they were all men. The circumstances in which human existence plays itself out according to one of realism's most celebrated figures – Thomas Hobbes – meant that life was 'solitary, poor, nasty, brutish, and short'. Or it was in a 'state of nature', at least. The solution to this unappealing and grim struggle for survival, Hobbes famously argued, was to create a Leviathan, or an overarching power with the capacity and the legitimacy to impose order. The social contract between individuals and a powerful sovereign actually created the conditions for civilized and secure existence, albeit at the price of some degree of political liberty.[30]

Given that Hobbes's own life was profoundly influenced by the English Civil War – *Leviathan* was written while he was in exile in Paris – it is perhaps unsurprising that the spectre of chaos, insurrection and disorder loomed large in his view of the world. Much the same observation might be made of Niccolò Machiavelli, another of realism's early leading lights.

Machiavelli not only lived in similarly troubled, violent and unpredictable times, but he subsequently offered political leaders unvarnished, amoral advice about how to stay in power. The phrase 'necessary evil' captures something of Machiavelli's thinking, as does the proposition that 'if an injury has to be done to a man it should be so severe that his vengeance need not be feared'.[31] Political advice has rarely been so callous and contingent – or so influential.

Order and anarchy

One of the key ideas that thinkers such as Hobbes bequeathed to his successors was the belief that in the absence of a Leviathan that was willing and able to impose order, anarchy would prevail. In Hobbes's case the notion of anarchy was not the abstract heuristic that it is generally seen as being today, but it is worth thinking about why this concept retains such a prominent place in realist theory, not least because it has direct empirical consequences: if policymakers and their advisors really believe they are involved in a war of all against all, in which security is achieved only through self-help, then they are likely to behave in ways that are consistent with such beliefs. And yet, in practice, as Hedley Bull influentially argued, the domestic analogy doesn't really work: international society not only exists – to some extent, at least – but it has different dynamics and drivers than the domestic variety.[32] Although followers of the 'English School' can be overly optimistic about the impact of norms and socialization, even at a time when there are real doubts about the stability of international order, interstate war remains the exception rather than the rule, and cooperation remains possible, if not likely. To be sure, there is no shortage of conflict, but this is generally associated with state failure and civil war.

In his pre-quantum incarnation, Alexander Wendt made an important contribution to this debate, too, when he famously argued that

> There is no 'logic' of anarchy apart from the practices that create and instantiate one structure of identities and interests

rather than another; structure has no existence or causal powers apart from process. Self-help and power politics are institutions, not essential features of anarchy. *Anarchy is what states make of it.* (Emphasis in original)[33]

Even if he might now argue that it takes a collapsing wave function to recognize it, the claim that there is nothing inherently deterministic about the 'structure' of the international order, or even that there *is* an international *order* of widely recognized rules and norms that states choose to follow, is a very different picture from the one painted by realists. As we shall see, this does not make difficult problems – such as addressing climate change – necessarily any easier to resolve, but it does suggest that the possibility of cooperation is not logically ruled out. The great paradox of environmental politics is that a failure to take advantage of the very real, albeit difficult, prospects for international cooperation may actually create the conditions for anarchy at the domestic level of a sort that Hobbes would have little difficulty recognizing.

And yet, it is precisely the claim that realists respond to the world as it is, rather than as we might wish it to be, which supposedly gives realist thinking its credibility and even policy relevance in the eyes of its adherents. Looking at the world with clear-eyed candour is the only way to recognize the forces that shape it, realists claim, and this argument can look soberingly persuasive when wielded by brilliant analysts, such as E.H. Carr. It is important to remember that when Carr wrote his most influential book, *The Twenty Years' Crisis*,[34] it was in the aftermath of the failure of the League on Nations, the idealistic limitations of which were painfully demonstrated by its failure to curb the rise of fascism and militarism in Germany, Italy and Japan. Carr had little time for 'utopians', such as Norman Angell (considered in more detail later), who he felt simply ignored the reality of great-power politics and the continuing divisions between the powerful and the relatively powerless. In this regard, as we shall see, he had something in common with critical Marxist scholars who continue to draw attention to the divisive and destabilizing impacts of political and economic inequality.

Carr was one of the relatively few British IR experts whose views directly influenced policymakers.[35] In the US, by contrast, the relationship between the policymaking and – at least some parts of – the academic community is generally closer and more institutionalized. No better example of this possibility can be found than Hans Morgenthau, a Jewish exile from Nazi Germany, whose views exerted a powerful influence over strategic thinking in the US as it came to terms with its new role as a hegemonic power in the aftermath of the Second World

War. Morgenthau's life experiences undoubtedly shaped his worldview, and he famously regarded many Americans as naive about the realities of, and fundamental insecurity generated by, the underlying dynamics of international power politics.

Morgenthau is frequently caricatured – as are many other realists past and present – by critics who pillory his 'scientific' approach to the study of international relations. To be fair, Morgenthau and his peers can be forgiven for not recognizing the possible significance of quantum theory, especially at a time when the overwhelming priority was winning the Cold War, not arguments about ontological reality. But it's not hard to see why his goal of detecting and understanding 'the forces that determine political relations among nations',[36] might strike at least some contemporary observers as fanciful, if not idealistic. The surprise is that the scientific principles of the Newtonian era still exert such an influence over so many realists to this day: if there is one thing that has become painfully clear over the last few decades it is that predicting the course of history, or even the forces that principally shape it, is still a very uncertain business.

As has been frequently noted, for example, realists were no better at predicting the end of the Cold War – perhaps the most significant development in the practice of IR in the period since the Second World War – than anyone else.[37] Interestingly, however, Morgenthau was very conscious of the fact that countries often behaved differently, even when confronted with the same 'exogenous variables', and that this might have cultural and historical explanations. He was also conscious of the possible significance of psychological traits in determining behaviour, even if he emphasized the pursuit of power first and foremost. As we shall see in Chapter 4, the psychology of leaders and decision making has become increasingly influential, especially when accounting for the policies that distinguish one country from another.

The limits of realism

This recognition of the possible importance of domestic politics and culture is important because broadly similar countries – at least when measured by material indices such as population, wealth or military capabilities – really do behave differently and have distinct national identities and domestic constituencies that incline leaders to favour some policies over others. North Korea is not Norway and domestic circumstances clearly help to explain the strikingly different policies that their respective leaders follow, *and* the way they are viewed and responded to by other states. Such observations may not strike the reader as terribly surprising or insightful, but this has not stopped some of the most prominent and influential 'neorealist' scholars from essentially ignoring national differences and treating states as 'like units'. As the principal advocate of the neorealist approach, Kenneth Waltz, famously put it, 'abstracting from the attributes of units means leaving aside questions about the kinds of political leaders, social and economic institutions, and ideological commitments states may have'.[38] The only noteworthy difference between states in this context is the amount of material resources or capacities they command, which ultimately determine what they can do.

Again, this might strike the disinterested observer as a rather extreme position, but in some ways this pared-back 'structuralism' captures a number of the key claims and principles that unite a range of scholars under the realist banner. In a self-help system with no overarching power to impose order (or justice), state leaders must rely on their own efforts to keep themselves secure, knowing that their counterparts are doing the same. This is the quintessential 'security dilemma', or the fear that potential foes may become too strong unless similar actions to increase defensive or offensive capabilities are undertaken. The best that can be hoped for under such circumstances – according to realists, at least – is a durable balance of power in which rational, utility-maximizing policymakers recognize that it is in their interest to preserve the status quo.[39] Or it is while they are not strong enough to challenge the reigning hegemon and dominate the system. It is precisely the idea that we may be at a moment of contestation for international leadership or even 'hegemonic transition' that preoccupies so many scholars and policymakers at the present moment.[40]

Unsurprisingly, given their focus on material resources and strength, realists think that redistributions of power in the system are liable to trigger conflict as dissatisfied rising powers challenge established but relatively declining hegemons. Hegemonic competition, or even 'transition', according to one of the most influential theorists of this idea, occurs when 'those actors who benefit most from a change will seek to alter the system in ways that favour their interests'.[41] It is precisely this sort of possibility and the growing friction between a rising China and a possibly declining US, which has led some observers to claim that 'a disastrous war between the US and China in the decades ahead is not just possible, but much more likely than most of us are willing to allow'.[42] Perhaps so, but much will depend on how such debates and decisions are refracted through the domestic political contexts of each nation. This possibility has led to the emergence of 'neoclassical realism', which has the advantage of taking such factors seriously and helps to account for consequential differences in national political systems and even cultures.[43]

While we might understand, if not necessarily endorse, the conclusions that Hobbes, Machiavelli and Carr came to about the times they lived in, the difficulty of survival or the limits of idealism, it is more difficult to see why such views persist today, when interstate war has become a comparative rarity, and violence of all kinds is in decline. To be sure, there is much to fret about in the world, but the chances of succumbing to casual violence, much less the state-authorized variety, are gratifyingly small – at least in the West.[44] Extrapolating from historical precedents, when the world was very different, and when the logic of conflict and conquest reflected that, looks a less persuasive and useful methodology. It is also an approach that downplays or ignores the possibility that the examples we draw on and the metaphors we employ may have the power to constrain contemporary policy options and influence the decisions of otherwise 'rational' policymakers. Even more importantly, perhaps, realist methodologies make untenable assumptions about the underlying nature and inherent dynamics of the world they claim to explain.

And yet, while some of the realist assumptions about the primacy of states and the drivers of collectively organized behaviour in the international system remain influential, there are signs that at least some realists are taking climate change in particular more seriously and rethinking the nature of the most pressing threats we actually face. Anatol Lieven's *Climate Change and the Nation State* is one of the more important contributions in this regard, although the competition for that accolade is not as intense as we might hope or expect. Central to Lieven's thesis is the claim that 'the world's great powers are far more threatened by climate change than they are by each other'.[45] In addition to the potentially catastrophic impact of environmental degradation of a sort that is considered in more detail in the next chapter, Lieven recognizes that this is likely to transform the nature of the threats states face. Internal destabilization and the collapse of democracies are possible outcomes of a warming world, especially as climate refugees try to move to the still viable parts of the planet. The only feasible response is a strengthening of the state, the inculcation of a progressive form of nationalism and the adoption of Green New Deal-type nation-building and economy-transforming activities.

Equally innovative, although from a more 'critical', anti-capitalist perspective, is the argument developed by Wainwright and Mann, which argues that a new, Hobbesian-style 'climate Leviathan' will emerge as a direct consequence of the need to preserve the conditions for capital accumulation in a rapidly deteriorating natural environment and an increasingly unequal social global social order. As a result, 'to address its contradictions – including the ecological contradiction that capital's growth is destroying the planet – capitalism needs a planetary manager, a Keynesian world-state'.[46] If nothing else, such arguments provide a reminder of how difficult it is to easily compartmentalize theoretical approaches in IR, even without the added complication of an underlying quantum ontology. Wainwright and Mann do share one thing in common with realism, however: a pervasive pessimism about the chances of avoiding catastrophe.

It is all the more surprising, therefore, that traditional realists don't take climate change more seriously. As one of the most influential realists in the world today pithily observes: 'Realism does not inspire a hopeful outlook on the future'.[47] Few would argue with that observation, at least. But Mearsheimer's scepticism about the ability of states to maintain stability and peace or create institutions to promote the common or even the capitalist good is based, he would claim, on a simple observation of 'the facts'.[48] In this context, it is equally surprising that traditional realists generally fail to take account of the most fundamental material circumstances in which international politics are played out. The same criticism might be made of Marxists, perhaps, but, to their credit, they do take the relationship between human beings and at least some aspects of material reality seriously. They are generally no more optimistic than realists about what this might mean – in the foreseeable future, at least – which is one reason for considering them together.

Marxism

Another reason for considering Marxism in conjunction with realism is that some scholars operating in a broadly Marxist or 'critical' tradition also recognize the importance of being 'realistic'. As Roy Bhaskar, one of the most important and innovative figures in the theoretical debates that bridge some of the more restrictive disciplinary divides that inhibit possible conceptual synergies puts it:

> The crucial questions in philosophy are not whether to be a realist or an anti-realist, but what sort of realist to be (an empirical, conceptual, transcendental or whatever realist); whether one explicitly theorizes or implicitly secretes one's

realism; and whether and how one decides, arrives at or absorbs one's realism.[49]

Not only did Bhaskar highlight that society was an ensemble of actively created relationships of interdependence in which normative beliefs and ideologies were historically and socially contingent, but he also recognized how dependent on and shaped by the natural environment human beings actually are. It is worth quoting him again:

> The social world is not a cut-off redescription of nature. Rather it is both inscribed within and in continuous dynamic causal interaction with (the rest of) nature. To fail to see this, and in particular that there are physical (natural) constraints on human life … is a charter for ecological disaster, if not indeed (species) suicide. (p 176)

This is arguably as 'realistic' a view of humanity's current dilemma as one might hope to see, albeit one that makes no claims about the underlying micro-level physical reality upon which the environment is predicated. As we shall see, more 'orthodox' thinkers operating in a broadly Marxist tradition have been at the forefront of identifying some of the 'contradictions' in the capitalist mode of production and the environmental problems that directly flow from it.

Socialism: sounds like a good idea?

Whatever the merits of Marxist ideas in theory, however, the historical track record of their application doesn't inspire confidence. Some readers will no doubt be surprised to find the paradigm being discussed at all, let alone in the context of a review of theories of security. Even if it is argued that Marxist principles have never been enacted 'properly' or as envisaged, ideas derived from this paradigm rarely feature in debates about security, or even in introductory textbooks that deal with IR more broadly. While this may be an understandable reaction to the declining practical and theoretical influence of Marxist ideas, I shall suggest that there is still something potentially useful to be learned from this broadly conceived approach. Indeed, when it comes to trying to make sense of capitalist development and its inner tensions, not the least of which is possible incompatibility of the world's dominant economic system and a sustainable environment, critically minded scholars have made important contributions. It is worth repeating that one of the key claims that animates this entire book is that, in the absence of an environmentally sustainable 'mode of production', even conventional forms of security will be unattainable, let alone those more intangible, psychological and even emotional forms of security that assume greater importance in societies where most material wants have been satisfied.[50] In countries where those wants and consumerist desires remain unsatisfied, Marxist thinkers have always claimed to have compelling ideas about why that might remain the case.

If there is one thing Marxist-influenced scholars – and Marx himself, for that matter, of course – can claim some expertise in, it's in their collective analysis of the origins and universal expansion of capitalism. It's worth pointing out that Marxists also have some things in common with all of the paradigms we have examined so far. Like realists, Marxist analysis takes the material conditions in which social life at any level unfolds as being profoundly influenced and ultimately constrained by material circumstances.[51] As Marx famously observed: 'Men make their own history, but they do not make it as they please; they do not make it under self-selected circumstances, but under circumstances existing already, given and transmitted from the past'.[52] In other words, human beings are involved in a dialectical relationship with what we might now call the biosphere and the trajectory of historical development that has occurred within it.[53] In the Marxist schema this means that progress through various modes of production – slavery, feudalism, capitalism and ultimately socialism – has a teleological inevitability, as human beings eventually resolve their internal contradictions.

Such 'grand narratives' are decidedly out of fashion these days, especially as a consequence of the historical failures of actually existing 'socialism' – if, indeed, that is what it was – in the Soviet Union and the PRC. Nevertheless, the idea that the fate and possibilities of human societies might be constrained and even determined by the material circumstances and constraints that we collectively confront looks surprisingly relevant to our own times. Indeed, Marx and Engels look remarkably prescient in their assumption that capital would become a global, ineluctably expansionary force that 'batters down all Chinese walls': 'It compels all nations, on pain of extinction, to adopt the bourgeois mode of production; it compels them to introduce what it calls civilization into their midst, i.e., to become bourgeois themselves. In one word, it creates a world after its own image'.[54] There can be little doubt that this is precisely what has happened, and that this is the essence of what we broadly and rather unsatisfactorily describe as globalization.

In that regard, at least, Marxists have much in common with liberals, despite the fact that Marx and Engels would have regarded the positive reading of capitalist development that liberals emphasize as a form of 'bourgeois ideology'.[55] As Marx and Engels put it, 'the ruling ideas are nothing more than the ideal expression of the dominant material relationships, the dominant material relationships grasped as ideas'.[56] While many modern observers would disagree with the deterministic nature of this relationship, or with the claim that Marxist theory might provide a way of escaping the sorts of 'false consciousness' that the power of the ruling class could create,[57] there are some interesting parallels with the manner in which contemporary constructivist scholars emphasize the social construction of reality. Some actors plainly *are* more powerful than others and able to manipulate the way some issues are understood.

The evolution of radical scholarship

The Italian political theorist and activist Antonio Gramsci is perhaps the most influential Marxist scholar in this context, and his ideas continue to have a very significant impact, especially on contemporary political-economists. Even the fact that we refer to political-economy as conjoined areas of mutually constitutive interaction is significant, as it captures something important about the way social outcomes are determined at both the national and transnational levels.[58] One of Gramsci's principal contributions was to provide a possible explanation for the failure of the proletariat to assume its historical role and end capitalism by overthrowing the bourgeoisie. Gramsci's followers have developed elaborate and not implausible explanations about the enduring power of capital, the attractions of consumerism and the declining importance and coherence of supposedly antagonistic class forces.[59]

Many contemporary observers – and notional members of one or other class, of course – find Marxist class analysis too crude, reductionist and improbably teleological. Even before the rise of identity politics made Marxism's highly generalized, structurally derived claims about social position look anachronistic, problems with class analysis were apparent.[60] The complex stratification of modern societies, the lack of resonance of class-based identity and language, and unconvincing accounts about the rather disempowering relationship between structure and agency have undermined the theoretical and practical status of Marxism. And yet recent developments have seen a renaissance of Marxist ideas as both an explanation of many of capitalism's various problems and susceptibility to crisis, as well as an alternative to business as usual.[61]

Thomas Piketty's surprisingly popular analysis of the problems of contemporary capitalism not only demonstrated the continuing theoretical utility of Marxist analysis, but it also persuasively explained why the world's dominant economic model is inherently crisis prone and liable to generate socially and economically unsustainable divisions of wealth and opportunity.[62] While many people may remain unconvinced by his explanation of the causes of the noteworthy growth in economic inequality in places such as the US and even the PRC, it is difficult to argue with the fact that wealth concentration has become a striking and potentially destabilizing part of the contemporary economic landscape. History demonstrates all too vividly that economic inequality is potentially a key driver of political instability, and consequently a fundamental cause of domestic and even international insecurity. After all, perceptions of economic exploitation were central drivers of the decolonization process, and continue to fuel unhappiness about the international financial institutions (IFIs) that are such a key part of the neoliberal institutional order.[63]

Given the emphasis that Marxist scholarship has placed on capitalism's historical role in creating a 'world system',[64] it is unsurprising that its adherents have much to say about globalization. Interestingly, however, there are important differences in emphasis among those working in a broadly Marxist tradition. On the one hand, are those observers such as William Robinson, who take a fairly orthodox Marxist view in which changes in the underlying mode of production cause a transformation of the social superstructure: 'The notion of a managerial elite at the apex of the global ruling class that controls the key levers of global policymaking captures the idea of a politically active wing of the global ruling class'.[65] In this depiction, class interests are transposed to a global level as members of a transnational ruling class cooperate with their counterparts elsewhere. On the other hand, influential observers such as Robert Cox emphasize the role of the US in creating a specific 'historic bloc' that shapes an institutionalized international order, and which America's capitalist allies ultimately benefit from and support.[66] As we shall see, however, it is far from clear that national forms of capitalism have succumbed to the inevitable homogenizing impact of global capitalist development, as some expected. On the contrary, varieties of capitalism and the growing importance of 'state capitalism' are striking features of the contemporary global economy, despite its high levels of interdependence and integration.

The continuing persistence of difference at the level of national political space is not simply noteworthy and surprising, therefore, but is also a potential source of conflict and insecurity. The continuing trade wars and clashes over economic policy, state autonomy and decidedly national interests are a striking feature of the contemporary era, and one with the potential to morph into outright conflict if they undermine or compromise domestic political and social relations. Marxist scholars have also been at the forefront of identifying the manner in which structural change in the economy can have transformational impacts on accepted social accommodations: the unravelling of the 'Fordist' mode of mass production and the breakdown of the post-war social settlement embodied in the welfare state are key examples of such possibilities.[67] David Harvey in particular has mapped the way 'neoliberal' policies have transformed social relations and economic orthodoxy in many of the 'advanced' industrial economies of the West:

> It has been part of the genius of neoliberal theory to provide a benevolent mask full of wonderful-sounding words like freedom, liberty, choice, and rights, to hide the grim realities of the restoration of or reconstitution of naked class power, locally as well as transnationally, but most particularly in the main financial centres of global capitalism.[68]

It is not necessary to accept Harvey's claims about the impact of economic and social theory to recognize that global capitalism *does* remain crisis prone, and this has implications for the legitimacy of the free market model and for its principal champion. Indeed, one of the most serious long-term consequence of the so-called 'global financial crisis' – which was primarily confined to the US and EU – was to undermine the standing and attractiveness of the American model of capitalism relative to its increasingly powerful and successful Chinese competitor.[69] While it remains to be seen quite how this will play out, there is little doubt that the US has experienced a relative decline in its material position and even ideational influence, and that this has potentially destabilizing consequences for the international system as a whole.[70]

The ability of Marxist scholars to place the now universal capitalist system in a global context – as well as identifying and offering explanations for its subsequent problems – is arguably what continues to give it distinctive analytical traction. Immanuel Wallerstein's model of core–periphery relations in a world systemic context, for example, continues to offer insights into the contradictory impact of global capitalism and the potential sources of conflict and insecurity it generates.[71] Recently, critical scholars have developed a sophisticated understanding of the historical consequences of 'combined and uneven development', which helps us to understand how different parts of the world are inescapably engaged in mutually constitutive social, political and economic relationships.[72] As Justin Rosenberg puts it:

> Differential development among societies impacts upon development inside societies through its consequences for political and military relations between them ... in this scenario – sovereign agents seeking to maintain their independence from outsiders – the unevenness of social development, on the one hand, and the context of multiple polities, on the other, are quite separate facts about the world.[73]

In other words, realists may be right to suggest that states, especially less-powerful ones that have less autonomy or capacity to control their domestic circumstances or the conditions within which IR play out, remain preoccupied with survival and protecting sovereignty. However, unless we can identify the historical forces and factors that determine the positions of very dissimilar states in what is an unambiguously hierarchical order, we will not be able to understand many of the key the causes of internal and external conflict and the endemic sense of insecurity that affects so many 'quasi-states' in the so-called developing world.[74] It is precisely this long-run historical process that recent Marxist-inspired scholarship has done much to illuminate.[75]

The uneven development of economic and state power becomes even more significant in the context of the emergence of new forms of imperialism, which Marxist scholars claim is becoming an entrenched part of the international order. Michael Hardt's and Antonio Negri's analysis of contemporary transnational social relations had a major impact when published, although subsequent events, especially phenomena such as the Arab Spring and other broadly based social movements, seemed to undercut some of their claims about the power of the US to control global civil society.[76] The rise of China and a number of other authoritarian powers has also cast doubt on the idea that the US retains the capacity to act as a unipolar imperial power – if it ever did. However, it is not simply the increasing importance of traditional great-power competition and geopolitics that has undermined the idea of uncontested American primacy, but the very material context in which the power of the

US is exercised. Marxists have also made a major contribution in highlighting this problem too.

Marxism and the environment

If there is one thing we can all agree on, perhaps, it is that the natural environment upon which we all ultimately rely for our survival has been profoundly affected by human activity. I shall discuss some of the causes and impacts of these changes and our collective efforts to deal with them in more detail in Chapter 3. The points to emphasize at this stage are that, first, the impact of human beings on the planet has become so great that we have a new word to describe our age: the Anthropocene.[77] The second noteworthy feature of the Anthropocene is that Marxist analysis has made some important – albeit rather gloom-inducing – contributions to explaining both the Anthropocene's origins and its underlying and potentially unstoppable dynamics.[78] Indeed, one of the most important claims that radical scholars make is that the evolution of a fossil fuel-based economy has not only led directly to our current environmental crisis, but has been inextricably bound up with the emergence and consolidation of capitalist social relations.[79]

As we might expect from a theoretical paradigm that is unambiguously grounded in material reality, the physical environment that we inhabit and ultimately depend upon is a natural extension of Marxist thinking.[80] That being said, it is important to note that the environmental records of and attitudes toward nature of both the PRC and the Soviet Union were truly appalling.[81] Both countries are still dealing with the legacy of earlier policies which saw the natural environment as lacking intrinsic worth, other than as something to be ruthlessly exploited as part of a drive toward 'modernization', industrialization and the geopolitical parity with the West that such things were expected to deliver. Contemporary Marxists might claim that neither the Union of Soviet Socialist Republics nor the PRC actually practised 'real' socialism, but the more fundamental point remains indisputable: capitalism is not the only way of wreaking havoc on the natural environment. It is, however, one of the most problematic and difficult to reform, as the active cultivation of consumerism and economic growth are integral to its continuity and 'success'. Some Marxist scholars are rather good at explaining why, even if their ideas about what might be done about it are rather less persuasive.[82]

The central problem that environmentally minded Marxists draw attention to is the fundamental incompatibility between an economic system that is based on endless expansion and consumption, and a finite planet with a limited capacity to support such a model. When Britain and 'the West' industrialized in the 19th century, their collective impact on the global environment was still relatively modest. As Charles Dickens, among others, pointed out, it's true that parts of Britain became hellish wastelands, but most of the world remained in relatively pristine condition.[83] Here was a case of uneven development if ever there was one. Worse was to follow from the perspective of the global environment and social justice, though, as the capitalist mode of production drew other parts of the world into its orbit. As Peter Dauvergne mournfully observes, the great paradox of 'successful' capitalist development is that a 'rising tide of consumption worldwide is swamping many of the gains from stricter environmental laws, higher environmental standards, and the creative energy of environmental activists and philanthropists'.[84]

In precisely the same way that colonial production structures and relationships created the sort of core–periphery relationship that Wallerstein identified, and which manifest themselves in a process of 'unequal economic exchange', contemporary Marxists argue that a similar process is happening in the natural environment. The essence of this conceptualization, as developed by Alf Hornborg in particular, is to recognize that 'the only adequate way to assess the occurrence of unequal exchange may be to look at the direction of net flows of energy and materials (concrete, productive potential), but *without* falling into the trap of equating productive potential with economic value'.[85] In other words, it is the exchange of real physical commodities or forms of energy that ought to be the focus attention, not the conventional abstract and intangible forms of economic exchange that are the principal focus of mainstream economics and measures of successful policy. Such an approach helps us to understand the environmental impact of core–periphery relations on would-be developing countries. Not only are the resources of such countries often plundered by core countries or the multinational corporations (MNCs) that are domiciled there, but such actions often have a devastating impact on the environments and long-term security of the exploited countries.[86]

An extreme example of this possibility can be seen in somewhere such as Nauru, which has been stripped of its only real resource – phosphate – and must now try to make a living as an off-shore detention centre for its richer neighbour, Australia.[87] A similar process has been at work in much of the Pacific, where MNCs from the likes of Japan have ruthlessly exploited the resources of their poorer neighbours.[88] It is no coincidence that Japan's domestic environment has improved significantly, as it is essentially able to export the impact of its own environmental footprint to the rest of the region. China's growing impact on East Asia is having a similar impact as it looks to establish similar ecologically unequal relations to service the needs of its massive, increasingly wealthy population.[89] The net effect of this process of unequal environmental exchange is to perpetuate the process of uneven development and exploitation that has distinguished relationships between different parts of the world:

> the existence of structural relationships ... facilitate[s] unequal material flows in which wealthier and more powerful Global North countries have greater access to both natural resources and the sink capacity for waste in countries within the Global South. In other words, Global South nations are structurally positioned as both a tap for resources and a sink for waste within the world-economic system of extraction, production, and consumption.[90]

For some observers, these sorts of outcomes are the entirely predictable consequences of the intensification of exploitation that has occurred as capitalism has evolved and political elites have promoted policies of neoliberalism.[91] Importantly, even in an era where capital has become increasingly mobile and financialized, territorial possession and control is intrinsic to a process of 'accumulation by dispossession'.[92] For many Marxist-inspired analysts, an expansionary capitalist system is simply incompatible with environmental sustainability. Whatever one may think about the actual chances of a socialist Utopia being realizable or even desirable, the idea that there are limits to growth has long been widely recognized, and not just by Marxists. What sets 'radical' scholars apart, however, is the idea that only a fundamental transformation of social relations and the incentive structures that individuals respond to can actually 'save the planet'. It is, according to Kovel, a choice between the end of capitalism or the end of the world.[93] In slightly less apocalyptic terms, Foster et al suggest that 'it is not a question of individuals seeking simply to withdraw from the capitalist economy but rather of creating a new ecological hegemony within civil society aimed at transforming the entire structure of production and consumption'.[94]

Sceptics might respond: good luck with that. Indeed, Marxists are much better at identifying problems with capitalism and contemporary social relations more generally than they are at coming up with plausible alternatives. One of the key problems most analysts fail to address – with the partial exception of realists – is that sheer demography threatens to undermine even the most sophisticated, equitable and well-intentioned of plans.[95] Whether or not human beings are succumbing to manufactured consumerist desires, there is little doubt that millions of people around the world would like nothing better than to experience the – highly desirable – life-styles enjoyed by at least some of the Western world's more affluent members. Without unimaginable attitudinal changes on the part of people around the world, it is difficult to see how the mismatch between the growing populations of the South and the privileged position of the relatively fortunate few in the North can ever be reconciled. While they remain in tension, realists in particular claim, there is a very real prospect that such frustrations and resentments will fuel conflict and intensify security problems in both the North and the South.[96]

Concluding remarks

Karl Marx famously believed that the point of philosophy was not to interpret the world, but to change it. Given the urgency of the combined, interconnected environmental and health crises that threaten to overturn all of our most influential assumptions about the way the world works, to say nothing about our expectations about the future, he would seem to have been right about that, at least. And yet there's still a role for thinking in theoretical terms – if only to understand how some people look at the world and why they come to the conclusions about it that they do. As we shall see in subsequent chapters, the assumptions that policymakers in particular make about the world have profound implications for their ideas about the best ways of pursuing security, too. For orthodox strategic analysts the world over, one of the unfortunate social realities is that, as the old cliché has it, if all you have is a hammer, everything looks like a nail.

And yet some forms of realist thinking that are actually attuned to the very real circumstances we actually face and the equally real security threats they generate look essential if we are to have any hope of addressing the environmental problems that threaten to unleash real anarchy and chaos if not addressed. The prospects for the sort of 'degrowth' strategies that involve 'a planned downscaling of energy and resource use to bring the economy back into balance with the living world in a safe, just and equitable way',[97] may look somewhat improbable in an era that remains dominated by a seemingly undiminished commitment to economic expansion. And yet Jason Hickel's arguments in favour of such a transformation look compelling, given our material circumstances; they may also chime with the intellectual temper of the times. Hickel suggests that 'the struggle before us is more than just a struggle over economics. It is a struggle over our very theory of being. It requires decolonizing not only lands and forests and peoples, but decolonizing our minds' (p 253). One man's mental decolonization might be another's collapsing wave function, but that might be another reason for a little theoretical and even political pluralism if we are to get out of an existential hole and embrace an existential whole.

2

Hope Springs? Peace, Progress and Pluralism

The possibility that our personal preferences, biases, values, psychologies and even emotions might influence the sorts of ideas we find attractive is not entirely surprising. The key question is whether we are drawn to less plausible or even inaccurate explanations of reality as a consequence. In other words, is it possible to claim that some ways of thinking about the world actually provide explanations that are closer to the 'truth', however unpalatable it may be? Even to raise such a question will be regarded as decidedly old fashioned in some circles, but if we are to make any 'progress' – another loaded and some would say outdated idea – in making ourselves and the world we inhabit more secure, then deciding on the best ways to think about our current collective predicament would seem wise. Indeed, thinking about thinking is arguably a necessary part of this, as we shall see in Chapter 4. At this stage, however, it is useful to consider some of the other more influential and potentially enlightening theories of IR to see if they can guide us toward salvation.

Given the historical development of intellectual traditions such as liberalism, which I consider first in this chapter, we might hope that the answer to this question ought to be 'yes'. After all, liberals generally take an essentially optimistic view of humanity's capacity for progress, problem solving and the conscious creation of a peaceful political order. At the very least, such uplifting expectations are being subjected to a rigorous examination by unforgiving empirical reality, not to mention the behaviour of a range of odious and/or incompetent political leaders around the world. If international cooperation, rationality and inclusiveness are the keys to progress and addressing some of the world's enduring problems, many of the most powerful people in the world – and not just those engaged in formal political practices either – have plainly not got the message.

One tradition that has focused on discourse, ideas and the social construction of reality – in which powerful people play a preponderant part – is constructivism, which is the other major paradigm considered in this chapter. Whether or not you think that collapsing wave functions are part of the explanation for the attractiveness or even accuracy of particular ideas, there is, to borrow another well-worn cliché, nothing like an idea whose time has come. The fact that not all governments and leaders recognize the importance of taking climate change seriously is a painful reminder of another sobering political reality: ideas are contested, and it's not clear that the 'best' or most accurate ones always triumph. It's not necessary to be a card-carrying Marxist, if such people exist anymore, to recognize that some people or even classes have a much greater ability to shape the conventional wisdom than others. It was ever thus, perhaps; it is doubly so in an era of fake news, well-funded and influential lobby groups and a general decline in efficacy of expertise and authoritative knowledge.

This is the second chapter devoted primarily to theoretical debates, but I should point out that, even so, I do not engage with a number of important approaches such as the 'English School',[1] nor do I address the debate about developing a more inclusive, global approach to the study of IR that has recently gained considerable momentum.[2] This is not because I think that such debates are unimportant or that I think that 'Western' IR is better. On the contrary, as I shall explain, none of the paradigms I discuss in this chapter or the preceding one is problem free, and the impact of Eurocentrism is evident in the discussions of China and East Asia, as we shall see later. What is important for my purposes, however, is that the models I discuss either are extremely influential (like realism and liberalism), or highlight issues that need to be taken more seriously if sustainable security policies and practices are to be developed (like Marxism and, to a lesser extent, constructivism). For readers who wish to engage more fully with the intricacies of these and other debates there is no shortage of excellent introductions.[3]

Liberalism

While liberalism is a relatively new conceptual paradigm compared to realism, it has also had a major impact on the IR discipline and has no shortage of high-profile proponents. Liberalism's association with the European Enlightenment has meant that it is perhaps the definitively 'Western' paradigm, and this has rather undermined liberals' claims about the potentially universal applicability of some of its ideas and principles. At a time when there is a concerted effort to broaden the epistemological, cultural and geographic scope of theoretical debates, any paradigm that is overwhelmingly centred on the historical experience of a small and unrepresentative part of the world is unsurprisingly vulnerable to accusations of Eurocentrism.[4] As we saw in the last chapter and as the environmental crisis reminds us, the case of intellectual and policy holism looks more compelling by the day.

Consequently, some of liberalism's fiercer and less forgiving critics argue that 'we should give up on the view of the liberal project as a prescription for an ideal regime and adopt instead a conception in which the pursuit of modus vivendi among incommensurable and conflicting values is central'.[5] The big question, of course, is whether liberalism can cohabit with other forms of government at the international level and even persist in the heartlands. This is much more of a challenge for liberals than it is for realists. After all, realists expect the worst. Liberals, by contrast, are inherently optimistic about individual human potential and the possibility of discernible social progress. What is significant about such ideas for the purposes of this discussion is that these beliefs also extended to the realm of security: certain ways of thinking about and organizing society are actually likely to make the world a less conflictual and more prosperous place.

In this context it is necessary to make a distinction between classical liberal political theory and the sort of 'neoliberal' economic (and social) policies that have become synonymous with the sort of political reform agenda that was so effectively promoted by former British Prime Minister Margaret Thatcher. This aspect of liberalism will be considered in more detail in Chapter 5. At this point it is important to note the very different assumptions about the world and the people who populate it that distinguish both the early and contemporary advocates of realist and neoliberal theories. If you believe the world can be made a better place, then you are more likely to make an effort to address problems such as climate change. If you think the necessary degrees of cooperation to limit climate change are too difficult to achieve, then you may think investing in national defence and free-riding are more 'rational' responses to looming crises and the inherent unreliability of other actors. As we shall see in subsequent chapters, one of the key factors shaping the interaction between the international system and state behaviour is 'the way that international interaction affects domestic struggles within states over the definition of the collective interest'.[6]

The liberal pantheon

The contrast between Hobbes's gloomy view of the human condition and the struggle for survival, and someone such as John Locke (1632–1704), who considered human beings to be rational and capable of reason and tolerance, is striking and instructive. One of the key features of the Lockean view of human nature is the belief that people are capable of cooperation; while everyone might have the right to 'life, health and liberty' in a state of nature, security is best obtained through the creation of a civil society in which these rights can be collectively protected.[7] Locke's ideas had a major impact in France and on the thinking of the 'founding fathers' of the US. The influence of his ideas can be seen in the American constitution and the emphasis on individualism and attitudes toward state power that persist to this day. Locke also had novel ideas about the economy, and his arguments about the right to property ownership had revolutionary implications in an era of absolutist rule and an emerging capitalist economic order.[8]

A concern with economic organization, its impact and potential benefits when appropriately organized was and is a continuing feature of liberal thinking. Nowhere was this belief more evident or influential than in the works of Adam Smith (1723–90). These days Smith is often invoked in contemporary ideological wars by those who believe that individual preferences working in response to market forces will produce the most 'efficient' economic outcomes, even for the environment.[9] There is little doubt that Smith's insights into the productivity-enhancing impact of an effective division of labour and specialization were and still are important. There is more debate about the possible merits of 'the invisible hand' and its capacity to produce the best of possible worlds if people are free to pursue their own interests, however, especially in the contemporary era where competitive advantages are often created by powerful interventionist states. But there is another, less well-known aspect of Smith's thinking, which preceded the celebrated *Wealth of Nations*, and which emphasized the 'mutual sympathy of sentiments that allows a form of socially constituted morality to develop within sentient and sensitive human society'.[10] Smith's vision is a long way from the anarchic struggle for existence that permeates much realist thought, and is conscious of the role that individual psychology can play in determining attitudes and ideas about what constitutes moral behaviour.

The other great figure in the development of liberal ideas was Immanuel Kant (1724–1804), a Prussian who lived through the tumultuous 18th century, but whose ideas are suffused with assumptions about human beings' capacity for rationality and even the successful pursuit of a permanent state of peace. In many ways, Kant was the quintessential product of the Western Enlightenment, and he argued that the implicit injunction of Enlightenment thought was for individuals to think autonomously, and to challenge the authority of the prevailing wisdom where necessary.[11] Again, given that the power of the church and absolutist rulers depended on inherited privilege, hierarchy and deference, these were potentially revolutionary notions. And yet, despite the incendiary nature of some of his ideas, one of his most important scholarly contributions for the purposes of this discussion was the idea of the 'perpetual peace'.[12]

Although realists tend to dismiss Kant's ideas as Utopian idealism, they are interesting and still worthy of our consideration for a number of reasons. First, and most obviously, they address the central question that informs this book: is security generally and peace in particular actually achievable? Second, some of the prerequisites Kant felt were essential if peace was to be realized – an international community of democratic republics, the international rule of law and the 'right to enjoy hospitality', or the free movement of people and goods between states – have never looked to be less likely than they do at this particular historical moment. I shall consider the implications of the rise of authoritarian powers, the possible demise of the rules-based international order and the pernicious impact of the administration of Donald Trump in subsequent chapters. The point to emphasize at this point is that Kant recognized the pivotal importance of states, but felt that under the right circumstances they could be critical elements of peace building rather than war fighting.

The emphasis that Smith, and to a lesser extent Kant, placed on the beneficial influence of trade for both its wealth-producing and its potentially pacifying effects was and remains a major and distinctive feature of liberal scholarship. Indeed, Mousseau has recently asserted that 'war among these states, even making preparations for war, is not possible'.[13] While this may seem implausibly Panglossian, at least much of the liberal contribution to political economy has the great merit of actually taking account of, and trying to explain, the way the world has actually changed. Two issues are especially important to consider in this regard. First, changes in the nature of international economic relations have also had a major impact on states and their ability to manage domestic economic activity. Indeed, the very idea that it is possible to draw a metaphorical line around the 'national economy' is much less certain than it was in Smith's time, when international trade, rather than production, was the principal driver of international commerce. The implications of this transformation are considered in more detail in Chapter 6. The point to make here, though, is that 'globalization' has had a transformative effect on interstate relations as well as international economic activities.

The second point to emphasize in the context of a discussion of liberal ideas about the impact of transnational economic relations, therefore, is that material changes in the international political economy have had a transformative effect on the state's role and capacities in the contemporary era. Not only has the power and autonomy of states been affected and very often undermined by the rise of powerful economic actors,[14] but the role of – at least some – states has changed as a consequence. In what Marxists might describe as a dialectical relationship, states are often involved in collaborative, institutionalized efforts to manage a highly integrated, interdependent and increasingly global economy.[15] The depth of this integration has become especially apparent, and to some extent fuelled by, the end of the Cold War and the development of a global system of capitalist production. But even before the Cold War abruptly and surprisingly ended, some of the more perceptive observers of IR had become conscious of the growing impact and importance of transnational economic relations.[16]

The fact that many realists continue to ignore or downplay the importance of political economy is surprising, given their supposed preoccupation with the real world. The world now is simply not one that E.H. Carr would easily recognize, let alone Thucydides. One of the strengths and weaknesses of academic endeavour is specialization, often to the point of wilfully ignoring contributions to the same topic from elsewhere, or assiduously protecting an area of interest and dismissing the efforts of those that are not immersed in its particular mysteries. One of the first people to draw attention to the dangers of creating intellectual silos was Susan Strange, who criticized the failure of political scientists and economists to talk to each other when both disciplines were – or should have been – trying to come to terms with transformative changes in what would become known as the international political economy.[17]

Interdependence theory

The implications of some of these changes for state, human and systemic security will be taken up in Chapter 6. At this stage, it is worth emphasizing how influential claims about the pacifying impact of trade have been, and to some extent still are. Long before Strange made her clarion call for the unification of economics and politics in the study of IR, Norman Angell had claimed that the era of interstate conflict was essentially over because the logic that drove it, and which may have made sense in an era of conquest, no longer did: 'If it [imperial power] remains military it decays; if it prospers and takes its share of the work of the world it ceases to be military'.[18] In other words, state power, development, prestige and influence were increasingly dependent on successful *economic* rather than military competition, and the calculus of state power and influence could be changed as a consequence. Angell famously published his book on the eve of the First World War, and subsequent events seemed to completely invalidate his claims and reinstate the dominance of realism of the sort propounded by Carr. Such ideas, or the logic that informed them, have never gone away, however.

One of the landmark publications that encouraged at least some IR scholars to take the economic dimension of international affairs more seriously was Keohane and Nye's *Power and Interdependence*.[19] A key insight of this book was that states are involved in much more elaborate, multidimensional webs of 'complex interdependence' than they had ever been before and that the realist understanding of sovereign states enjoying the power to autonomously enact policy was over and inaccurate. This surprisingly idealized view of state power had only ever applied to a limited number of states anyway. But by the 1970s it was becoming increasingly apparent that military force was becoming a less consequential determinant of national welfare and security, and that any straightforward idea of the 'national interest' was becoming highly problematic. The potential importance of this insight has only become clearer over the intervening years, as the Trump administration's difficulty in 'winning' the trade war with China reminds us.

Keohane was also at the forefront of attempting to understand the way that international organizations (IOs) were becoming more important parts of the governance of the international system, especially but not exclusively in the economic arena. Indeed, Keohane argued that there was an increasing 'demand' for such bodies and the regimes they helped to manage, as states found themselves incapable of governing an increasingly interdependent international economic order on their own, or even collectively for that matter.[20] There was, in short, a need for new entities to supply the sorts of collective goods that had traditionally been associated with more state-based and realist forms of hegemonic leadership. What is worth emphasizing at this stage is that the 'neoliberal institutionalism' of the sort Keohane helped to develop was entirely in keeping with a liberal tradition that emphasized the normative and practical benefits of an 'open' economic order.

Significantly, however, it was not only the possible attractions of a well-functioning liberal economy that made American leadership attractive but, according to some prominent liberals such as John Ikenberry, it was the way that the US *agreed* to be bound by the very institutions it did so much to create in the period after the Second World War, when it assumed the mantle of hegemonic leadership – in the Western world, at least.[21] What Ikenberry calls 'strategic restraint' refers to the manner in which the US refrains from exploiting its hegemonic advantages and potential by abiding by the rules and principles it created. Not only does this make the hegemon's position more legitimate and widely supported as a result, Ikenberry suggests, but it also makes it more difficult for rivals to supplant its leadership position.[22] This claim is especially important, given that there are currently a number of so-called rising powers that are neither liberal nor enthusiastic supporters of American leadership.[23] In this context Ikenberry argues that if there is a transition occurring, hegemonic or otherwise, it

> represents not the defeat of the liberal order but its ultimate ascendance. Brazil, China, and India have all become more prosperous and capable by operating inside the existing international order – benefiting from its rules, practices, and institutions, including the World Trade Organization (WTO) and the newly organized G-20. Their economic success and growing influence are tied to the liberal internationalist organization of world politics, and they have deep interests in preserving that system.[24]

Testing the validity of this claim and its implications for the contemporary security order will be one of the recurring themes of this book. But it is not just the reality of American hegemony that makes US leadership so significant – although, as Ruggie perceptively pointed out, this is what defines the international order after the Second World War[25] – but the fact that it led to the expansion of capitalism becoming the default economic order around the world. True, there are some very different forms of capitalism to be found in the PRC, or even in Western Europe for that matter,[26] but the greater levels of international economic interdependence that are such a distinctive feature of *any* form of capitalism in a global era are of enormous potential significance. Or they are if liberals are right about the pacifying effects of international commerce, at least.

One of the major claims of economic liberals is that policymakers everywhere have come to realize that some forms of economic organization are more 'efficient' than others. Not only is capitalism capable of delivering the goods consumers crave but it also confers a degree of political legitimacy on those that oversee it.[27] Even more important, in the context of a discussion of international security in particular, though, is the possibility that rational policymakers will realize that they have too much to lose by jeopardizing the wealth-enhancing potential of international commerce. In the contemporary era, in which global production is organized primarily by non-state actors, the role of states is increasingly seen as being to ensure a stable international political environment in which commerce can flourish. To be sure, some states are keen to ensure that they still have a capacity to shape such processes, and some parts of the world benefit from such processes far more than others, but the basic liberal claim is that international activity is a process from which all countries benefit to some extent and that this influences the way policymakers think about their own roles, and their attitude to their counterparts elsewhere.[28]

This rather idealized view of the international political economy is often frequently at odds with the lived experience of many people in the poorer 'less developed' parts of the world, as we shall see, but the basic claim is an important one: 'the historic impetus to territorial expansion is tempered by the rising importance of intellectual and financial capital, factors that are more expediently enticed than conquered'.[29] In other words, in a world of mobile capital and growing transnational economic integration, governments cannot be seen to be hostile to a broadly liberal economy or blind to the benefits of successful economic development or the factors and strategies that are most likely to support it.[30] The remarkable pacification of Western Europe in the aftermath of the Second World War is arguably the most important vindication of the argument that economic interdependence promotes peace and cooperation and transforms the thinking of policymakers and even of the broader European population, to a point where war between the states of the European Union (EU) is virtually unthinkable.

To be sure, there are currently major questions being asked about the EU's capacity to deal with internal region-wide economic, social and strategic crises, let alone provide leadership for the wider world on environmental issues. Nevertheless, the absence of war in Western Europe and the development of an institutionalized 'security community' is a striking and historically unparalleled achievement. It is equally noteworthy and instructive that other parts of the world have been less successful in reproducing the extent of the EU's institutionalized modes of cooperation, or overcoming the sorts of historical animosities that once distinguished Western Europe. The contrast between the rehabilitation of Germany and the enduring tensions between Japan, China and South Korea is instructive, despite the high levels of economic interdependence that exist between the latter countries. Yet, even if we accept the possibility that liberals may overestimate the amount that economic integration can transform the attitudes and beliefs of people about their neighbours, one thing seems clear: the nature of transnational production in particular does seem to have transformed the political and economic calculations of policymakers. As Stephen Brooks puts it, 'the globalisation of production has greatly lowered the economic benefits of conquest in the most economically advanced states, and hence among all of the current and future great powers'.[31]

Even if there is still some unresolved debate about the causes and durability of the closely related democratic peace theory, which claims that democracies rarely go to war with one another,[32] the possibility that economic integration has fundamentally changed the long-standing logic and incentive structures associated with war is profoundly important[33] – if true. What is most noteworthy, perhaps, is that changes in behaviour on the part of policymakers and even people more generally seem to have as much to do with ideas and beliefs as they do with any 'structural' variables or changes in the distribution of power. The possibility that ideas, norms, cultural sensibilities and even individual consciousness play an important role in deciding international political outcomes and the likelihood of war and peace might be an anathema to some realists,[34] but it is the principal interest of constructivists.

Constructivism

Compared with liberalism and, especially, realism, constructivism is a new paradigm and doesn't have quite the sort of common core of knowledge that other theoretical approaches have.[35] Nevertheless, there are some consistent themes in constructivism that revolve around questions of identity and the possible importance of socially produced norms. For the purposes of this discussion, norms can be thought of as 'a standard of appropriate behaviour for actors with a given identity'.[36] One of the key claims that unites scholars who consider themselves to be constructivists and who are interested in the forces that shape the international system is that 'the character of international life is determined by the beliefs and expectations that states have about each other, and these are constituted largely by social rather than material structures'.[37] In other words, the interests of states, the way that they pursue them, their relations with other states and the principles to which state policymakers may (or may not) subscribe are *socially* determined by contingent factors, and not the product of 'timeless', structurally determined imperatives as realists would have us believe. Although some of the most prominent constructivist scholars might agree with realists and liberals about some of the basic constituent parts of the international system, they are alert to the possibility that they operate and develop in different ways at different times.

Although the idea that the specific form that social relations take is the result of the interaction of human beings in a particular time and place is a long-standing and widely accepted idea in sociology,[38] its acceptance among IR theorists has been much more controversial and uneven. A key insight that sociologists developed was not simply that social reality is a product of human actions, but that a central part of this process is the creation of 'institutional facts', especially the regulative or constitutive rules which effectively govern our individual and collective behaviours.[39] The institutionalized logic of appropriateness can be just as compelling as the logic of consequences; social sanctions and norms can be just as effective as the legal or formal variety. One of the most influential and sophisticated elaborations of the social and active construction of social reality was developed by the French sociologist Pierre Bourdieu, whose notion of the 'habitus' captured something important about the 'dynamic intersection of structure and action, society and the individual'.[40]

The social construction of security?

We are already a long way from the sort of structural realism advocated by Kenneth Waltz and his followers, which is interesting and revealing in itself. Perhaps the greatest claim to importance of the constructivist approach is that its advocates take seriously the social context that shapes the human condition, as well as ideational influences on the construction of domestic and international orders[41] – possibly too seriously for some of their more parsimoniously minded colleagues. Rather paradoxically, in light of the physical basis of consciousness, ideas and action revealed by quantum theory, realists are far less willing to grapple with the ideational implications of structural reality at its most fundamental levels. To their credit, constructivists are interested in the contingent nature of social reality, even if they often studiously ignore its scientific basis and the questions this may raise about the possible limits of agency.

Despite these possible shortcomings, the significance of control of the means of organized violence to which realists pay such attention was given its contemporary conceptual importance by another sociologist, Max Weber.[42] Given the crucial place that the potential use of violence occupies in realist thinking, it is surprising that constructivists don't pay more attention to the conditions under which it is deemed to be legitimate. It was Weber more than anyone who highlighted the potential importance of socially accepted of norms, especially when embodied in a state-sanctioned legal framework: the legitimate use of violence is one of the defining features of effective state authority and capacity.[43] Where such legitimacy is challenged, or where alternative centres of power exist within the notional confines of state boundaries, many of the foundational assumptions about the state as a unitary actor, which are such a prominent feature of realism and (to a lesser extent) liberalism, break down.[44]

One of the most important contributions of constructivism in this context is to draw attention to the circumstances in which states can (or cannot) operate effectively at either the domestic or international level. To be sure, there is no simple demarcation between these spheres these days, if there ever was. Nevertheless, there is little doubt that some states are more 'sovereign' than others,[45] and that some issue areas are either more susceptible to effective management or deemed to be so important to the most powerful states of an era that they become intensely engaged in efforts to exercise influence or even control.[46] As Nicholas Onuf, one of the founders of constructivism, suggested, 'rule is an effective exercise of influence – effective in some measure because of a political formula which helps to make rule a routine and acceptable activity'.[47] In other words, effective expressions of state – or non-state, for that matter – power are not solely dependent on material or coercive power. On the contrary, in the absence of outright conflict, processes of socialization and influence assume much greater significance.[48]

The other critical insight that sociologists and those interested in the active construction of society and the principal institutions that govern *and reflect it*, such as the state, is that there are fundamental discontinuities between people in different historical periods that cause them to think differently about themselves, their relationship with society and the most fundamental belief systems that underpin it. As Anthony Giddens points out: 'What separates those living in the modern world from all previous types of society, and all previous epochs of history, is more profound than the continuities which connect them to the longer spans of the past'.[49] Simply put, the world that Thucydides and Hobbes inhabited is fundamentally different from that of the contemporary period, and so is our understating of its most fundamental properties. To be sure, the transmission, understanding and even authority of science is anything but universal. Indeed, it is not necessary to believe in an inevitable 'clash of civilizations' to recognize that very different belief systems, normative values and cultures continue to exist in the world, the prominence of 'Western' assumptions about the nature of modernity and science notwithstanding.[50] But neither are alternative belief systems necessarily uniform or unchallenged either. What 'globalization' seems to be causing, as Peter Katzenstein perceptively points out, is that any possible clash between belief systems or civilizations is 'occurring *within* rather than between civilizations' (emphasis added).[51]

One of the problems of treating states as essentially similar unitary actors is that we are in danger of missing the factors that make one state very different from another in terms of its internal architecture of governance and its foreign policy. As Chris Reus-Smit points out, at different moments in history what the English School of IR describes as international society is bound together by specific and *different* constitutional structures that help to determine what states consider to be appropriate behaviour. Importantly, these 'constitutional structures' are, Reus-Smit argues, composed of 'coherent ensembles of intersubjective beliefs, principles, and norms that perform two functions in ordering international societies: they define what constitutes a legitimate actor, entitled to all the rights and privileges of statehood; and they define the basic parameters of state action'.[52] Put differently, states don't operate as or in timeless, unchanging abstractions. On the contrary, states – or the most powerful, at least – exist in a mutually constitutive, dynamic interaction with other states, and their historically contingent, changeable material circumstances. The way that state elites in particular think about the specific challenges they face is a reflection of these circumstances and a shifting calculus of 'state interests'. The big question in this context is how effective processes of socialization actually are at the international level.

Normative suasion and socialization

The potentially tangible, even transformative impact of norms and principles was clearly demonstrated by Japan's adoption of the 'Western standard of civilization' during the 19th century.[53] Craving acceptance from the great powers of Europe, Japanese elites embraced the principles of European diplomatic practice, not to mention some European technological innovations and ideas about public policy.[54]

Unfortunately, Japan also copied European ideas about the merits of imperialism and attempted to colonize Southeast Asia and parts of China, with disastrous results for Japan itself and the region more generally.[55] While the story of Japan's epic strategic miscalculations and its eventual military defeat at the hands of the US may be widely known, the role of norms and questions of national identity is less well recognized.[56] Constructivists argue that unless we do recognize them we shall miss important drivers of state behaviour. Indeed, Ruggie argues that 'within their theoretical terms, neorealism and neoliberalism are capable of explaining the origins of virtually nothing that is constitutive of the very possibility of international relations'.[57]

Evidence to support claims about the potential importance of norms in particular is, constructivists argue, apparent in the way a series of new issues have appeared on the international agenda, to which many states feel obliged to at least pay lip-service. The remarkable change in attitudes toward human rights and the willingness of liberal democracies in particular to make the recognition of common principles part of their foreign policy is one important example of the impact of normative influences, peer pressure and a broader process of socialization. Risse and Sikkink argue that 'the diffusion of international norms in the human rights area crucially depends on the establishment of networks among domestic actors and transnational actors who manage to link up with international regimes, to alert Western public opinion and Western governments'.[58] As we shall see in subsequent chapters, there are limits to how much impact these sorts of socialization processes may have on policymaking elites in authoritarian regimes and in generating cooperation on common challenges such as global warming. Indeed, there is currently a major competition between the US and China in particular about the sorts of norms, models and principles that ought to shape behaviour in the international system.[59]

Nevertheless, there have been a few noteworthy successes that constructivists can point to when claiming that transnational advocacy networks and the norms and issues they champion can influence state behaviour in consequential ways. Heightened environmental consciousness is one area where transnational activism and non-state actors have plainly played an important part in drawing the attention of policymakers to a problem that they might have been – and in many cases still are – reluctant to confront.[60] Although sceptics might argue that there is a major gap between rhetoric and reality in this issue area, in some less technically and ideologically fraught contexts, discernible progress has been made. Banning the use of landmines is frequently cited as one key example of effective advocacy by non-state actors that directly impinged on a traditional security arena and the state's supposedly most fundamental sovereign responsibility.[61] Johnston argues that the effectiveness of any socialization process 'ought to depend a great deal on what kind of institutional social environment leads to what kind of socialization microprocess'.[62]

Some policymaking arenas and issue areas would intuitively seem to be more receptive to normative influence and peer pressure than others. Plainly, there are limits to how much influence non-state actors and normative suasion can have, especially in the security domain. The long-running campaign to ban nuclear weapons, for example, has had little real impact. To be sure, treaties have been signed that attempted to limit the number and spread of such weapons, but the limited success they achieved was primarily a consequence of elite preferences in powerful states, and the limited impact of the normative rhetoric of non-state actors. This is not to say that constructivists are simply wrong about the persuasive influence of ideas, however. On the contrary, major transformations have occurred in the sorts of economic policies states pursue, not least because of the successful lobbying and proselyting of well-placed think-tanks and prominent intellectual champions.[63] The shift from Keynesianism to monetarism is another frequently cited example of a 'paradigm shift' in policy thinking that occurred in large part because of the actions of non-state actors.[64]

The implications of these economic ideologies will be explored in more detail in Chapter 6, because one of the frequent criticisms of 'neoliberalism' is that it has failed to promote economic development in the 'South' and that this has direct negative consequences for human security as a result. The point to emphasize at this stage is that constructivists are clearly right to draw attention to the possible importance of ideas, norms and values in the construction of policy agendas and even national identities. The EU is the best example of an institution that has had a major socializing impact, and where the 'logic of appropriateness' exerts a powerful influence over member's behaviour and identities.[65] Indeed, one of the consequences of the sort of increased interdependence and integration that liberals emphasize is that national interests and national identities are far more malleable and less clear cut than they once were, as we shall see in Chapter 4. The concerted opposition to participation in the war in Iraq across Europe, Australia and even North America is a reminder of how fractured opinion can be even when it comes to questions of national security. More recently the perception that governments might have 'lost control' of national borders in the face of unauthorized migration flows has fuelled a rising tide of populism whose leaders claim to have better policy responses to new security challenges.

Concluding remarks

Ideas matter, no matter what their origins. Whether they are the result of individual brilliance, the influence of powerful vested interests, the ill-informed paranoia of the less powerful and left-behind, or even an expression of structurally determined neurological activity, they will help to determine our collective fate and ability to act. As we have seen, liberal ideas continue to underpin important assumptions about the benefits and impacts of particular policy initiatives – especially in the economic arena – but they also help to inform the wider belief systems from which policies emerge. As we shall see in Chapter 5, the assumption that the promotion of economic liberalism would be geopolitically advantageous for the US's overall strategic position and hegemonic influence was plainly part of the logic of American grand strategy in the period after the Second World War, when it assumed the leadership of the 'free world'.

The idea that ideas, beliefs and norms might matter is hardly a novel one, but their significance has been mapped and demonstrated in part by the rise of constructivism. It is no coincidence, it seems to me, that constructivist scholarship rose to prominence in the period following the Cold War, when the structural foundations of the international system proved to be a good deal less rigid than many had assumed. It is hardly surprising, then, that many – but certainly not all! – analysts, commentators and even some policymakers chose to rethink some of their foundational assumptions about the relative importance of policy issues in an environment where interstate war seemed significantly less likely. As we shall see, the growing interest in, and the practical importance of, 'geoeconomic' strategy and thinking has been one of the more noteworthy consequences of this period, despite the occasional disastrously misconceived efforts to exert old-fashioned coercive power in the Middle East.

Perhaps the most important potential conclusion that emerges from a comparative review of theory – for those that are open to new ideas, at least – is that none of the theoretical positions we have considered is entirely lacking in merit. Even Marxism has its uses, especially when it comes to thinking about the causes of economic inequality and the potentially unsustainable nature of a global capitalist system. If Marxists are correct about some of these consequences, this has major implications for liberals in particular and the basis of security more generally. It is because no theoretical paradigm is entirely without merit that some scholars have suggested taking an 'analytically eclectic' approach to theory, which attempts to synthesize some of the more useful and illuminating insights from different paradigms.[66] If we are interested in trying to make theoretically informed progress, we might do worse than to follow Berenskötter's suggestion that 'deep theorizing is concerned with how political actors view and organize their situatedness in (social) space and time, how they shape and are shaped by their spatio-temporal reality, and how they work with or against this condition through particular forms of (inter)action'.[67] Such an approach seems useful, not least because we need to understand why policymakers take the positions they do, which is often a more subtle, context-specific process than some would have us believe. And there is no more compelling, materially consequential context than the natural environment, upon which we all depend for our continuing existence.

3

Environmental Security

Whatever you may think about the various models of IR theory that have been developed to conceptualize security, one thing is clear: the very possibility of achieving security of any sort is highly dependent on the context in which it is pursued. Even the best-intentioned and most enlightened of policymakers must play the hand they are dealt by history. Providing a degree of security for the citizens of Singapore, for example, is a very different challenge from trying to do the same thing in Burkina Faso. History, geography and implacable biophysical realities constrain the options available to even the most capable and uncorrupted of leaders. But where leaders *are* incompetent, ignorant, self-serving and/or corrupt, the likelihood of even the most naturally blessed of countries achieving sustainable security outcomes becomes significantly less.[1]

My own adopted homeland, Australia, illustrates this point rather clearly. Despite a host of natural advantages, a combination of mediocre political leadership and the geopolitical constraints that inevitably confront a 'middle power',[2] the overall security context has unambiguously deteriorated. Although most analytical attention from Australia's strategic elites in this context continues to focus on traditional security threats such as the rise of China and a shifting distribution of power in the region, these are arguably not the principal threats that faces the people of Australia. On the contrary, the wildfires that attracted global attention in the summer of 2019–20 highlighted just how vulnerable the people and economies of even the most prosperous of countries now are to changes in the natural environment. Significantly, surveys of opinion in Australia now indicate that not only has the number of people describing themselves as feeling 'safe' declined from over 90% to less than 50% in only ten years, but pandemics and water shortages are also now seen as more important causes of insecurity than the threat posed by foreign powers such as China.[3]

Changing the minds of professional strategic analysts about the environment and relative importance of threats is a major challenge, not least for cultural and psychological reasons, as we shall see in the next chapter. More prosaically, some scholars argue that environmental issues should not even be considered as security threats, as this makes the definition of security too wide to be analytically useful.[4] Either way, one might be forgiven for thinking that, given the apparently incontrovertible evidence of the impact of climate change generally and global warming in particular, political leaders everywhere would be doing everything they could to address this immediate and distressingly tangible threat to the safety and well-being of their citizens. But such an assumption overlooks the inevitable degree of institutionalized path dependency and inertia that influences the policies and prospects of different countries everywhere. Even if one accepts the rather self-serving argument that grand strategy and questions of national security are best left to specialists, it's increasingly clear that they haven't been doing a terribly good job; there is currently a growing epidemic if *in*security, if not despair, especially among the young.[5]

Such initial observations may not be terribly novel, but they merit repetition for a number of reasons. First, the fact that these points are well understood is a reminder of the reality that we have known about the possible links between human activity, climate change, diminished security and the natural environment for quite some time. Thomas Malthus famously fretted about the natural environment's capacity to support an ever-expanding human population as early as 1798.[6] It will come as no surprise to the reader to learn that there has been a long-running academic debate about this issue and other possible environmental consequences of human activity ever since.[7] Consequently, a second point to emphasize is that an absence of agreement about the nature and impact of environmental problems has made collective action – even at the national, let alone the international level – much more difficult.[8]

As a result, much of this chapter is taken up with explaining just why it has proved so difficult to achieve international cooperation at the international level, the creation of a number of organizations and processes that are intended to do precisely that, notwithstanding. The paradox is that, despite a heightened consciousness about, and understanding of, many of the environmental problems we collectively face, it has proved extraordinarily difficult to address them, despite their growing unambiguous impact on our security. Before doing this, however, I shall make some brief remarks about both the nature of nature and the fact that the environment has become such a feature of the contemporary political horizon, even if political leaders seem to be incapable of addressing the challenges it poses.

An environmental perspective

IR scholars have a very mixed track record when it comes to thinking about the environment at all, let alone as the defining security challenge of the era. Even when they do, the conclusions they come to about what could or should be done about environmental problems are often strikingly different and reflect the assumptions of paradigms various scholars embrace.[9] One thing that those observers who focus on the social construction of reality have usefully drawn attention to, however, is that the way many of us think about the natural world upon which life depends – not least our own – has undergone a profound transformation. For many people the distinction between human life and an external natural world that was traditionally seen as ours to command and exploit no longer makes a great deal of sense. Simon Dalby, for example, argues that understanding the nature of contemporary security problems requires us to collectively 'shift away from an understanding of environment as the external context of humanity to a recognition of life as interconnected within a changing biosphere'.[10] The psychological implications and feasibility of this sort of intellectual shift are taken up in more detail in the next chapter. What is noteworthy at this stage is that there *has* been something of a revolution in the way that the natural environment is viewed and valued, even if only by some of the population.[11] It's not necessary to believe that this is a function of quantum effects and a material expression of 'the world in its open-ended becoming',[12] to recognize that this is novel and potentially important.

Part of the reason for the limited nature of change in thinking about the environment thus far can be explained by the very different economic circumstances that determine people's priorities in different parts of the world. The persistence of poverty means that the so-called environmental Kuznets curve – which suggests that as living standards improve, so concern about the environment will also increase – is unlikely to ever apply in many parts of the world.[13] The other reason why thinking about environmental problems hasn't changed as much as we might expect, of course, is that some people actually benefit materially from the status quo – in the short term, at least. Equally importantly, powerful, well-funded business lobbies are able to influence politicians and the general public to shape policy debates in ways that favour their economic interests and ideological biases.[14] The Koch brothers in the US and the Murdoch empire everywhere are some of the more well-known and consequential illustrations of this possibility.[15] As we shall see in the next chapter, the net effect of efforts to cast doubt on the value of scientific expertise and evidence is to politicize an already challenging problem and add to a pervasive sense of anxiety and insecurity about complex public policy issues and the ability of policymakers to manage them. As Frank Fischer points out, the net effect of such partisan readings of 'the facts' means that 'knowledge that does not contribute to a move in a particular ideological direction, while possibly true, is seen to be either of no interest, irrelevant or problematic'.[16]

Undermining the credibility of scientific expertise can have baleful consequences, not least for personal security. The strikingly inept handling of the COVID-19 epidemic in the US owes much to the incompetence and beliefs of former President Trump, no doubt. But the widespread scepticism among his supporters about the significance, origins and impact of the pandemic also contributed to its devastating and outsized impact in the US, which may yet have significant domestic security consequences. Some of the underlying cultural and psychological drivers of such behaviour and beliefs are considered in the next chapter. The point to emphasize here is that attitudes towards COVID-19 are similar in many ways to those of climate deniers and invariably found in the same people. The consequence, as Peter Jacques observes, is that such beliefs have wider ramifications:

> the challenge from climate deniers has also created acute democratic and civic problems. One problem is a science trap, where elites and masses cannot differentiate between authentic controversy in scientific literature, and manufactured controversy outside of the literature, in part because one has to be an expert in that literature to know the difference.[17]

Given the creation of disinformation and the politicization of what ought to be a technocratic discussion, the fact that there has been *any* change in the priorities of people, be they individual consumers or some of the most powerful policymakers on the planet, is both noteworthy and mildly optimism inducing. Before considering why this may have happened and what obstacles confront those trying to turn new ideas into action, it is important to say something about the environment itself and our collective understanding of its role and importance.

Planet A

An increasingly common sign held up at environmental protests these days proclaims that 'there is no Planet B'. As pithy slogans go, it is hard to beat. It makes it all the more important to consider what has happened to 'Planet A', and why such protests are considered necessary in the first place. Of course, not everyone accepts that we are actually facing an environmental threat, but for the moment let's just assume that the 97% or so of people who identify (and are recognized by their peers) as climate scientists actually know what they are talking about. The major claims made by such specialists and the reasons why the rest of us ought to be concerned about our future safety are well-enough known, but merit brief repetition.

At the outset, it is important to recognize that, as disconcerting as much of the analysis made by climate scientists may be, it is also a cause for celebration. The scientific method that underpins such claims, in which induction, empirical observation, falsification and rigorous peer review have a demonstrated capacity to generate knowledge, even 'facts', is a major collective achievement. As we have seen, the natural sciences are subject to the occasional revolution in which the conventional wisdom is overturned in a 'paradigm shift',[18] but new evidence and more plausible theory becomes the basis for the new prevailing wisdom. As such, it may not be completely 'true' or unchallengeable, but it is the best explanation the smartest people working in that area have come up with thus far. The comparison with those of us working in the social sciences is not flattering. I am not alone in experiencing a degree of 'physics envy': many in the social sciences – especially in economics, but increasingly in IR, too – have a similar affliction, which is manifest in the increasing dominance of quantitative-based work and conceptual approaches.[19] Yet, despite the social sciences' pursuit of 'rigour', as we saw in the last chapter there are striking differences even about what constitutes the primary research agenda for professional IR scholars, to say nothing about the best ways of studying it. Whether this makes us any less worthy of being taken seriously, I leave it to the reader to judge, but the experience of our colleagues in the natural sciences suggests that being right about things doesn't mean you will be listened to, much less be asked to advise on policy.

Although the analyses of climate scientists may not have had as much influence on policymakers as some of us might hope, they have had an impact on what might very loosely described as 'popular consciousness' – or they have in many of the privileged outposts of Western consumer capitalism, at least.[20] The fact that 'the environment' has become such a taken-for-granted part of the political and social discourse is not insignificant, even if there are still great differences about what – if anything – to do about it. That being said, it is also important to note that some of the first people to draw attention to the growing environmental impact of human beings on the natural environment were individuals and activists, rather than the governments who are notionally responsible for security in all its forms.

The American marine biologist Rachel Carson, for example, is widely acknowledged as one of the first prominent voices in what would eventually become a growing international chorus of alarm and protest.[21] More organized and transnational expressions of such concerns became part of the inspiration behind the likes of Greenpeace.[22] Significantly, much of the IR community was slow to recognize the impact of such 'non-state actors' and the causes they championed on the conduct of domestic and international politics. The rise of transnational activism was one of the principal reasons why a growing number of IR scholars felt that traditional distinctions between 'inside' and 'outside' and a preoccupation with the state as the principal focus of analytical attention no longer made much sense in an age increasingly characterized by transnational forces, actors and relationships.[23] Indeed, the growth of non-state transnational actors led many observers to believe that a form of 'global civil society', which extended the more familiar domestic variety across national borders might be emerging, and could play an important role in promoting and even managing environmental issues.[24] Despite this, much theoretical analysis and public policy practice remains relentlessly focused on national interests and the belief that they can be successfully pursued – if the state in question is powerful enough, at least.

If there is one thing that climate science ought to have made even the most fervently nationalist politician realize, however, it is that environmental security is *the* quintessential collective action problem. Tackling what Garret Hardin famously described as the 'tragedy of the commons',[25] or the inherently selfish approach that individuals and even politically demarcated communities have to the exploitation of common pool resources, is a problem that cannot be addressed without unprecedented levels of cooperation between states and other actors.[26] To be fair, the historical record in this context is far from encouraging, which is why realists who do take climate threats seriously tend to think of dealing with them through rather conventional means: states must accumulate power to defend what they have in the face of 'the coming anarchy'.[27] The possible justification for, and utility of, such thinking is taken up in Chapter 4. At this stage, it is useful to outline what climate scientists consider to be the key consequences of human activity on the planet, and why they are now so consequential that it makes sense to describe our era as the Anthropocene.

Some words seem to capture the *zeitgeist*, or the spirit of a particular era. 'Globalization' was the widely accepted shorthand for a complex set of interrelated processes that seemed to define a new phase of economic expansion and cross-border integration. Even though many IR specialists studiously ignored the potentially transformative impact and implications of such processes, the very idea of globalization seemed to capture something important and distinctive about the post-Cold War era. A similar process seems to be at work in the environmental arena.

There is little doubt that heightened consciousness of humanity's impact on the natural environment has become one of the defining features of our time,[28] even if there is continuing debate about quite what it might mean or what – if anything – to do about it. For climate and social scientists alike, the recognition of our collective impact on the biosphere seemed to set our era apart from what had gone before and require a new way of thinking about and describing this relationship, as a consequence.[29] Hence, the Anthropocene, which 'represents a new phase in the history of both humankind and of the Earth, when natural forces and human forces became intertwined, so that the fate of one determines the fate of the other'.[30] The Anthropocene, in short, is a convenient linguistic expression of the idea that the actions of human beings have become so consequential that they are quite literally transforming the planet itself.

Marxists might argue that this is the dialectic of historical materialism writ large, as our collective interaction with the biosphere reshapes the natural environment and the context in which we exist. IR, especially the theoretical variety, might seem like a rather unimportant aspect of such epochal change, and no doubt it is. Or it is unless policymakers decide to take some of its ideas and arguments seriously. Given that policymakers and influential commentators tend to be realists, the consequences of such thinking are – to put it delicately – not likely to generate useful ideas about the development of sustainable forms of cooperation and environmental management. On the contrary, as we have seen, much IR scholarship and public policy is predicated on short-term, overwhelmingly militaristic, nationally based responses to long-term problems.

If climate scientists have achieved nothing else, they have provided a detailed analysis and explanation of the causes of climate change, and some plausible-sounding best guesses about what such changes might mean for the biosphere upon which we ultimately depend. The contents of such analyses are increasingly well known and understood, even by sceptics and denialists, who choose not to accept the opinions and advice of recognized authorities in the area. This unwillingness to accept our best collective understanding of the evidence is in part a psychological response to the problems we face and is discussed further in the next chapter, as it illustrates a wider set of issues that bear on environmental insecurity. At its heart though, the idea of the Anthropocene is so profoundly challenging because, it is argued, it 'cancels the peaceful and reassuring project of sustainable development'.[31] At this juncture, therefore, it is worth briefly reminding ourselves about what the climate scientists have been telling the rest of us for decades, and why their claims are so difficult for many to accept.

What climate science tells us about our future security

Global warming and its possible consequences is the most widely discussed and recognized aspect of the scientific consensus on what is causing climate change, and is raising unsettling questions about our collective future. The basic science underlying the 'greenhouse effect' is well known and sufficiently widely accepted that even those who are opposed to transformational change feel obliged to pay grudging lip-service to its existence. The build-up of greenhouse gases, of which the most problematic is carbon dioxide (CO_2), has played a crucial role in absorbing the sun's radiation, causing average temperatures around the world to rise. One positive aspect of the growing environmental crisis has been the mobilization of some of the world's leading climate scientists to examine the problems and try to forecast what the likely consequences of unmitigated global warming might be. The Intergovernmental Panel on Climate Change (IPCC) is arguably the very model of the much-invoked 'international community' responding to a common problem. The IPCC's views are uniformly discomforting for policymakers everywhere, though:

> Global atmospheric concentrations of carbon dioxide, methane and nitrous oxide have increased markedly as a result of human activities since 1750 and now far exceed pre-industrial values determined from ice cores spanning many thousands of years. The global increases in carbon

dioxide concentration are due primarily to fossil fuel use and land-use change, while those of methane and nitrous oxide are primarily due to agriculture.[32]

Simply put, human activities, especially the transformative and seemingly beneficial processes associated with the Industrial Revolution and – for some, at least – the global expansion of capitalism, have been the principal drivers of global warming and a number of related environmental problems.

The phrase 'environmental problems' seems a rather feeble way of describing predictions that – if only partially accurate – have potentially apocalyptic implications.[33] The point to emphasize at the outset is that the acute, survival-threatening aspects of environmental change are rapidly gathering pace. What Steffen et al refer to as the 'great acceleration' refers to 'the holistic, comprehensive and interlinked nature of the post-1950 changes simultaneously sweeping across the socio-economic and biophysical spheres of the Earth System, encompassing far more than climate change'.[34] In addition to overall global warming, which remains the most threatening and potentially irremediable problem we collectively face, there are a number of other intersecting or resultant environmental problems that have the potential to create destructive negative feedback loops and possible tipping points that make achieving any sort of human security difficult, even in the wealthier, better-resourced parts of the world.[35]

One of the most unfortunate consequences of global warming, however, is that it is having an especially dramatic impact on the so-called 'developing world', which has not only done the least to cause the problems, but which is unlikely to ever achieve the levels of economic development enjoyed by the North.[36] Global warming is increasing the number of droughts (and floods) experienced in various parts of the world, but this is having an especially pernicious impact on Africa, which is historically vulnerable to famine.[37] Apart from the obvious impact on human health, declining agricultural productivity can exacerbate underlying ethnic, civil and interstate conflicts.[38] In addition, the melting of the Arctic ice cap means that rising sea levels will inundate some of the most impoverished parts of the world, such as Bangladesh.[39] Bangladesh, like much of South Asia, is also threatened by the very real prospect of some of the region's main rivers drying up as the glaciers that feed them in the Himalayas disappear.[40]

'Water wars' have the potential to be a major source of insecurity and contribute to the sorts of traditional security problems that occupy the minds of policymakers and strategic experts.[41] In this context, the realists have a point: powerful countries such as China have used their economic and strategic leverage to exploit the resources provided by the Mekong River that it shares with its neighbours, who can do little more than complain.[42] Being upstream is a crucial geographical advantage, as Ethiopia's rather grandiose dam-building plans demonstrate.[43] The diminishing water levels in the Nile, not least because of its centrality in Egypt's agricultural output, are already creating enormous tension between neighbours who understandably put national imperatives ahead of international obligations. It is not necessary to subscribe to some form of environmental determinism to recognize how such forces might exacerbate underlying tensions over scarce resources. Indeed, even among rich countries, grievances about access to fishing grounds have become a greater source of irritation as stocks rapidly diminish, as we saw in Britain's exit from the EU.[44]

At the risk of depressing and/or trying the reader's patience with this unrelenting tale of environmental woe, a couple of other issues are worth mentioning in brief. The threat to marine life is not simply due to overfishing: pollution and the acidification of the oceans threaten the very basis of marine life, with potentially catastrophic consequences for communities that rely on fish as a source of protein, not to mention income.[45] One of the greatest contributors to global warming itself is deforestation: trees are irreplaceable 'carbon sinks' which release vast amounts of CO_2 when burned. Apart from robbing our fellow creatures of their habitats and directly contributing to species loss, the clearing of forests for agricultural purposes, such as palm oil plantations, is causing alarm among climate scientists who fear that Brazil's rainforest may become a savanna, with dire implications for both its climate and the world's.[46] Given a still expanding global population that is generally intent on replicating the privileged life-styles of readers of a book such as this, plausible solutions to such problems are in short supply. More importantly, perhaps, some of the most powerful people in the world either do not believe they are needed or argue that they are best left to 'the market' to sort out even if they do exist.[47]

Despite the efforts of some politicians and climate denialists to downplay the seriousness or immediacy of environmental problems, however, the outbreak of COVID-19 has provided the proverbial wake-up call for policymakers everywhere. Even leaders such as Donald Trump and Boris Johnson, who initially dismissed its significance, found it increasingly difficult to escape responsibility for their respective countries' woeful efforts to deal with a problem that has been long predicted, but studiously ignored.[48] However, what the pandemic has highlighted, Fukuyama argues, is that it is not regime type that matters so much, 'but whether citizens trust their leaders, and whether those leaders preside over a competent and effective state'.[49] In that regard, the Trump administration's catastrophically mishandled response also undermined the US's claims to global leadership, an issue that ought to worry even mainstream security analysts.[50] COVID-19 also highlights two other issues that are powerful reminders of the security implications of environmental problems and our failure to address them, no matter what type of regime we individually live under.

First, the links between human encroachment on the natural environment, the commodification of animals and their subsequent unnatural juxtaposition in so-called 'wet markets' have made the development and transmission of new pathogens and viruses like COVID-19, SARS, MERS, Ebola and many others much easier than they were before. In other words, it has become painfully apparent that human beings' collective neglect of the biosphere and the creatures that inhabit it is causing increased blowback as natural barriers and cycles are upended.[51] As Sonia Shah points out, 'when pandemics unfold, it is not just because particularly aggressive pathogens have exploited passively oblivious victims or because we're inadvertently provided them with ample transmission opportunities. It's also because our deeply rooted, highly nuanced capacity for cooperative action failed'.[52]

The second issue that COVID-19 has highlighted is the impact of human economic activity on the very air we breathe. One of the paradoxical and unexpected consequences of effectively closing large parts of the global economy, shutting down major cities and drastically reducing the amount of domestic and international travel people could undertake was a dramatic fall in CO_2 emissions and pollution levels. For what may prove to be all too short an interlude, we were collectively presented with a glimpse of what the world could look like.[53] More to the point, this is what the world *has* to look like if the worst, life-threatening impacts of climate change are to be avoided. In this regard it is difficult to overstate the nature of the threats we collectively face.[54] On the contrary, climate scientists are now criticized for having *understated* the nature of the problems. The good news, such as it is, may be that COVID-19's immediacy and direct impact will actually spur policymakers to act on the even larger, more enduring and implacable challenge of climate change.

The implications of some of these views are taken up later. As we shall see in the next chapter in particular, though, the psychological consequences of the Anthropocene are increasingly evident, but generally ignored by security specialists. There is a relatively small group of IR scholars who are paying increased attention to the impact of psychology and even emotions in shaping the way people think about and respond to a rapidly evolving natural environment, however.[55] Likewise, some policymakers are at least trying to develop strategies that might keep global warming to what is considered to be a 'manageable' overall increase of less than 2°C. The fact that they are not making much progress is likely to add to the anxieties and insecurities of the young in particular. It is worth thinking about why international cooperation is proving so elusive, and whether – however deflating it may be to contemplate – realists might have a point about why individual states find it so difficult to cooperate even when the need to do so and the potential benefits seem quite so obvious.

Why is international cooperation so difficult?

As we saw in Chapter 1, liberal theorists such as Robert Keohane have long argued that there is a demand for the creation of international organizations and regimes: states as rational actors will realize that they have no choice other than to cooperate to solve collective action problems. While this proposition sounds intuitively plausible and is supported by the remarkable growth in intergovernmental organizations, especially since the Second World War, things are more complex in reality. One of the key constituent features and goals of effective regimes is, as Stephen Krasner famously argued, to develop 'sets of implicit or explicit principles, norms, rules, and decision-making procedures around which actors' expectations converge in a given area of international relations'.[56] Even in those areas of IR practice where we might expect functional necessity to be an especially compelling driver of international cooperation, however, agreement on quite how to go about it, and equally important questions about who actually benefits, have often proved difficult to answer.

In many ways, the creation of an interlinked, deeply integrated global economy would seem to be the quintessential expression of global cooperation intended to create a system from which participants benefit.[57] While this benign picture has some merit, as we have seen, Chapter 5 details the highly uneven nature and impact of economic development and the chronic sense of insecurity it has generated in some parts of the world as a result. One important point to keep in mind is that even in the economic sphere, where there were undoubtedly many beneficiaries of, and advocates for, increased liberalization and integration, hegemonic influence was required to embed the new international economic order that emerged after the Second World War. In other words, many of the 'rules and principles' that distinguished the American-led capitalist system were not the spontaneously adopted choices of similarly rational actors, but reflected the normative preferences of the most powerful state in the world. In this context it is important to recognize that 'the US, too, is subject to rules; it is merely that the network of rules and institutions governing the dynamics of international finance is heavily biased in favor of the US'.[58]

There are some fairly obvious differences between the current era and the Cold War period, when the US was able to persuade, cajole or even compel weaker states to go along with its goals. First, the US currently does not have anything like such a coherent grand strategy or set of goals to give direction to its own policies and actions, let alone those of other actors in the system.[59] Second, the US occupies a significantly diminished position in the international system and can no longer simply impose its preferences or vision of world order, even if they were coherently articulated or rose above a simple mantra of 'America first'.[60] Third, the Trump administration's deeply hostile attitude toward multilateral organizations actively worked to undermine them, even when the US seemed to have been one of the principal beneficiaries of their existence.[61] President Joe Biden has pledged to rebuild America's relations with multilateral institutions and allies, but there is a good deal of damage to repair. On the plus side, however, the appointment of John Kerry as a 'climate envoy' suggests that the Biden administration will take a more constructive attitude to the environment than its predecessor; it could hardly do otherwise, of course.

The potential damage that an unsympathetic and uncooperative regime can cause to an already under-performing international institutional architecture was vividly displayed by the Trump administration's decision to stop funding the World Health Organization (WHO).[62] As many people have pointed out, for all its possible failings the WHO has been the only body with the capacity to coordinate a global response to the COVID-19 pandemic, especially in the absence of American leadership. IR scholars ought to be concerned about this, as it gives China yet another opportunity to exert its influence through its 'Health Silk Road'.[63] Finally, of course, Donald Trump is a climate change denialist who saw little need for international cooperation to address environmental change and was deeply protective of American industry and sovereignty; views that have potentially profoundly negative consequences for the established international order.

The big question that the Trump regime in particular threw into sharp relief, therefore, was whether American leadership matters in quite the way it once did.[64] Even in the event that American policy under Biden does become more coherent and purposeful, will it make a significant difference for better or worse as far as climate change in particular is concerned? Keohane had a prescient and optimistic answer to this question, too: 'nonhegemonic cooperation is possible, and it can be facilitated by regimes'.[65] In other words, even in a period of hegemonic decline, or in the context of a counter-productive foreign policy agenda from the hegemon of the era, the potential ability of regimes to facilitate international cooperation and reduce transaction costs will continue to make them an attractive and functionally necessary part of the international order.

When we look at the history of international cooperation and the proliferation of international organizations and regimes that underpin it, Keohane appears to have a point. Most analytical attention about the role of IOs has focused on American post-war hegemony generally and the operation of the Bretton Woods institutions (BWIs) in particular. But it is important to recognize that the creation of IOs and the perceived benefits that might flow from institutionalized cooperation in which non-state actors played a great role is a trend that has been in place for well over a century. Some of the original IOs founded in the mid-19th century, such as the International Telegraph Union and the Universal Postal Union, had clear links to technological innovation and compelling functional qualities.[66] Even before that, however, other regimes had developed in less-technical issue areas as a consequence of the perceived need to manage what were seen as collective problems. The most important of these was the 19th century Concert of Europe, which not only institutionalized hitherto unprecedented forms of cooperation but did so in ways that impinged on national sovereignty and autonomy. What is worth emphasizing here is that some consider the Concert as an important illustration of 'collective intentionality among states'[67] and a precursor of the more elaborate forms of 'global governance' that would follow in other issue areas, especially economic.

Although many 'critical' scholars are concerned that the sort of 'global polity' that has emerged as a consequence of greater transnational integration is simply an extension of the influence of the most powerful states, perhaps it is the fact that an increasingly transnationalized sphere has emerged at all that is the noteworthy development. The growth in the number of IOs after the Second World War was especially significant, particularly in the economic arena, where the need for technical expertise in operating increasingly important institutions such as transnational money markets encouraged a shift of responsibility and authority to the private sector.[68] Indeed, it is worth noting in this context that not only was this outsourcing of regulatory responsibility actually something that was facilitated by states, but it was an expression of an overarching grand strategy designed to entrench capitalism's position as the default economic model.[69] As Mazower, puts it, 'the Cold War did not derail the project of internationalism; rather it redefined it and established its limits and goal and its relationship to American power'.[70]

But it is one thing to develop transnational connections and institutionalized infrastructure; it is quite another to utilize them to address problems of any sort, let alone the greatest challenge the human race may ever have faced. No doubt that will strike some readers as hyperbole, but how else are we to describe something that threatens the underlying basis of economic, political and social life – not to mention life itself? No less a figure than the UN Secretary General, António Guterres, has argued that our collective actions are 'suicidal' and part of a 'war on nature'.[71] And yet, despite the urgency of the problem, effective responses have so far been in short supply, especially where they involve coordinated action.

Institutionalizing good intentions

The rapid expansion in the number of IOs in the international system really gathered pace as a consequence of American grand strategy, and its commitment to creating an open international economic order. Unsurprisingly, perhaps, IFIs have attracted the most attention, not least because of their ability to influence the behaviour of less-powerful states, as we shall see in Chapter 5. But economic institutions were not the only feature of the post-war international order. On the contrary, some of the most important and enduring intergovernmental organizations, such as the United Nations (UN) and what would eventually become the EU, were direct products of the Second World War itself, and the desire to try to place security on more stable, institutionalized foundations. For all their manifold faults and current problems, it is not unreasonable to suggest that they have largely been successful in this endeavour.[72] If nothing else, this is a telling refutation of some of the more pessimistic claims of realists.[73]

The UN is the quintessential, well-intentioned, intergovernmental organization charged with maintaining and promoting peace. It was established in the immediate aftermath of the Second World War and reflects not only the compelling geopolitical realities of the period but also a very Western commitment to the protection of human rights by rational actors. From the outset this goal was complicated by the Cold War and the ideological contestation that often played out in the UN Security Council (UNSC), an increasingly anachronistic-looking institution which is a reflection of the distribution of power in the immediate post-war period. The history – and problems – of the UN are sufficiently well known to not need exhaustive delineation here,[74] but a few points are worth highlighting.

First, an already ambitious initial mandate has expanded over time, and the UN has major responsibilities in the areas of economic development, healthcare and international justice, in addition to its primary peace-keeping and conflict-prevention mandate. Second, the unrepresentative and veto-wielding nature of the UNSC has often meant that agreement about key policies has proved impossible, something that has been exacerbated by ideological and other differences.[75] Third, the gap between heightened expectations and an expanding range of responsibilities has undermined the authority and effectiveness of the UN.[76] Fourth, a lack of support, if not open hostility from the US, in particular, has undermined and politicized the UN's role. Fifth, limited resources have restricted what the UN can actually accomplish and added to claims about bureaucratic inefficiency.[77] Finally, the general criticisms that are made about the unrepresentative, undemocratic nature of intergovernmental organizations apply to the UN and are heightened by the relative powerlessness of the General Assembly as compared to the UNSC.[78] Similar claims are also frequently levelled at the EU as well, of course. Nevertheless, what is significant for the purposes of this discussion is that the UN has also taken an increasingly high-profile role in debates about environmental sustainability and about how to deal with global pandemics.[79]

The UN Environment Programme was established in 1972 to help developing countries to establish sustainable environmental practices. The fact that it was established when it was is a reflection of the heightened consciousness that was developing about the possible importance of the environment, although it is also telling that initial efforts to address this problem were directed toward the developing world, which had done the least to create them.[80] The most important development in recent times has been the creation of the IPCC, which was established under UN auspices in 1988 to provide scientific evidence about the impact of and risks associated with human-induced climate change.[81] Despite much criticism from those hostile to the UN and/or the role of the international scientific community in trying to develop a clearer understanding of the extent and likely course of anthropocentric climate change, the IPCC reports are generally regarded as being credible and independent.[82]

In tandem with, and driven by, the work of the IPCC, the UN sponsored a series of major international conferences designed to bring together member states in an effort to develop a coordinated response to what was increasingly seen as the threat posed by unmitigated climate change. Beginning with the so-called Earth Summit in Rio de Janeiro in 1992, a series of summits have occurred with the intention of coordinating government actions with the goal of reducing the amount of greenhouse gases entering the atmosphere. The UN Framework Convention on Climate Change (UNFCCC), adopted at the Rio Summit, established non-binding limits on greenhouse gas emissions and established the idea of 'common but differentiated responsibilities and respective capabilities'.[83] The Kyoto Protocol, concluded in 1997, attempted to give more concrete expression to the principles established under the UNFCCC, primarily by establishing legally binding commitments for the so-called Annex 1 Parties, or the developed industrialized economies. From the outset, however, the goals established at Kyoto were undermined by opposition from the US and allies such as Australia,[84] and by widespread concerns that the 'South' was expected to do more than was reasonable or fair, given its limited role in causing many of the world's environmental problems. As Roberts and Parks argue:

> When powerful states consistently treat weaker states like second class citizens in areas where they possess structural power, they run the risk of weaker states 'reciprocating' in policy domains where they possess more bargaining leverage. Since climate change is a problem that requires near-universal participation to solve, North–South negotiations have suffered this fate.[85]

Unfortunately, it is not only the structurally embedded asymmetries of power and influence between North and South that have contributed to the difficulties of achieving cooperation on climate change mitigation. Policy debates and negotiations within the UNFCC itself, for example, are compromised by underlying national interests so that, as Dryzek and Stevenson delicately put it, they 'perform weakly against the standards of authentic deliberation'.[86]

Just how difficult getting agreement on possible responses to environmental problems could be was demonstrated at the Copenhagen Summit of 2009. Despite the noble intentions of the organizers and the personal efforts of key international leaders such as Barack Obama, meaningful agreement proved impossible to achieve. Although participants agreed to 'take note of' the subsequent Accord, in reality little of substance was achieved. As Falkner et al note, 'rather than promote a global solution in the interest of climate protection, the major powers focused narrowly on securing their own national interest and avoiding costly commitments to emission reductions or long-term funding for adaptation'.[87] The Copenhagen meeting also demonstrated not just the continuing prominence of national interests, but that China would have to be an active partner in any agreement because it had the capacity to veto any agreement it did not like.[88]

The failure of the world's great powers to agree on what should or could be done was not a simple illustration of clash of interests, much less of civilizations. It is important to remember that even as recently as 2009, when the Copenhagen Summit took place, the PRC was still something of a diplomatic neophyte and very much in learning mode when it came to articulating, let alone asserting, a clear international position. As noted China watcher David Shambaugh observed, 'China is *in* the community of nations but is in many ways not really *part* of that community; it is formally involved, but it is not normatively integrated'.[89] What made China's position especially difficult and inflexible at that time was that 'the Chinese domestic system leaves virtually no scope for positions to be significantly adjusted on the spot during international negotiations'.[90] In other words, the same sort of policy paralysis and uncertainty on the part of provincial officials that many think badly affected the PRC's initial response to the coronavirus outbreak in Wuhan[91] can also affect members of the diplomatic corps.

The foundations of global environmental governance?

Given the disappointing outcome of the Copenhagen conference in particular it might seem quixotic to suggest that global governance of the environment is either likely or possible. Even those who argue that 'environmental solidarism' has become an embedded principle of international diplomacy are forced to concede that 'environmental multilateralism is more a procedural than a substantive norm'.[92] In this context there is no doubt that the sceptics have some powerful evidence to deploy. The fact is that all of the problems about which the 'international community' is supposedly concerned – with the noteworthy and instructive exception of the hole on the ozone layer[93] – continue to get worse. And yet, hope springs eternal; so, too, do well-intentioned international conferences designed to encourage collective responses to the increasingly evident dangers of unmitigated climate change. The latest iteration of this UN-sponsored process was COP 21, which was held in Paris in 2015. The Paris Agreement, which emerged from the conference, was regarded as a 'political success', and something of a triumph for climate-oriented diplomacy;[94] and, to be fair, the stated intention of limited global warming increases to 1.5°C was appropriate and a potentially vital contribution to addressing the problem.

Getting some of the most powerful states in the world to agree in principle to cutting CO_2 emissions was no small achievement in itself, perhaps; getting them to actually live up to their commitments in the face of domestic political imperatives has proved to be an altogether more difficult challenge. For all the talk about global civil society and the emergence of a common set of objectives and security concerns, the reality has been that national interests continue to dominate the policy agenda of individual states. Despite China's remarkable commitment to developing its renewable energy capacity, it is still the world's largest emitter of CO_2, and coal still accounts for nearly 60% of its overall energy production.[95] Given that the legitimacy of the Chinese Communist Party (CCP) is largely dependent on its ability to keep delivering rising living standards, as well as economic and social stability, this is unlikely to change rapidly. Despite the fact that social stability may actually be jeopardized by environmental problems,[96] in the short term development takes priority. India is another major producer of greenhouse gases and is actually increasing its reliance on coal, despite having some of the most polluted cities in the world.[97] The reality is that the domestic imperative to provide energy with which to fuel continuing economic growth trumps all other considerations.

The possibility that transnational commitments remain hostage to domestic politics became painfully clear in the wake of the Paris talks, but not quite in the way we might have expected. On the one hand we saw the emergence of populist leaders, such as Jair Bolsonaro whose policies have resulted in a rapid increase in the exploitation of the Brazilian rainforest that plays such a pivotal role in the planet's overall climate system. In response to concerns expressed by outsiders aghast at the implications of unrestricted logging operations, Bolsonaro questioned the evidence and bluntly asserted that 'the Amazon is ours, not yours'.[98] Whatever the rest of the world may think of Bolsonaro or his policies, he does have a point: all countries have tended to exploit 'their' resources as part of the developmental process, and rising powers such as Brazil, China and India are no different from their predecessors in Europe. The real difference, of course, is that when

Britain industrialized, its impact was on a smaller scale and not part of a global process. Be that as it may, the argument about the 'need' to exploit domestic resources is not easily refuted, especially where economic development remains an urgent priority.

However, where a degree of economic development has already occurred, we might expect to see heightened consciousness about both the importance of preserving the environment and minimizing some of the consequences of its exploitation, such as the pollution that has become such a problem in China and India. This is, after all, precisely what advocates of the environmental Kuznets curve would have us believe.[99] There is also a large body of political theory which suggests that as people's incomes rise, the prospects for democratic transition increase, and reformist political pressure from civil society will grow as a consequence.[100] Yet, Brazil's and India's environmental problems suggest that there is no simple relationship between democracy and sustainable ecological outcomes. As with the overwhelmingly Western IR theory examined in Chapters 1 and 2, political theory has not proved to be very good at predicting national political outcomes in what is still sometimes rather patronisingly described as the developing world, not least because it is assumed the periphery will replicate the experience of the core.[101]

The limits to convergence

The most famous example of this possibility, of course, is Francis Fukuyama's claim that in the wake of the Cold War's ending, history was effectively over. By this he meant that, given the end of ideological competition and the absence of any credible alternative model of economic and political order, an expanding global middle class would demand a form of democratic liberal capitalism.[102] As we now know, things haven't quite turned out that way, but it's not hard to see why Fukuyama – and many others – thought we were about to enter an era of public policy and ideational 'convergence' under the auspices of American hegemony and grand strategy. Indeed, some observers were convinced that even environmental policies were converging on international best practice as a consequence of globalization and policy learning.[103] The most consequential deviant from the path of liberalism and democratization, of course, is China. While the PRC may be communist in name only these days, it remains resolutely undemocratic, and there is little sign of this changing, despite a rapidly expanding middle class. Although there has been a significant increase in awareness and concern about environmental issues in China – at this stage, at least – civil society remains firmly under the control of the CCP. As Jessica Teets puts it, 'China, although unique in many ways, has increasingly converged with other nondemocratic regimes in developing a new relationship with civil society – one that allows autonomous civil society more participation in the policy process while creating new tools of state control.'[104]

Given that democracy of any sort is currently in retreat around the world,[105] the possibility that the influence of civil society will be either constrained or even negative is a real challenge for those who wish to promote international cooperation. The very idea of 'global environmental governance' suggests a form of world politics that is no longer confined to nation states but characterized instead by the 'increasing participation of actors that have so far been largely active at the subnational level'.[106] The rapid emergence of authoritarian and/or populist leaders around the world has meant that there is an inherent hostility toward multilateralism and perceived threats to national sovereignty. When questions of environmental security are actually addressed, it tends to occur through a predominantly national frame of reference. More than that, the prospects for the sorts of deliberative democracy which some take to be vital parts of developing domestic and ultimately international climate policies look remote indeed. On the contrary, those advocating 'progressive' climate policies have to reckon with the political reality that many people have little sympathy with such proposals or the evidence that informs them.[107]

The most consequential example of this possibility, of course, was the rise and election of Donald Trump. While there have been many attempts to analyse and account for his popularity, especially among poorly educated, white, working-class Americans,[108] a number of things are relatively uncontroversial. First, although his supporters may not necessarily be in the majority, there were enough of them to see him elected. Many of his supporters are unconcerned about Trump's profound ignorance, propensity for lying, striking conflicts of interest, questionable personal morality or his affinity with authoritarian leaders.[109] On the contrary, this is seen as part of an authentic anti-elite narrative. The fact that this is also demonstrably at odds with reality, or that his administration was packed with and supported by plutocrats, is not the key issue in this context. More pertinent was Trump's status as an ardent nationalist who was inherently dismissive and suspicious of international cooperation: if the president of the country that has done most to rhetorically champion the so-called rules-based international order has lost faith in it, then this bodes ill for the future of multilateralism. This is especially the case when there is a growing contest between China and the US for international influence, in which multilateral institutions may continue to play a significant part. It is far from clear that the Biden administration will necessarily adopt a more cooperative attitude toward China, to judge from the new president's earlier rhetoric.[110]

A competitive environment

In this context, even mainstream observers of America's overall position are concerned because they worry that China's version of 'environmental authoritarianism'[111] may be better equipped to deal with future challenges than the US's standard-bearing democracy. As Campbell et al suggest, 'among political systems, authoritarian ideologies would certainly be the "winners." One way or the other, severe climate change will weaken the capacity of liberal democratic systems to maintain public confidence'.[112] Significantly, these observations were made before Trump began to systematically undermine some of the celebrated checks and balances that have distinguished democracy in the US, or before the profound shortcomings of America's healthcare system were laid bare by the coronavirus. America's unfavourable comparison with the Chinese response was widely noted and did little to repair the damage to its already diminished soft power.[113] The possible long-term implications of this shift in the reputational standing of the world's major powers in this regard is highlighted by Hobson, who argues that

> At a time when the ideational ascendency of liberal democracy may be starting to falter, how climate change is perceived to be handled by different regime types could influence the democracy–authoritarian balance in the world. Democracies coming to address climate change in a more comprehensive and satisfactory manner – relative to their capabilities and historical responsibilities – would be good not only for the environment, but also for the 'brand' of this form of government.[114]

In this context, one of the great attractions of the East Asian-style 'developmental state' tradition pioneered by Japan is that it offers a way of mobilizing national – and, theoretically at least, transnational – capacities to directly address a range of environmental problems.[115] The idea of leaving major policy problems and goals to 'the market' to resolve was never popular in East Asia; in the wake of the region's economic success and the travails of American capitalism it has become even less so.[116] It is not just environmental and economic problems that are causing doubts about the supposed superiority of the American way, however; nor are such doubts exclusively held in places such as East Asia.[117]

While the calamitously misconceived invasion of Iraq, rather than climate change, may have been initially responsible for diminishing its standing and influence, the abrupt change in America's fortunes and the rapid emergence of other centres of power has had a profound impact on the US itself. The possibility that leadership – even the currently unfashionable individual sort that used to figure prominently in the 'great man of history' theory – might matter ought to have been evident even before President Trump appeared. After all, the nightmarish impact of the Great Depression was largely seen by realist advocates of hegemonic stability theory as evidence of a failure of leadership.[118] If the Trump administration did nothing else, it ought to have made it clear that individual leaders can make a difference – for better or worse – and that foreign and domestic policy is not simply a function of the structure of the international system.[119] That being said, of course, the profound domestic problems and constraints that have been revealed in the US system will make Biden's job all the more difficult, no matter how well intentioned he may be.[120]

This is not to say that international influences or pressures do not matter. On the contrary, even the most powerful countries are profoundly influenced by the actions of their counterparts, or the potentially adverse impacts of greater international integration, be they economic or environmental. The coronavirus pandemic and the panicked response of publics and policymakers everywhere has been a timely reminder of the multiple levels of interconnection that characterize the modern world and the difficulties that instinctive nationalists like Trump had in responding to it. This will not stop populist leaders from claiming that they can, of course, or trying to apportion blame to foreigners or others who do not fit easily into the caricatures of populist rhetoric. It is hardly controversial to suggest that these are less than optimal conditions in which to be trying to encourage greater levels of international cooperation to tackle unprecedented threats to human security.

Indeed, it has been persuasively argued that American hegemonic decline, leadership failures and the perceived failures of multilateralism have all worked to undermine the efficacy of and prospects for environmental cooperation.[121] This is not just a problem for those concerned about the prospects for addressing climate change, though: a failure to generate the necessary forms of international cooperation with which to address environmental degradation also has the potential to transform the global security environment. Importantly, it will not only be the South that feels the effect of unmitigated climate change. On the contrary, the idea that the world can be divided into sustainable zones of peace and conflict,[122] and that the rich world can insulate itself from the sorts of problems that afflict the poor, looks increasingly fanciful as the transitional impacts of climate change make themselves felt across the world.

The EU: the last, best hope?

A geopolitical context that is potentially less conducive to cooperation is a particularly important consideration for the EU. The EU represents the most enduring and *successful* example of long-term, institutionalized cooperation across national borders that the world has yet seen; it consequently has a talismanic status, given its role in attempting to address climate change. Not only has the EU replaced the US as the most influential actor and exemplar of effective environmental policy,[123] but it has also made significant progress in encouraging member states to sign up to binding agreements the implementation of which is overseen by the Institute for European Environmental Policy. One of the more potentially interesting aspects of the EU's approach to encouraging members to adopt environmentally sustainable policies is what has been described as 'obligated policy transfer', in which member states are cajoled by the EU into adopting best practice policies. While there is understandably some debate about the success of this approach, it arguably represents the most ambitious attempt to coordinate international responses thus far. If it fails, or if its goals are significantly wound back, as some claim has already happened,[124] then this will be a major blow for the prospects of international cooperation more generally, and for the EU's possible 'normative power' in particular.[125]

Unfortunately, there is every chance that this is precisely what will happen. The negative impact of the rise of uncooperative populist governments among the EU's member states has, ironically enough, been compounded and fuelled by environmental problems. While not all the asylum seekers trying to enter Europe have been driven by environmental problems, some have, and their numbers are likely to increase, given the rapidly deteriorating environmental conditions in part of Africa. Ironically enough, as Held points out, because 'multilateral governance has been gridlocked over climate ... it is not unreasonable to expect climate change to become an ever more powerful cause of migration'.[126] Whatever the legitimacy of displaced people's claim to sanctuary may be, they are creating an enormous political problem for the governments of the EU, and undermining solidarity and a sense of collective responsibility to the point where it threatens to derail the entire European project.[127] Some observers claim that 'for some low-fertility Western European countries that have poorly integrated Asian and African immigrants, the rapid growth of these minorities could erode social cohesion and promote reactionary politics'.[128] As a consequence, the protection of national borders and the restoration of sovereignty in the name of supposedly diminished national security has once again become a key issue in European politics, something that Britain's exit from the EU epitomized.[129]

Some of the EU's problems are arguably of its own making and spring from the fact that political ambition and the perceived importance of expanding the EU project for geopolitical reasons created economic problems and tensions that culminated in the euro crisis, which has never been satisfactorily resolved. The rapid expansion of EU membership, and the inclusion of economies into the euro mechanism that were plainly ill prepared, not only created an economic problem but also paved the wave for populists with little sympathy for the grand European project.[130] These unresolved political and economic tensions have made the already difficult job of collectively addressing climate change, which many see as a second-order issue, that much more difficult. As Burns et al suggest, 'it is clear that the combined effects of enlargement and the economic crisis have reduced the EU's appetite for ambitious environmental policy'.[131]

The great paradox of the EU generally and of its response to climate change in particular, therefore, is that on the one hand it demonstrates that institutionalized cooperation in pursuit of international collective goods is possible, while on the other hand it reminds us how difficult it is to construct effective and enduring organizations to oversee and implement cooperation. Even states with a history of cooperation and powerful incentives to continue 'remain firmly in control, deciding how they will permit other actors to help them govern'.[132] The increasingly fraught internal policy discussions within the EU over environmental issues and their consequences may help to explain why encouraging policy convergence has proved to be more problematic than some expected, given its importance and the EU's history of effective action.[133] Even with well-designed and powerful institutional mechanisms that have a demonstrated history of policy achievement and innovation, providing leadership is complicated, especially where there is a general underlying hostility to supposedly unresponsive, unrepresentative elites.[134]

In short, the EU highlights many of the problems that confront the world more generally. The fundamental problem is that environmental problems are hugely challenging threats to security that cannot be seen or addressed in isolation. The capacity and willingness of even the most powerful and capable of organizations will be determined by contingent economic and geopolitical factors, as well as the complex dynamics that exist between sovereign nations embedded in institutionalized frameworks of cooperation.[135] Given the continuing importance of economic inequality and uneven development within even the most affluent parts of the world, there are also some sobering implications about addressing economic insecurity in parts of the world that are also wracked with profound environmental problems. As Peter Hall observes of the euro crisis, perhaps the biggest lesson in this context is about the limits of cooperation:

> the torturous politics of the Euro crisis betrays the difficulty the member governments have had coming to grips with the prospect that the survival of the Euro will require substantial transfers of resources, at least temporarily, across national borders ... the crisis has thrown the limits of European solidarity into sharp relief.[136]

If the Europeans with all their advantages cannot begin to create stable, equitable economic relations and practices within a regional context, then the prospects for doing so at a global scale in the forbidding time frames available look problematic indeed.

Concluding remarks

Despite the overwhelming evidence about the realty and impact of climate change and global warming, some people – including some of the most powerful people in the world – remain in furious denial about the changing natural environment upon which human life ultimately depends. This would be unfortunate at any moment, but it is especially problematic when the time remaining to keep global warming to possibly manageable levels is alarmingly short. One thing we can say with some confidence is that changes in the natural environment will inevitably have a major impact on the way that we live and upon broadly conceived IR. The fact that the global coronavirus pandemic had its origins in our collective impact on, and mistreatment of, the natural environment demonstrated this, if nothing else.[137] The prospects for developing a more cosmopolitan outlook and a sense of global citizenship as the basis for transnational cooperation, as many academic observers hope,[138] do not look good, however. On the contrary, a resurgence of nationalism and the rise of populist leaders across much of the world has raised major and urgent questions about the capacity of individual nation-states, let alone the international system as a whole, to manage the consequence of profoundly destabilizing, intersecting political and environmental forces.[139]

Even the few international institutions that have been created in an effort to manage the sorts of tensions that realists rightly draw attention to are in trouble.[140] Confidence in national political elites to manage complex public problems is generally declining, although people still seem to value their international counterparts in principle, despite their problems. The EU is emblematic of all of these contradictions, not least because it has been such a remarkable success story, until relatively recently, at least. Not only has the EU been primarily responsible for bringing peace and security to one of the most violent, blood-soaked parts of the planet, but it also helped to create a geopolitical environment in which economic development rather than grand strategy could become the focus of policymakers across the region. Indeed, so successful was the European project that it is quite simply unimaginable for many young Europeans that they would ever go to war with their neighbours.[141] Despite continuing doubts about the EU's ability to act collectively internationally, the creation of a genuine security community within Western Europe is a remarkable achievement, nevertheless.[142] It is not hard to see why so many European intellectuals might think that they really have been part of a paradigm shift in the way people interacted and conducted relations between what had formerly been frequently hostile sovereign territories. If nothing else, the EU has been an important demonstration that the international system is not inherently anarchic and profound shifts in the consciousness of leaders and peoples are possible in the right circumstances.

Such beliefs no longer look as assured, however. It is no longer outlandish to contemplate the break-up of the EU itself as it struggles to deal with a multitude of political, social, economic and environmental pressures that seem beyond the ability of policymakers to resolve.[143] 'Performance legitimacy' may not be everything, but the success of the EU in underpinning peace and prosperity is plainly one of the reasons it assumed such a dominant and seemingly irreplaceable position in Europe's collective destiny. If the EU does succumb to its manifold challenges, not the least of which is a growing lack of popular support and a loss of legitimacy, then this will be a major blow for everyone who believes that effective international cooperation is the only way to address urgent problems that transcend national borders and are beyond the scope of individual states. To be sure, some states are more drastically affected by climate change and COVID-19 than others, but no state will be able to insulate itself from the impact of environmental transformation in the long term. This increasingly undeniable reality, especially if unaddressed, is likely to have a profound impact on the way people think about their prospects, their governments, even themselves as they are forced to confront the very real prospect of a world characterized by very real, very different sorts of insecurity.

4

The Psychological and Cultural Dimensions of Security

Security is ultimately a very personal thing. If you don't actually *feel* secure for one reason or another, then it is not unreasonable to ask whether this is a measure of the failure of public or strategic policy and the ability of our leaders to keep us safe. The chances of feeling secure are also still significantly greater in some parts of the world than in others: who your parents are, where they live and the sorts of cultural beliefs they seek to pass on to you are all key determinants of our life chances, our expectations about what it means to be secure and – most importantly of all – the chances of actually achieving it. To be sure, the percentage of people living in absolute poverty around the world had demonstrated a pleasing decline – until COVID-19 struck, at least – but the chances of living a long and fulfilling life are still notably lower in sub-Saharan Africa, for example, than they are in most other parts of the world.[1] This is bound to affect the way people view the world and their place in it. Lots of people feeling unhappy about their situation is not a recipe for domestic or international harmony, especially if they are young.[2]

Yet, despite this rather banal truism, the psychological aspects of security have not been given the attention they deserve. This is simultaneously rather surprising and entirely predictable. Given that most security specialists tend to focus on the traditional aspects of the pursuit of security – crudely put, guns, bombs and other strategically significant, material indicators of power – it is unsurprising that the way people feel should be of next to no interest to them. To be fair, as we will see, some IR scholars have taken some of the insights of psychologists seriously, but primarily to explain how and why leaders may make the decisions that they do.[3] Even this is something of a fringe interest in a discipline that remains dominated by realists of one sort or another, who either ignore what goes on in people's heads altogether or assume that people are driven by a narrow range of motivations that spring from the struggle for survival or the pursuit of narrow self-interest. This is a major and relatively new oversight and lacuna. After all, one of the founding fathers of realism, Hans Morgenthau, recognized that individual behaviour might reflect what a 'particular culture considers to be desirable', even if this had an 'irreducible minimum of psychological traits and aspirations'.[4]

Yet, even if we concede that the pared-back approach favoured by neo-realists in particular may have some heuristic value in explaining the behaviour of policymakers and even national populations at times, it entirely overlooks the way that the very idea of security may or may not be experienced by individuals. If people don't actually feel secure, then simply buying ever more exotic forms of military hardware is unlikely to change the way they view the world and their place within it. On the contrary, it is worth remembering that the 'security dilemma' not only highlights the futility of attempting to 'solve' security problems by endless innovation and spending, but may actually contribute to a sense of existential anxiety about a world that remains constantly on the brink of nuclear war. Anyone who grew up during the Cold War will probably remember a pervasive sense of unease about the stability of the bipolar order that underpinned the nuclear stand-off.[5] It is worth emphasizing at the outset that the peaceful end of the Cold War owed as much to what people thought and felt about that unique historical moment as it did to rational calculation about the feasibility of one grand strategy or another. If the border guards on the Berlin Wall had decided to shoot rather than ignore the people flooding in from East to West, things might have turned out rather differently. Quantum models of cognition and decision making may have something to tell us about precisely this sort moment of unpredictable, highly contingent decision making.[6]

The way people act, think and feel in particular circumstances is not entirely predictable, especially at moments of crisis, and this may lead to entirely new and unexpected outcomes. Lucia Seybert and Peter Katzenstein argue that such moments may enable a new form of 'protean power', or 'the effect of improvisational and innovative responses to uncertainty that arise from actors' creativity and agility in response to uncertainty'.[7] At the very least such analyses, and the profoundly important historical examples that have informed them, should make us recognize the limits of approaches that rely heavily on the supposed rationality of individual and collective actors, or the constraining impact of structures. To be sure, structural constraints and the actions of powerful actors *are* important, but, as Stephen Bell points out, on some occasions 'instead of power shaping ideas, it is ideas that shape power'.[8] In other words, agency matters, and not necessarily just at moments of crisis, although great uncertainty about the status quo can provide an especially permissive environment for paradigm changes to occur. The escalating deterioration of the natural environment is potentially providing precisely the sort of context in which new ideas may emerge, although this is no guarantee that they will be 'progressive' or appropriate, of course.

This chapter explores the context in which decision making occurs and the factors that help to determine the sorts of choices that people make at a number of levels, not the least important of which is that of the individual. It is striking that spontaneous forms of mass mobilization have become increasingly common and have the capacity to actually change the minds of policymakers and power holders in surprising ways at times. The so-called 'Arab Spring' may have ultimately been snuffed out – for the moment, at least – but at its height it threatened to overturn the established order in some parts of the Middle East and give the lie to some of the cultural stereotypes about attitudes in Islamic countries. Equally noteworthy has been the rise of environmental activism in the face of a growing threat to the very survival of human civilization everywhere. Understanding such developments, and their capacity to transcend national borders, involves thinking about psychology and even emotions as much as it does about conventional notions of military security.

The psychological turn

Rather fittingly, these days IR scholars are always having 'turns' of one sort or another: cultural, ideational, sociological, practice-oriented, quantum, relational and even psychological. Whether this is a healthy sign of interdisciplinary cross-fertilization and debate, or a collective inability to decide what to study and how to study it, is partly a subjective judgement, no doubt. Either way, it is important to know what the various schools and approaches to the formal study of IR are saying and contributing if we hope to account for some of the most complex and consequential patterns of behaviour that determine our collective fate. And, yes, there was a behavioural turn in IR as well.[9] Interestingly enough, behavioural approaches rather went out of fashion, but are currently making something of a comeback, driven in no small part by the desire to make sense of the Iraq War and its aftermath.[10] At the very least, the rise and fall of various paradigms and their sheer multiplicity is another reminder of the possible value in adopting an eclectic approach to the study of international politics.

In this context what is interesting and important is that scholars seeking to incorporate psychological understandings of human behaviour are seeking to embellish existing approaches to the study of IR, rather than replace them. The possible importance of such approaches was demonstrated by Graham Allison's landmark and highly influential study of the Cuban missile crisis, which provided a forensic analysis of decision making under the most extreme personal pressure imaginable.[11] When faced with the seemingly real prospect of nuclear Armageddon, the idea of rational actors making judicious calculations about the best way of pursing the national interest seems almost comically at odds with reality. As Lebow notes, 'irrational consistency can leave its mark on every stage of the decision making process ... policymakers are more responsive to information that supports their existing beliefs than they are to information that challenges them'.[12]

As a result, the assumption that is made by neo-realists in particular, that domestic politics and individual leaders are of no great concern when explaining or even predicting international political behaviour, looks even less compelling in the light of recent events. Not only are we seeing a remarkable and troubling re-emergence of authoritarian 'strong men' leaders around the world who are often determined to transform domestic political institutions in ways that entrench their power, but the last two American presidents also provide both a striking contrast in personal qualities and abilities, and a useful illustration of just how important individual leaders continue to be. To put it in the language of American political science, 'presidents are not just dependent variables; they are significant independent variables as well'.[13]

In their account of political psychology's growing influence in IR theory, Kertzer and Tingley suggest that this is explained by three factors. First, what former British Prime Minister Harold MacMillan famously referred to as 'events', such as 11 September 2001 or the outbreak of global pandemics: conventional explanations cannot explain why George W. Bush surrounded himself with neoconservative, ideologically motivated advisors who were determined to pursue highly risky, even irrational policies in response to Al Qaida's attack on the US.[14] Moreover, given that 'charismatic' populist leaders in the US, Britain and Brazil have been spectacularly inept in their ability to deal with the COVID-19 pandemic, explanations that fail to consider the personal qualities of leaders look deficient, at best.[15] Likewise, the willingness of many people in the US to continue offering support to a leader such as Donald Trump whose policies directly impacted on their personal security at a number of levels, takes some explaining, not least because the effects and consequences of ineffective leadership have been felt well beyond American borders.[16]

The second development spurring a growing interest in psychology, Kertzer and Tingley argue, is a general growth of 'micro-level' approaches to the study of IR. One example of this phenomenon that they note is the study of combat veterans in particular, and the exposure to violence more generally; people who have witnessed the horrors of war are notably less enthusiastic about using organized violence as a possible problem-solving mechanism. It is a striking feature of recent American political history that neither George W. Bush nor the majority of his key advisors had actually seen active combat.[17] On the contrary, Bush, like Donald Trump, had managed to engineer an exemption. This is not to suggest that there is a direct causal relationship between exposure to violence and its renunciation – as the number of people struggling with post-traumatic stress disorder suggests – but it is noteworthy that combat veterans tend to be more cautious about the application of coercive power than those who have never seen its effects or the uncertainties associated with warfare generally.[18]

Finally, and most importantly from the perspective of IR theory, there is a growing awareness of the need to understand and account for the psychological dimensions of 'agency', which is leading to a questioning of the foundational assumptions of rationality. At one level, this relates to the difference between 'thinking fast and slow', or routinized versus deep thinking.[19] More fundamentally, however, the very notion of rationality has been called into question by insights drawn from the behavioural sciences:

> The rational paradigm tends to assume a 'deep, conscious, thoughtful thinker'. In reality, most operations of the mind are automatic and subconscious. Not only is this a necessary cognitive trait, but it is also an efficient and powerful way of processing information and making decisions. … the process of 'cognition' – the dynamics of the mind – produces the 'beliefs' and constructs (such as 'images' and 'schemas') that allow us to make sense of our environment.[20]

The idea that more intangible factors such as emotions might play a part in determining the actions of decision makers, and that such factors should be integrated into understanding policy outcomes, remains an anathema to many IR scholars. And yet, one of the consequences of the rise of a new generation of autocratic leaders who have concentrated power in their own hands and who are unconstrained by institutional safeguards is that policy decisions are even more closely bound up with the personalities and psychological dispositions of a single person. Xi Jinping is currently the most consequential example of the 'bad emperor syndrome',[21] in which the personal fallibilities of a single leader may have a disastrous impact on the wider polity and society of which he – or, much more rarely, she – is the most important part. Such developments ought to be of immediate interest to IR scholars if only because they are contributing to the possibility that 'the long-standing dominance of a set of consolidated democracies with developed economies and a common alliance structure is coming to an end'.[22]

When leaders fail

The ascendance of autocrats and the importance of individual leaders is not a problem that is confined to states with no or little history of democratic rule. On the contrary, the presidency of Donald Trump provided a compelling case study of just how much difference the personal failings of a powerful individual can make to both domestic and foreign relations, even in countries that are famed for the 'checks and balances' of their political systems. Predictably enough, perhaps, given Trump's long-standing opposition to regulation and his support of the fossil fuel industry, his administration actively sought to wind back many of the environmental reforms of the Obama administration. Indeed, it is widely believed that 'Obama remains something of an obsession for Trump; the subject of a political and personal inferiority complex'.[23] That he was able to act upon his personal feelings with little regard for the damage this did to the social or natural environment was due in no small part to the support of the Republican Party, which offered strong support for a figure many initially reviled and rejected.

Dispiriting as such developments may be, they can be explained by some of the standard forms of political analysis in which winning is what matters and principle often comes a poor second. What was more remarkable about Trump, however, was his personality, and the very plausible claim that was made about his evident failure to mature psychologically. It is not necessary to agree with Daniel Drezner's description of Trump as the 'toddler in chief' – although it seems plausible enough to me – to recognize that his character flaws, especially his notorious narcissism, lack of empathy, self-obsession, impulsiveness and short-attention span, are more commonly found in small children than mature adults. One of the most important consequences of this limited emotional and intellectual development is that Trump 'lacks the necessary metacognition to know what he does not know'.[24]

Unfortunately, this was not a problem that was confined to the President; many Republican voters in particular are sceptical about the value of scientific expertise.[25] It is the supposed ability of populist leaders such as Trump to connect with 'real' people and give voice to their feelings, anxieties and grievances that are otherwise ignored by self-serving, out-of-touch elites, that constitutes the very essence of populist appeal, of course.[26] Indeed, whatever one thinks about populist politicians and their capacity to address problems such as climate change or global pandemics, it is important to recognize that part of their appeal is anything but that of a 'rational actor'. On the contrary, it is visceral and emotional. As Mudde and Kaltwasser point out, 'the key strength of a populist social movement relies on its capacity to interpret a widespread feeling of anger with the establishment and to convincingly propose that the solution lies in the sovereign people'.[27] Interestingly, the manifest failure of leaders such as Trump, Britain's Boris Johnson or Brazil's Jair Bolsonaro to actually deal with health crises such as COVID-19 and implement effective public policy has not – at the time of writing, at least – fatally undermined them politically. In Trump's case, his supporters have seemed entirely impervious to glaring failures in competence or even personal probity and morality.[28]

Given the increasing numbers of populist leaders around the world, this is no longer a niche interest for students of comparative politics. Recognizing that Trump was a populist with a remarkably limited understanding of grand strategy, the US's historical international role, or the complex interdependencies that underpin the contemporary international political economy, is – or ought to be – an absolutely vital consideration when trying to make sense of America's foreign policy and the legacy of the Trump era. It is also important to recognize that a susceptibility to populist impulses is not uncharted territory for the US, as the history of the 19th-century social movements reminds us.[29] What is equally noteworthy in this regard is that such impulses plainly endure and, most importantly for the purposes of this discussion, have the capacity to influence the conduct of contemporary IR. Iskander Rehman argues that 'there is a clear historic lineage to the Trumpian vision of foreign policy. Its roots are burrowed deep in the dark undersoil of American reactionary thought. It is a nervous and conspiracy-driven worldview – one that depreciates alliances, scoffs at multilateralism, and accommodates authoritarianism'.[30]

The rise of identity politics

If this analysis is correct, which I think it is, this means that IR can simply no longer neglect the historical, sociological, cultural and even identitarian forces that help to shape distinctive national attitudes to domestic and foreign policy. The national context that allowed Trump to become president is not just important when trying to explain domestic politics, but is also an important indicator and driver of significant structural changes in the international order in which the US remains the most important actor. In this context, the changing nature and consequences of 'globalization', which I discuss in more detail in Chapter 6, are not simply some of the most important material changes in the international system, but they have a major impact on the way people think about themselves and the economic, political and social orders of which they are a part. As Michael Sandel points out, 'the hard reality is that Donald Trump was elected by tapping a wellspring of anxieties, frustrations, and legitimate grievances to which the mainstream parties have no compelling answer'.[31]

The sense that life is unfair, that some are profiting from unwelcome and unsettling change while others fall behind, is hardly a new phenomenon. At times of significant economic change or crisis social movements are one broadly based form of response to events that seem both disorientating and inequitable.[32] The US is especially vulnerable to the destabilizing effects of such broadly based economic changes and social dislocation because they highlight long-standing underlying racial and geographical differences. What the Marxists used to call the 'labour aristocracy' was largely white and dependent on the sorts of manufacturing jobs that Donald Trump claims have disappeared overseas. His promise to bring them back and restore the fortunes of his 'base' may have been at odds with economic reality, but this did surprisingly little to undermine his popularity.

Trump managed to undermine further an already polarized and increasingly dysfunctional political system. So incendiary and destabilizing have his actions been that serious commentators wonder whether the fabled checks and balances of the American political system will be able to cope with the impact of Trumpian populism, or even whether democracy itself can survive. Levitsky and Ziblatt argue that 'the traditions underpinning America's democratic institutions are unravelling, opening up a disconcerting gap between how our political system works and the long-standing expectations about how it ought to work. As our soft guardrails have weakened we have grown increasingly vulnerable to antidemocratic leaders'.[33] Likewise, Nobel prize-winning economist Paul Krugman has suggested that the US may be on the verge of a second civil war as the country struggles to come to terms with, much less respond effectively to, entrenched racism and disadvantage.[34] One of the consequences of the Trump presidency has been to highlight neuralgic, racially based pressure points and exacerbate underlying disadvantage and ideological difference. The net effect, Eric Kauffmann argues in a controversial but persuasive book, is that 'culture wars are increasingly displacing economics as the central axis of politics'.[35] It is not clear that the more inclusive and conciliatory approach of the Biden administration will be able to unite a country that is now so bitterly partisan and divided.

In some ways this is unsurprising. Despite widespread expectations – especially among economists – that the forces associated with globalization would bring about forms of 'convergence', this has not happened, especially within national boundaries, as I shall explain in more detail in Chapter 6. The point to emphasize at this juncture is that, far from encouraging a process of public policy harmonization, the destabilizing influence of global forces has actually reinforced the attractions of national, ethnic and religious identities, often sparking important forms of resistance and pushback in the process. The most consequential manifestation of this policy for scholars of IR, of course, has been the rise of radical Islam and its violent rejection of what are seen as alien norms and practices, and the imposition of a widely resented form of American hegemony. Whatever the possible economic benefits of globalization – and these are by no means uncontested, as we shall see – the social impacts have often been disorienting, resented and actively resisted in 'traditional' societies where other patterns of social organization are stubbornly resistant to change.[36]

Nor is it only 'pre-modern' societies that have not been overturned or transformed by the thoroughgoing impact of globalization. As I explain in Chapter 5, 'China' has not been reconfigured by its incorporation into a global capitalist economy, even if its people have been powerfully affected in many ways. Nationalism remains a powerful motivating force and source of social cohesion in the PRC, just as it was in Europe during the 19th century, when the continent was coping with profound social and economic change. In China's case the persistence, even the resurgence, of nationalist sentiment is helping to legitimate its grand strategic ambitions, as we will see. Somewhat paradoxically, it is the most 'advanced' or 'developed' Western democracies that are struggling to deal with the consequences of economic restructuring at the national and transnational levels, and the social transformation this is bringing in its wake, not least because migration has made these debates internal and immediate.

Populism is one manifestation of this phenomenon as the losers of globalization look for answers to the anxiety-inducing impacts of often radically transformed social circumstances. The Brexit phenomenon in the United Kingdom (UK) is one of the clearest examples of the way in which questions of identity and concerns about high levels of immigration have coalesced into a visceral revolt against distant elites and a possible loss of sovereignty.[37] The fact that politicians such as Boris Johnson may have opportunistically latched onto a cause for which he had no great belief or answers, does not make his impact and the rise of populist politics any the less important. On the contrary, not only is Britain's place in the international system significantly reduced as a result of its exit from the EU, but the very future of the UK as a cohesive political unit is in real doubt.[38] Paradoxically enough, however, Britain has some of most ambitious environmental goals in Europe.[39] It remains to be seen whether the Johnson government can actually deliver on them, of course. Either way, though, the idea that we can simply ignore the domestic drivers of such outcomes at the level of individual states or the international system more generally looks highly implausible.

Identity and political transformation

It is not necessary to believe there is such a thing as the 'postmodern geopolitical condition' to recognize that some of the familiar ways we have thought about ourselves, our identities and even our sense of loyalty to what is ultimately an arbitrary, geographically determined group are less certain and more contested. Many of the most irresolvable and enduring conflicts around the world are fought over contested borders and rival claims to sovereign authority, and driven by seemingly non-negotiable questions of identity, ownership and ethnicity. It was ever thus, perhaps. The remarkable feature of the 'rise of the West', in retrospect, is that the creation of the nation-state seemed to have gone some way to resolving some of these questions for some time in some places, at least. That in itself is no small achievement. What is surprising at this moment in history is that the stability and future of even such an apparently foundational piece of institutional architecture is no longer assured.[40] One of the more important factors that is undermining its centrality – in some parts of the world, at least – is the seemingly declining commitment of the people who ultimately constitute it as a distinctive the nation-state. Ultimately, loyalty to a state and its particular identity involves a process of socialization, which seems to be less effective. In a world where other sources of identity are becoming more important and confidence in national political elites and economic structures in the West in particular is in decline, the implications for domestic and international order are potentially profound, especially where achieving consensus on climate action is concerned. There are signs, however, that even in the likes of the US and Australia, which are notorious laggards on climate action, popular opinion and sentiment is shifting decisively.[41]

If the rise of identity politics is significant and revealing in an already diminished power such as Britain, how much more important are such forces in the case of the reigning hegemon, which is also convulsed by radically opposed views about the future of the nation. As with the UK, there are now serious and sober discussions about whether the US can, or even should, remain a single political entity.[42] It is frequently observed, for example, that on its own California is one of the largest economies in the world, and subsidizes other American states which have little sympathy for its liberal values and life-styles. California is also synonymous with the rise of an influential form of identity politics that is eroding more traditional forms of social identification and consciousness, which is directly impacting on traditional political alignments and forms of mobilization. Francis Fukuyama argues that this is an especially difficult challenge for more traditional forms of mass mobilization associated with class consciousness, but which are now being supplanted by debates about gender, ethnicity and narrower sectional interests: 'The problem with the contemporary left is the particular forms of identity that it has increasingly chosen to celebrate. Rather than building solidarity around large collectivities such as the working class or the economically exploited, it has focused on ever smaller groups being marginalized in specific ways'.[43]

Whatever one thinks about the merits of this argument, there is little doubt about the polarized, increasingly toxic nature of America's domestic politics and the very real impact this is having on internal stability and the US's role in the world more generally. Indeed, there is a growing interaction between internal and external aspects of American political and strategic behaviour. As I've pointed out in other chapters, many scholars of both IR and international political economy have long argued that the division between domestic and foreign policy has never been clear cut and the boundaries have always been somewhat arbitrary and porous. Yet national security did seem to be one area in which such a notional division made some sort of sense, as the 'security of the nation' was ritually invoked by policymakers everywhere as their primary responsibility, no matter what form of government they were a part of, and how instrumental and self-serving the rhetoric of national security was for the elites that articulated it.

Now, however, even this notional distinction looks less certain. While we might intuitively expect that this makes sense when thinking about the likes of the PRC, where an autocratic government exercises direct control over the military and its actions, or even Indonesia, where the military has played a prominent role since the inception of the nation, it is more surprising in mature democracies where civil–military relations are clearly defined and seemingly uncontroversial. And yet, in the US under the leadership of Donald Trump, such distinctions became less clear cut, and there were growing concerns about how the military might act in the event of a major political crisis over the result of a disputed election, for example.[44] In part, no doubt, this is a consequence of the fact that the US has been at war for the vast majority of its history, and the military has assumed a prominent part in the life of the nation as a result. More troublingly, however, it is argued that 'as police departments increasingly use military tactics, weapons, equipment, and even apparel, domestic policing has come to look more and more like war'.[45]

The plausibility of this claim was on vivid display during the so-called 'Black Lives Matter' protests that erupted in the US in the middle of 2020. Not only was the military employed in a domestic policing role during the widespread civil unrest, but President Trump further inflamed existing racial, attitudinal, identitarian and class tensions with his notably divisive rhetoric.[46] No doubt a more thoughtful, less polarizing figure than Trump might have handled things more effectively. But it is important to recognize that, as we saw in the last chapter, the Trump administration has also been responsible for hollowing out America's state capacity, especially and not only in the area of environmental protection and regulation, but also in other areas, as has become brutally clear during the COVID-19 crisis. As Daron Acemoglu suggests, 'by relentlessly attacking the norms of professionalism, independence, and technocratic expertise, and prioritizing political loyalty above all else, Trump has weakened the federal bureaucracy to such an extent that it is now beginning to resemble a "Paper Leviathan"'. By this Acemoglu means the sorts of

> autocratic states that offer little room for democratic input or criticism of government – and exhibit paper-thin policymaking competence as a result. Bureaucrats in these countries get accustomed to praising, agreeing with, and

taking orders from the top rather than using their expertise to solve problems. The more American bureaucrats come to resemble autocratic yes men, the less society will trust them and the less effective they will be in moments of crisis like this one.[47]

This is not simply a concern about the erosion of institutional infrastructure, however, although that is important enough in itself, as America's health problems and constraints demonstrate all too vividly. Perhaps the most enduring damage will be to the overall political culture of the nation, the growing tribalism, polarization and the loss of faith in governments and those with specialist expertise. The numbers of Americans who think that the COVID-19 epidemic is exaggerated, the result of a conspiracy, or who will refuse to be vaccinated against it, is alarming and revealing.[48] The sort of political capital that is thought to distinguish high-trust societies and provide a key dimension of overall social and personal security has long been in decline in the US;[49] the Trump administration accelerated a process that was already in train, but which now threatens the very basis of social stability in what was formerly seen as the world's leading democracy.

As a result, the internal security of the most powerful country in the world has been threatened in a way it had not been for decades, if not since the Civil War, and this plainly has potentially major international implications, too. At a time of heightened international instability caused by great-power competition and a major health crisis, the chances of accidents, miscalculations and ill-conceived strategic opportunism destabilizing the international order are very real. Old-fashioned interstate rivalry and competition have also directed attention, energy and resources away from the greatest security threat humanity has ever faced, of course. All of which raises questions about the forces that were actually fuelling greater insecurity at both the domestic and international levels, and about the way we understand them.

Culture: strategic, national and international

These sorts of transformations in the nature of national politics and even personal identities are not just important considerations for students of domestic politics. Nor is it only the likes of the late Samuel Huntington that ought to be alert to the significance of different cultures as manifestations and sources of values, ideas and policies. On the contrary, competition between the US and China in particular is likely to be about their very different visions of how the international system should be ordered and the sorts of principles that should inform state behaviour. Richard Higgott suggests that 'at the level of ideas and philosophy on the one hand and policy and practice on the other, the 21st century's new Great Game will now be contested across [a] much wider threefold paradigmatic domain of economics, politics and security, and culture and society'.[50] Culture is invariably an under-appreciated aspect of IR practice and this has potentially major consequences for the way we think about key collective goods problems. As Jack Goldstone argues, 'cultural frameworks act with particular power at times when states are rebuilt or revised at times of state breakdown or crisis'.[51]

Clifford Geertz famously defined culture as 'an historically transmitted pattern of meanings embodied in symbols, a system of inherited conceptions expressed in symbolic forms by means of which men communicate, perpetuate, and develop their knowledge about and attitudes toward life'.[52] While this may sound relatively uncontroversial, problems arise when different and potentially incompatible ideas are promoted or imposed by powerful states, or even come to inform their respective grand strategies, as we shall in the next chapter. At one level, the entire history of Western imperialism generally and American hegemony in particular can be read as a process of attempted ideational colonization in the same way the more familiar economic variety can.[53] In reality, of course, it is rather difficult to separate them, as incorporation into a transnational capitalist economic order inevitably brings about profound changes in the societies on the receiving end of such processes.

What is most noteworthy in this context, perhaps, is not that existing cultural values and practices are impacted upon by powerful external forces, but that indigenous ideas often prove so resilient.[54] China is clearly the most important example of a state where distinctive national attitudes and values have been shaped by hundreds, if not thousands, of years of continuous history; especially the 'one hundred years of shame' that occurred as a consequence of European imperialism.[55] The subsequent 'struggle for status' and peer recognition that has driven foreign policy since the reunification of China under Mao Zedong has to be an essential part of any explanation of contemporary domestic attitudes and foreign policy.[56] The widespread support for Xi Jinping's increasingly assertive and grandiose foreign policies is indicative of just what a powerful force nationalism is in China.[57] Indeed, it is important to remember that when Mao was attempting to reunify the country during and after the civil war, nationalism was a more powerful unifying doctrine than the abstractions of Marxist ideology.[58] It still is.

National culture matters

While it is now increasingly accepted that culture matters, not least to a country or people's developmental experience, some of the differences are worth spelling out, not least because they are generally neglected or ignored by mainstream IR theory. First, national cultures reflect specific historical experiences that can even have an emotional content. The period in which China experienced dynastic collapse, civil war, the violation of its sovereignty and the overturning of traditional values is not known as the century of shame for nothing. As Richard Lebow's pioneering analysis of culture's role in IR theory reminds us, a sense of humiliation and fear, to say nothing of the pursuit of honour and recognition, can powerfully influence the conduct of policymakers and even entire nations. Indeed, Lebow argues that cultural, psychological and emotional factors are 'the principal cause of the breakdown of orders' as 'actors to fear for their ability to satisfy their spirit and/or appetites, and perhaps for their survival'.[59]

Examples of the possible significance of individual and collective psychological traits influencing the behaviour of states are numerous and often glaring, which makes the failure to take them seriously all the more noteworthy. Kaiser Wilhelm's role in creating the conditions within which the First World War erupted has been widely documented and highlights both the dangers of autocratic rule and the potential importance of the personal qualities of national leaders where institutionalized constraints are ineffective or inadequate. Significantly, foreign and domestic policy preferences can also have a degree of contingent path dependency that reflects distinctive national circumstances. For example, North Korea's '*Juche*' policy of national self-reliance may be an extreme manifestation of this possibility, but given the Kim dynasty's destabilizing impact on the security of Northeast Asia, it is hardly an insignificant one as far as IR is concerned.[60] Nor is the impact of poor national leadership confined to 'rogue' states, as the eccentric decision making of Donald Trump vividly demonstrated.

The US also illustrates the importance of national perspectives about what individual states could or *should* do. The sense of national 'exceptionalism' that is such a distinctive feature of the national self-image in the US has played a powerful role in shaping American foreign policy and grand strategic objectives, as we shall see in the next chapter. The idea that the US might have a God-given duty to act in particular ways to fulfil a special purpose is not just self-righteous flummery. On the contrary, the extraordinarily high level of defence spending on conventional threats that distinguishes American foreign policy can be explained in no small part by the perceived need to achieve 'full spectrum strategic dominance', in which the US dominates the air, land, maritime, space and information environment.[61] Even more strikingly, aspects of the increased militarization of foreign policy are now becoming evident in the domestic sphere too, as the heavy-handed response to the 'Black Lives Matter' campaign reminds us.[62] Given that at least one former American president – Dwight D. Eisenhower – was concerned about the potentially pernicious, self-serving impact of what he famously called the 'military-industrial complex', it is surprising that the political influence on, and even cultural impact of, security policy is not given greater attention when accounting for national strategic and public policy.

Despite the prominence of realist thinking in the US, it is noteworthy that the possible influence of nationally specific strategic doctrines has long been part of the study of *other* countries' policies. It is worth remembering that America's entire grand strategy after the Second World War, when it was immediately plunged into a potentially even more dangerous confrontation with the Soviet Union, was profoundly influenced by George Kennan's 'Long Telegram', in which he highlighted what he saw as the fundamental, historically contingent, culturally embedded drivers of strategic policy: 'At bottom of [the] Kremlin's neurotic view of world affairs is [a] traditional and instinctive Russian sense of insecurity'.[63] In other words, despite the rhetoric of Marxist ideology (and in much the same way as China) national attitudes in the Soviet Union were shaped by deep-seated fears and anxieties and commonly held, inherited worldviews that owed much more to historically ingrained cultural attitudes and values than they did to the rational calculations of grand strategists.

One of the key insights that can be drawn from psychology, therefore, is that 'identity ultimately determines attitudes by weighting certain information as more important or better than other information'.[64] Significantly, this claim can be made about the supposedly dispassionate architects of grand strategy as well as the 'ordinary' men and women who are, for better or worse, on the receiving end of their master plans. The impact of such grand strategizing outside of policymaking communities is considered later; the point to note at this juncture is that even policy elites are part of distinctive intellectual and social milieus that are highly contingent and anything but identical. Robert Jervis has been at the forefront of applying insights drawn from psychology to explain the way that intense pressure on decision makers and the need to simplify vast amounts of information can create 'serious discrepancies between the perceived and the actual environment'.[65] One of the reasons why interest in the possible importance of different strategic cultures has grown is because of their potential to explain different ideas about nuclear strategy and deterrence during the Cold War.

This focus on the social construction of reality is, as we saw in Chapter 2, part of a more general growing interest in the way in which 'cultural environments affect not only the incentives for different kinds of behaviour but also the basic character of states'.[66] The significance of this trend when thinking about the factors that influence strategic behaviour is that states have distinctive identities, too, and this may influence the way they behave in the same 'structured' environments.[67] Perhaps the most noteworthy, counter-intuitive feature of the international system in this regard is not only that state behaviour is frequently shaped by rules and norms that make it anything but anarchical and atomistic, but also that states are designated by their peers as actual or potential friends and enemies. One of the striking examples of countries that are unambiguously 'friends' and often formal allies is the so-called 'Anglosphere' countries whose close ties, Vucetic argues, 'are racial rather than liberal-democratic'.[68] Whatever the merits of that argument, it is evident that some states *do* develop enduring ties, and even the capacity to form 'security communities', such as those that exist in Western Europe under the North Atlantic Treaty Organization (NATO) and – to a lesser extent – in the Association of Southeast Asian Nations (ASEAN). Compatible ideas about identity, values and security and 'dependable expectations of peaceful change' are part of this process.[69] So, too, are the strategic cultures that shape national preferences.

Strategic cultures

Of all the factors that shape strategic policy and ideas about security one of the most neglected is the impact of the distinctive intellectual, social and cultural milieus in which national policy emerges. As we've seen, neo-realists are the most extreme proponents of the view that the actions of policymakers and populations at the national level can be ignored, as strategic policy is essentially driven by the imperatives of regime survival. While there may be some merit in this claim, the reality is that some countries go about the pursuit of national security in very different ways, and this has major consequences for their behaviour as international and strategic actors. Even at the height of the Cold War, when the behaviour of the two principal protagonists appeared to be profoundly influenced by the bipolar structure of the international system, it became apparent that the Soviet Union and the

US had significantly different views of the world and their respective places in it, and that this might influence the way they behaved as a result. Such insights are not confined to traditional security issues. On the contrary, the priority given to environmental issues as a potential threat is also profoundly affected by the relative importance attached to competing and often incompatible policy goals.[70]

Even though Allison's seminal analysis of the Cuban missile crisis was still grounded in the 'rational actor paradigm', it recognized that some individuals and their ideas about strategic reality played pivotal roles in deciding how states could and should behave. The possibility that rationality might be 'bounded' by the 'physical and psychological limits of man's capacity as alternative generator, informational processer, and problem solver', and that this might 'constrain the decision-making processes of individuals and organisations', was an important development, even if the language was rather formulaic.[71] This basic insight was developed by Colin Gray in particular in another influential contribution that drew attention to the different 'strategic cultures' that existed in the US and the Soviet Union. Gray argued that the influence of distinctive national strategic cultures had the effect of socializing members of national strategic policymaking elites into particular ways of thinking, even about seemingly deterministic, structurally decisive issues such as nuclear weapons.[72]

Invariably, therefore, the way governing elites think about broadly similar problems – the security of the nation and the kinds of strategic policies that might best achieve it – can differ significantly and affect the sorts of decisions policymakers take. The most dramatic examples of this possibility are so-called 'rogue states', such as North Korea, which seem to deviate from 'normal' forms of behaviour. But history is replete with examples of policymakers making bad decisions because of intense pressure and the consequent failure to understand and accurately interpret the intent of potential or actual adversaries. This is why the idea of different strategic cultures, or what Glenn describes as 'a set of shared beliefs, and assumptions derived from common experiences and accepted narratives (both oral and written), that shape collective identity and relationships to other groups, and which influence the appropriate ends and means chosen for achieving security objectives',[73] can be such an important 'intervening variable'.

It is not necessary to cite examples of radical outliers such as North Korea to see the potential value of strategic culture as an explanatory tool. On the contrary, Australia provides one of the best illustrations of a country whose strategic options and thinking are profoundly influenced by its unique history, its geography and its policymakers' congenital sense of vulnerability. The decision to support the US in its disastrously ill-conceived invasion of Iraq – despite Australia having no obvious strategic stake in the Middle East – becomes easier to understand in the context of its distinctive ideational and normative inheritance. As Bloomfield and Nossal argue, Australia's distinctive strategic culture not only accounts for past policy preferences but helps to explain the continuity in strategic policy thinking, despite the radical changes that have occurred in the region of which it is a part.[74] Even the highly unpredictable behaviour of its principal ally and notional security guarantor under the erratic leadership of Donald Trump did little to change Australia's basic security posture. On the contrary, Australian policymakers have gone out of their way to demonstrate their fealty to the US, even when this negatively impacts the country's relationship with China, its largest trade partner.[75]

It might be argued that the options for a 'middle power' like Australia are far more constrained than those of a great power such as the US or China. Plainly there is something in this argument, and the rise of both China and Donald Trump provides a major test for any theory that hopes to explain, much less predict, how the US or any other country will behave in an era characterized by an agglomeration of health, environmental, economic and strategic challenges. And yet there is no doubt that the idea of distinctive strategic cultures can explain why some ideas and orientations to strategic policy have persisted in China,[76] and the particular manner in which even the US, as the most powerful state in the world, has employed its unique capabilities. As Bradley Klein suggests, the notion of strategic culture helps to explain

> the state's war-making style, understood in terms of its military institutions and its accumulated strategic traditions of air, land and naval power. But strategic culture is more than mere military style, for it emerges from an infrastructure of technology and an armaments sector. Most importantly, it is based upon the political ideologies of public discourse that help define occasions as worthy of military involvement.[77]

The big question in the context of contemporary international and domestic politics is whether Joe Biden will prove capable of repairing the damage of the Trump years, allowing the return of diplomatic and strategic business as usual, as so many hope. It's important to recognize, however, that the norms and values that have been traditionally associated with American grand strategy have been responsible for

America's involvement in numerous wars, often to the detriment of the US itself. These issues are taken up in more detail in the next chapter, but a few preliminary points may be made here that are directly relevant to the role played by ideas, culture and even the strengths and weaknesses of individual leaders. As I shall explain, the potential consequences of bad leadership and the persistence of inappropriate ideas are not confined to the international level, or even the realm of formal domestic politics.

Cultural concatenation

One of the reasons why at least some IR scholars have drawn on the insights of psychologists, sociologists and even anthropologists to explain decision making and the persistence of national policy differences is because more 'parsimonious' approaches are not capable of explaining some of the most significant developments in the practice of international and domestic politics. The failure to predict the peaceful end of the Cold War and its aftermath is perhaps the most egregious example of this possibility. Equally importantly, some of the more traditional approaches to IR theorizing are uninterested in and/or incapable of explaining the social and even ideational transformations that underpinned epochal events. For example, a loss of faith in Soviet-style communism was clearly a major contributing factor to its downfall, especially outside the Soviet Union itself.[78]

The sorts of epochal shifts in the polarity of the international system that occurred at the end of the Cold War as it dramatically shifted from a familiar bipolar, super power-dominated order to something else, are exceptional and infrequent. Trying to decide how much weight to place on the actions of individuals and how much on longer-term structural transformations and shifts in the relative balance of material forces is no easy task. On the one hand, individuals such as Ronald Regan, Mikhail Gorbachev and even the Polish trade union leader Lech Wałęsa, played prominent roles in the downfall of the Soviet empire.[79] On the other hand, the long-term inability of the Soviet model of development to match the levels of economic development in the West created the conditions in which leadership, or even protean power, could be decisive. What we can say, perhaps, is that shifts in consciousness on the part of key actors — and on the part of the individuals who make up different societies more generally — can make the difference between change and continuity. The most dramatic example of this possibility was the dramatic and instantaneous collapse of the authority and infrastructure of power that surrounded the Romanian dictator, Nicolae Ceaușescu.

While 'Ceaușescu moments' may be infrequent, they are a reminder that significant changes in domestic and international orders are invariably turbulent, rather than linear progressions. In a seminal contribution to our understanding of such processes James Rosenau distinguished between three different 'parameters' within which national and international change unfolded. In addition to a 'structural' parameter composed of regimes, alliances, legal conventions and other formal arrangements, he suggested that a 'relational' parameter composed of hierarchal authority relationships, such as national class structures and patterns of international dependency, formed an overarching framework in which change occurred. Importantly for the purposes of this discussion, however, Rosenau also emphasized the crucial role played by what he called a 'micro parameter', or the 'predispositions and practices by which people relate to higher authority, a cluster that includes their loyalties, legitimacy sentiments, compliance habits, analytic skills and cathectic capabilities'.[80]

It has long been noted that in the more affluent enclaves of the global capitalist economy, post-material values are becoming more commonplace and even influential, especially in connection with heightened consciousness about environmental problems. For Marxist scholars, such as David Harvey, this 'dematerialization' of the economy has essentially structural causes that reflect the irreconcilable internal contradictions of capitalism.[81] As we have seen, these are exacerbated by the biophysical limits of the planet itself and its ability to support growing numbers of people aspiring to consumption-oriented life-styles. In this context, however, it's worth re-emphasizing that the dilemmas of 'postmodernity' and the 'cultural dominance of late capitalism'[82] are arguably good problems to have – at least when compared to the struggles for existence that continue to confront so many people around the world. The implications of global inequality are taken up in more detail in Chapter 6. The point to stress here is that just because the 'postmodern condition' and the rise of identity politics might strike some readers as slightly self-indulgent 'First World' problems, this does not make them any less real to those that endure them. On the contrary, if security is to be meaningful, even the heightened sensibilities of the so-called 'snowflake generation' will have to be addressed.[83] Even more importantly, perhaps, if and when such insecurities become the basis for political mobilization, they can impact on some of the most important countries in the world, even when such states are anything but democratic.[84]

As we saw in Chapter 3, environmental politics, especially in the West, is becoming an increasingly prominent part of social activism, even if it has failed to transform the way human beings generally interact with the natural environment. Nevertheless, what Appadurai calls 'culturalism' is an increasingly prominent 'feature of movements involving identities consciously in the making'.[85] Although a good deal of recent analytical attention has been paid to the increased prominence of solipsistic individualism, it is important to recognize that collective identities remain potentially important sources of state behaviour. As Goldgeir points out, 'public perceptions based in large part on issues of identity are crucial, and any notion of in-group and out-group, who is legitimate and who is a threat to national culture, is heavily driven by psychological needs to simplify the world and maintain group solidarity'.[86] The possibility that the identity and self-perception of populations may have important cognitive and even emotional impacts has become an increasingly prominent part of at least some IR scholarship as it attempts to explain otherwise aberrant social realities and their potential impact on national policy.[87]

Identity and emotion

The possible importance of traumatic and emotional collective experiences is most apparent in the contexts of war and its aftermath. The idea that nationalism has fuelled conflict since it became such a prominent part of the international system in 19th-century Europe is uncontroversial. The possibility that national sentiments, identities, emotions and fundamental insecurities might shape domestic politics and foreign policy was starkly demonstrated in very different ways by their impact on those on the losing side of the First and Second World Wars. The perception within Germany that it had been unfairly treated after the First World War helped to create the febrile domestic atmosphere that led to the rise of fascism and all the well-known horrors that accompanied it. Unsurprisingly, perhaps, after the Second World War the trauma of defeat and the pervasive sense of shame that surrounded revelations about the Holocaust exerted a powerful influence on post-war politics in Germany. Ironically, Germany is now criticized for not acting like a 'normal' country and developing a military capacity in line with its economic importance. Mainstream IR theory struggles to explain such apparent anomalies.[88]

Nor is Germany unique in this regard. Japan, the other defeated power in the Second World War, became even more emphatic in its rejection of the sort of militarism that ultimately culminated in disastrous and deeply traumatising defeat. It is one thing to lose a conventional war, it is quite another to be the only country in history to be subjected to attack with nuclear weapons. Little wonder, perhaps, that the entire country seemed eager to repudiate the past and concentrate on rebuilding the shattered economy. In this regard Japan was even more successful than Germany and pioneered a new form of 'trading state' in which economic development was privileged over more conventional and discredited forms of power and a norm of anti-militarism became deeply embedded across much of Japanese society.[89] Despite the efforts of a later generation of policymakers such as Abe Shinzō to turn Japan into a 'normal' country, it has proved difficult to make fundamental changes to Japan's celebrated 'peace constitution', which forbids it from taking offensive military action. The point to emphasize, as Crawford suggests, is that 'fear and other emotions are not only attributes of agents, they are institutionalized in the structures and processes of world politics'.[90]

It might be objected that Japan and Germany are exceptions to a more generalized rule about state behaviour. In some way they are, of course, as few countries have experienced anything like the physical and psychological devastation that they did. Although the Soviet Union lost nearly 17 million people or 15% of its population during the Second World War, first Stalin and now Putin have been able to turn this into an epic tale of noble sacrifice in defence of the nation that ended in decisive victory.[91] Much the same story could be told about China's even more traumatic experience during the Second World War, in which some 20 million people perished; this has not stopped the current PRC leadership from turning this into a similarly triumphalist discourse.[92] Significantly, in both countries the discursive construction of a narrative about an ultimately triumphant collective effort is still utilized as a source of nationalist identity. It is precisely the potential importance of in-group and out-group identities, and their potential utilization in nationalist causes, that has been highlighted and explained by political psychologists.[93]

Seen in this context, nation-states have an ambiguous position in debates about security. On the one hand, they are – potentially, at least – one of the most important mechanisms for overcoming the sense of vulnerability and fear that confronts human beings living in a supposedly anarchical state of nature, which underpins so much conventional thinking about international and domestic politics. The state has proved itself to be especially adept at solving collective action problems such as the defence of sovereign territory. On the other hand, however, they can entrench and exacerbate the divisions between nations that determine which states are deemed as possible friends and enemies, an idea famously propagated by the Nazi ideologue and political theorist Carl Schmitt.[94] In this sense, states are more than simply paradigmatic bureaucratic entities, judicial systems and controllers of organized violence. Even if we put to one side the extent of state capacity that distinguishes one country from another, there is still the all-important question about the purposes to which such potential is put.

Alexander Wendt – before his quantum epiphany – argued that in order to explain differences in state behaviour, goals and even the sorts interests they pursue, it makes sense to think of states as 'real actors to which we can legitimately attribute anthropomorphic qualities like desires, beliefs, and intentionality'.[95] Germany before the Second World War was a very different country than it was after the war, and it was perceived as such by other states. How else do we explain the pivotal role played by former foes Germany and France in the creation of a united Europe? At the same time, however, the German experience is a salutary reminder of the fact that a nationalist and racist ideology can make states a danger to not only the rest of the 'international community' but also to their own populations. Indeed, one of the more striking features of the state's role in contemporary international politics is that it is often the greatest potential threat to the people it claims to represent.[96] The form that states assume and the purposes to which state power are put are far from inevitable, and this has major consequences for the practice of IR. It also helps to explain why domestic security can be so varied and elusive even where states possess the capacity to provide ample conventional security. Such differences and the contradictory impulses that inform them have been painfully exposed in the COVID-19 crisis.

COVID-19: the new face of insecurity?

If the coronavirus pandemic has done nothing else, it has caused many people – and not just in the scholarly or policymaking communities – to think seriously about what it means to be secure and the nature of the threats that are actually likely to impact directly on people's lives. One of the most strikingly incongruent features of the COVID-19 crisis has been the shocking lack or preparedness on the part of policymakers and even specialist health officials in the West, where a noteworthy degree of complacency had developed about the possible impact of 'Third World problems'.[97] It hardly needs to be pointed out that no similar nonchalance about possible security threats existed in more conventional strategic arenas, as rich and poor nations alike continued to ramp up spending on expensive weapons systems that seemed increasingly unlikely to be used – against other states, at least. The militarization of domestic security, by contrast, continues unabated, even in those countries that thought of themselves as role models of good governance.[98]

Given the dominance of conventional ideas about the nature of security and the sorts of dangers that even the most 'developed' countries face, the overwhelming focus on the security of the nation-state is both unsurprising and unforgivable. Many health specialists – and even the likes of Bill Gates – had been warning that the outbreak of the pandemic that affected the North and South alike was inevitable at some stage, and it was incumbent upon governments everywhere to prepare. The abject failure of governments to do so was both an indictment of public policy and testimony to the impact of 'neoliberal'-style policies on public infrastructure generally and the healthcare system in particular. The shortcomings of a chronically underfunded and inequitable American system were thrown into especially sharp relief and compared badly with China's rather brutal but ultimately effective authoritarian response.

The impact of economic policies and pervasive inequality will be taken up in more detail in Chapter 6. What merits emphasis at this point is that many observers had become increasingly convinced of both the theoretical shortcomings and practical failures of conventional thinking about security long before COVID-19 laid bare the inadequacy of the rich world's response to a crisis from which there was seemingly no escape. The notion of 'human security' had first been promoted by the United Nations Development Programme (UNDP), in a landmark report in 1994.[99] The UNDP's key contribution was to shift the focus away from the state and the conventional preoccupation with interstate war and/or domestic stability, and toward seven new categories: political, personal, food, health, environmental, economic and community security. In short, as Edward Newman points out, human security 'seeks to challenge attitudes and institutions that privilege so-called "high politics" above individual experiences of deprivation and insecurity'.[100]

Despite a growing body of academic literature that utilizes the human security concept and which draws attention to the 'power structures that determine who enjoys the entitlement to security and who does not',[101] as we saw in the last chapter, it has not had a significant impact on the way most analysts think about security issues. To be sure, there is a growing recognition among security planners and strategists that global warming is real and having an impact on the potential causes of conflict, but the focus remains predominantly on the way that *states* will be affected. Deciding how to respond to threats to the sovereignty and security of the nation–state, not to the individuals who ultimately constitute such entities, remains the principal focus of attention and government spending.[102] It is important to note that although it is dawning on security analysts that state security is actually threatened by climate change, there is little recognition of, much less preparedness to deal with the consequences of, the complex interaction between humans and the natural environment. The emergence of COVID-19 is widely thought – conspiracy theories notwithstanding – to have resulted from our growing impact on the habitats of animals that subsequently interact with humans and other animals in 'unnatural' ways that generate new pathogens as a result. This is yet another feature of the Anthropocene that is threatening our collective security and raising fundamental questions about our national and international priorities as a consequence.

Or it ought to be. Perhaps no more significant illustration of the failure to take new problems seriously can be seen than the omission of health issues on national and international security agendas. Part of the problem confronting those actors who are trying to encourage greater policy coordination and preparedness in this issue area is the same as that confronting climate change: the transnational and novel nature of the problem means that collective action is complex. As Adams et al point out, 'biosecurity requires consideration of the critical relationships among economic systems, transportation systems, quarantine, and control systems and, above all, the international relations mechanisms that may be called into play when negotiating transborder biosecurity'.[103] Put simply, even with the best political will in the world, the immediacy and complexity of the problem make international cooperation inherently difficult.[104] What is more surprising, perhaps, is that possible cooperation has been undermined by the politicization of the problem and its consequent role in interstate competition and diplomacy. Even more remarkably, there were suggestions from both the US and China that the availability of any possible vaccine would be restricted to their own populations or those of key allies.[105] Even human health, it seems, can be weaponized.

A very national malaise?

The COVID-19 crisis is highlighting the failures of more than comparative national health policies and even the leadership qualities of the people who are ultimately responsible for them. While many might agree that the performance of the Trump administration generally and the president in particular were startlingly incompetent and inept, some of these failings can be ascribed to distinctive national characteristics. Not only are many Americans incapable of recognizing the shockingly inadequate and inequitable provision of basic healthcare in the US, but there is an inability or unwillingness to draw lessons from international best practice, especially in the midst of an intensifying rivalry with China. Jeremy Konyndyk argues that

> The catastrophic U.S. response to COVID-19 is not primarily the result of scientific or medical deficiencies. Rather, it is the product of an insularity in U.S. politics and culture. American exceptionalism – the notion that the United States is unique among nations and that the American way is invariably the best – has blinded the country's leaders (and many of its citizens) to potentially lifesaving lessons from other countries.[106]

As the US continued to lead the world in terms of the numbers of its citizens that had succumbed to the pandemic, there was evidence that it was finally dawning on even some of Trump's fabled 'base' that things were not going well, and that their own security was directly threatened by the president's incompetence, ignorance and an inadequately funded healthcare system. Whether this will be sufficient to transform either the toxic polarization and paralysis of America's domestic politics or the scepticism about – even hostility toward – expertise is another question altogether. In part this reflects another failure of American public policy: the fact that the US provides either the world's best or some of the world's worst forms of education.[107] Under such circumstances it is hardly surprising that many citizens find it hard to understand complex issues like climate change, the origins of pandemics and the complex effects of 'globalization'. Even some of us who study such things for a living do.

What is less forgivable is that powerful, self-interested actors have been able to influence public policy debates in the US in ways that suit their interests, and which consequently make any objective analysis of 'the facts' about issues such as climate change or the best way to deal with environmentally generated threats such as pandemics all the more difficult. That vested interests might seek to influence public policy debates in ways that suit their interests will surprise no one, perhaps. Even the fact that lobbying in the US has become such an integral, influential and seemingly indispensable part of the American political system and the policymaking process is either a widely accepted reality or poorly understood by those who might be most adversely affected by its consequences. The role of 'Big Pharma' is the quintessential example of this possibility, and one that has been thrown into sharp relief during the recent pandemic.[108]

There are two interconnected points that merit emphasis about such developments that have consequences that go beyond the coronavirus pandemic. First, without adequate regulation, or – even more problematically – with the active complicity and support of government, private interests will inevitably benefit at the expense of the public good. As David Rothkopf observes, 'history demonstrates that when the power of the state is reduced, with alarming regularity, it does not benefit average citizens so much as it does private sector actors well positioned to swoop in and take best advantage of the opening'.[109] When the state is actually intent on winding back regulations that 'discourage' business investment, incentives and entrepreneurship, the potential problems are multiplied. The sort of nexus between private capital and an accommodating political class became even more entrenched under the Trump administration, with the result, as Robert Reich points out, that 'there is no longer any significant countervailing power, no force to constrain or balance the growing political strength of large corporations, Wall Street, and the very wealthy. The middle class and poor – and the economic interests they encompass – have little or no agency'.[110]

The second consequence of the growing spread of disinformation and special pleading by vested interests is increasing uncertainty and anxiety about the nature of public policy problems and the best ways of addressing them. The COVID-19 pandemic and climate change are the most immediate and consequential examples of this possibility. Difficult, 'unprecedented', 'wicked' policy problems have been rendered even more intractable by the fact that many people have diminished confidence in the value of expertise or specialist knowledge.[111] Climate change is the definitive example of an issue area where the findings and conclusions of experts specializing in the topic have been routinely dismissed and discredited by sceptics or those who choose to ignore the overwhelming scientific consensus because it suits their interests to do so. No doubt such political and epistemic realities will be understood by anyone having read this far through a book like this. And that, of course, is part of a very paradoxical problem: the consumption of information in an age where it has never been so readily available is either not happening or selective, biased and ideological.[112] Indeed, in another irony, we live in anything but a post-ideological age, and this has potentially important consequences for effective democracy.[113]

The consequences of these institutionally embedded changes are especially pernicious, self-destructive and evident in the US, which Tom Nichols describes as 'a country obsessed with the worship of its own ignorance'.[114] While this may seem a little harsh, supporting evidence for this thesis is not hard to find. Only half of Americans said they would get vaccinated against the coronavirus, should a vaccine be developed.[115] The number of Americans who continue to support Donald Trump, despite the fact that he is manifestly unqualified intellectually and morally for the position he held, and that most of his policies did little to advance the interests or material position of his base, might be cited as another example, and one with potentially far-reaching consequences for the international system, of course, as we shall see in the next chapter. The point to stress here, which is generally ignored by most mainstream approaches to IR, is that much of Trump's success, like that of populists everywhere, can be attributed to a visceral response that owes little to the idealized rhetoric that accompanies ideological claims about the superiority of democracy generally and the American version in particular. On the contrary, the outcome is doubly damning where 'emotion is an unassailable defence against expertise, a moat of anger and resentment in which reason and knowledge quickly drown'.[116]

The world after Trump

The great expectation among many commentators and scholars, as well as America's friends and adversaries, is that under Joe Biden normal service will be resumed as far as the domestic and foreign policies of the US are concerned. But even if this proves to be the case, the pathologies that have been revealed in the American political system and the growing prominence of authoritarian alternatives have raised serious and plausible questions about the durability and even the utility of democracy.[117] Unthinkable as such a possibility remains for many American observers, democracy was in trouble before Mr Trump arrived, not least because the possible rationality and knowledgeability of the voting public seems to have been seriously overestimated. It is important to remember that a record number of people voted for Donald Trump, and they and their grievances are not going to disappear. As Achen and Bartels point out, 'voters, even the most informed voters, typically make choices not on the basis of policy preferences or ideology, but on the basis of who they are – their social identities'.[118]

Given the pivotal role that the nation–state has played in recent human history and the central place it assumes in IR theory, the social construction of very different national identities occupies a surprisingly small part in mainstream thinking, or is entirely absent. And yet, not only are such intangible, non-material factors potentially important even at the best of times, but they become especially critical at moments of crisis when familiar, reassuring patterns of existence are suddenly overturned and replaced by fear and anxiety about the most personal and existential of questions. Under such circumstances, laudable and altruistic ideas about possible responsibilities to others, at either the individual or the state level, begin to look problematic, to say the least. Intergovernmental institutions such as the EU, which are already wrestling with increasingly resisted questions of regional identity, are especially vulnerable to such challenges, as the increasingly less-generous treatment of would-be migrants demonstrates. Even more problematically for those who see the EU as a pioneer of alternative, more cosmopolitan forms of governance, Greenhill argues that 'citizens of any given EU member state would only be able to strengthen their sense of EU identity to the extent that the boundary between the EU and the rest of the world is accentuated'.[119]

In the meantime, at times of stress and in the face of major challenges, people look to states to protect them and reinforce their security. Consequently, questions of belonging, identity and membership of in- and out-groups assume greater importance as we are reminded that 'politics is the effort to define oneself with the nation or some other cultural grouping'.[120] In such circumstances the state is not simply a technocratic instrument with which to resolve collective action problems, but an expression of personal feelings and a threatened sense of identity. Krastev and Holmes's perceptive analysis of the success of populist figures such as Viktor Orbán in Eastern Europe makes it clear that part of his appeal lies in the fact that many people resented the imposition of foreign values and the implicit criticism of their former identities. They suggest that 'a refusal to genuflect before the liberal West has become the hallmark of the illiberal counter-revolution throughout the post-communist world and beyond'. Moreover, Krastev and Holmes suggest that:

> Shame at reshaping one's preferences to conform to the value hierarchies of foreigners, doing so in the name of freedom, and being looked down upon for the supposed inadequacy of the attempt – these are the emotions and experiences that have fuelled the anti-liberal counter-revolution ... that has now metastasized worldwide.[121]

While the US is not Hungary, and has never been on the receiving end of such externally imposed demands for reform, it is striking how much of the support for populist leaders such as Trump and Boris Johnson has come from people whose sense of identity and security has been threatened by unwelcome and seemingly unmanageable social change.[122] The impact of global forces and growing economic inequality is considered in more detail in Chapter 6, but it is worth emphasizing that many of the factors that allowed Trump to rise to power have not gone away and may continue to exert an influence on America's engagement with the rest of the world. In other words, Trump is arguably a symptom of wider long-term effects with which his successor will have to deal. Analysts who emphasize the importance of 'structural' influences on the conduct of IR may have a point; but the way such long-running transformations and changes in the distribution of power play out is anything but inevitable.

The possibility that ingrained habits of thought, perceptions and assumptions might render policymakers incapable of addressing new realities is, perhaps, unsurprising. The difficulty many British people and policymakers have had in coming to terms with that country's reduced status and importance is one of the more noteworthy examples of this possibility.[123] More consequentially, there is a continuing debate about the influence of what has been described as 'the Blob', or the foreign policy elites who influence the conduct and content of American foreign policy, and whether they, too, are incapable of recognizing the changed circumstances with which the US must contend. One of the key questions in this context is whether the Trump presidency has inflicted permanent damage on the reputation, authority and capacity of the US as a foreign policy actor. Equally importantly, will a re-empowered Blob prove anymore capable of reconfiguring American foreign policy priorities under Biden than it was under his predecessors?

This is not simply a question of theoretical interest to the IR community. For some observers, the US policy-making elite 'is not the problem. It is the solution'. Brands et al argue that

> the foreign policy establishment is an American strength rather than weakness. It is more open-minded and accountable than its critics allow. It acts as a storehouse of accumulated professional wisdom, providing intellectual ballast to the ship of state. On balance, the establishment's practical track record has been impressive, with some well-known fiascos outweighed by many quiet successes.[124]

But even sympathetic observers would have to concede that the 'fiascos' have been massive in both the strategic and economic arenas. Equally importantly, perhaps, no matter how the Blob's performance is judged, the idea that America's policymaking elites and institutions can survive the Trump presidency intact is anything but certain. As Emma Ashford points out, 'Trump's administration is not replete with incompetents because he questioned the foreign policy status quo; he has been unable to staff his administration because many capable people concluded that they could not in good conscience serve this president, while others' willingness to criticize him barred them from service'.[125]

While there is little question that Trump's administration had a destabilizing, if not a corrupting, influence on the foreign policy establishment and its guiding assumptions,[126] it is far from clear that even if American foreign policy returned to a more 'normal' and familiar pattern this would necessarily be a good thing. As we shall see in more detail in the next chapter, the grand strategy of the US has not always been unambiguously synonymous with 'America's national interest', no matter how this loaded and socially constructed term is defined. As Ted Hopf persuasively argues, ingrained habits and the dominance of conventional wisdom can have pernicious consequences that fly in the face of many of the foundational assumptions of IR theory: 'Since habit is automatic and unreflective, it is not rational, not even boundedly rational, as there is no deliberate consideration of even one alternative to what is automatically perceived and practiced'.[127] Unfortunately, the routinized and unchallenged acceptance of conventional wisdom applies to many advocates of mainstream IR theory as much as it does to members of strategic communities who share similar assumptions and worldviews.

Concluding remarks

This chapter has paid a lot of attention to the US and the Trump presidency, not simply because the US is still the world's most powerful state but because there is still a very real possibility that its internal political struggles over identity, justice and power may transform not just its domestic politics but its role as an international actor as well. The implications of America's repudiation of many of the international institutions it helped to create are perhaps the most consequential and noteworthy example of this possibility, which is explored in more detail in the next chapter. What we have seen in this chapter is that the personality of any president, the cultural traditions and self-image of any nation, and dominant ideas about the nature of security and the way it ought to be pursued not only influence strategic policy but may differentiate it from that of other countries. This is especially consequential in the case of the world's most powerful state. It is no exaggeration to say that inherited notions about a country's perceived role and place in the international order can contribute to what Ringmar describes as a 'public mood', which provides the surprisingly malleable context within which even the grandest of strategies arise.[128]

Indeed, a widely held view of the nation as an actor on the world stage and the sort of role it *ought* to play helps to explain why countries such as the US and China take themselves quite so seriously: it is an expression not simply of their material capabilities but also of the sort of role their leaders feel they should play in international affairs. Chinese people's apparent resentment of foreign criticism, their continued loathing of Japan, the determination to retake Taiwan and restore national unity and pride, can be more easily understood if we think of the country as having an identity, self-image and collective view about how the country should act.[129] To be sure, as Gries rightly points out, 'like all peoples, Chinese are neither innately pacifist nor hardwired for conflict. Instead, history and culture shape how individual Chinese will construe the events of world politics'.[130] But this does not mean that widely held attitudes are not influential or even potentially subject to change. The hostility between China and Japan persists to a surprising degree – especially when compared to former foes Germany and France – despite both societies having changed profoundly since the Second World War, and this suggests that other forces are at work in maintaining the animosity.

Domestic politics continue to play a major role in Sino-Japanese ties, as they do in so many other relationships. What is noteworthy about the current international situation is not simply that 'strong men' and supposedly powerful leaders are back in fashion, but that they are having an increasingly visible effect on the foreign policies of the countries they lead. While this may be relatively unsurprising in an authoritarian regime such as China, it is still rather surprising – even shocking – that this occurred in one of the world's leading democracies where institutionalized constraints on presidential power are supposed to ensure foreign policy continuity and guard against megalomania and/ or gross incompetence. At the time of writing the effectiveness, even the durability, of distinctively American forms of political behaviour look less certain than they have for many years – the election of Joe Biden notwithstanding.

The once unthinkable possibility that democracy in the US might be in real danger and nothing like as secure as many had assumed is not simply an American problem. If Mounk and Foa are correct in their claim that 'the long-standing dominance of a set of consolidated democracies with developed economies and a common alliance structure is coming to an end',[131] then this has potentially profound consequences for the international order that the US did so much to create. It is not only the international impacts of such a development that are likely to prove seismic and transformative, however. On the contrary, the way people in the US think about themselves, their society and the political order that has assumed such an important practical and symbolic importance in everyday life may well be overturned as well. Whatever else this may or may not do, it is likely to undermine further the sense of personal and national security that had already been battered by a series of economic, social, strategic and health shocks.

(Not So?) Grand Strategy

Realists are right about one thing, at least: by definition, great powers have more capacity to influence the behaviour of other states in the international system than do their less-powerful counterparts. Indeed, in the case of so-called 'super-powers' their actions can shape the system itself, even if that was not their intention. The surprisingly peaceful dissolution of the Soviet Union is the quintessential recent example of this possibility. Not only was this development entirely unexpected, not least by the Soviet leadership, but it had the effect of transforming the structure of the international order from bilateral to something else – although there is still some debate about what it actually is.[1] What we can say with some confidence is that no one really saw this coming, not even the structural realists who, as the name suggests, focus intently on the principal 'poles' of the prevailing system. There are plainly limitations to an atomistic, Newtonian worldview when it comes to thinking about IR, even if it's not clear that any other perspective is likely to give a more accurate explanation of current, much less future, behaviour.

These initial observations are not intended as yet another argument for taking domestic politics seriously – although they are inevitably that, too, of course – but as an illustration of the limits to the conscious, goal-oriented power of even the most consequential of countries. They also illustrate how difficult it can be for policymakers and analysts everywhere to recognize underlying changes in key parts of any system, and the possible impact these may have. Because the Cold War balance of power looked so stable and such a fixture of the international order, change seemed almost literally unimaginable for many observers, including – perhaps especially – policy-making elites and security analysts in the Soviet Union and the US. As we saw in the previous chapter, the existence of the Blob at the heart of

American policy-making has created a degree of intellectual inertia. Consequently, some observers persuasively argue that not much has changed in the way the world is viewed and the sorts of threats that are taken seriously: 'the foreign policy establishment's very existence is a barrier to strategic adjustment'.[2] The belief that policymakers in notionally powerful states can control events and exert their will takes some shifting, in part because it so psychologically gratifying to the ego of those calling the metaphorical and literal shots.

Because some nations and the individuals that determine strategic policy clearly do have more capacity to exert influence than others, their thinking, plans and attitudes inevitably assume greater significance. Adolf Hitler is the quintessential example of this possibility, of course. Although it is possible to dismiss Hitler and his henchmen as the mad, drug-addled and aberrant products of an especially unfortunate set of domestic and international circumstances, while he was at the apex of German power Hitler was able to implement his own grand strategic vision, with all the well-known horrors that embraced. While this story is well-enough known, we tend to forget that Hitler was regarded as a 'rational actor' by peers such as the unfortunate Neville Chamberlain.[3] If ever there was a failure to take distinctive domestic contingency seriously enough, this was it.

The point of this historical digression is to highlight a number of important initial comparative possibilities: first, not all grand strategies are alike and they simply cannot be read off from the 'structural' properties of the international system. As we shall see, ideology was such an important and distinctive feature of the Cold War in part because the leaders of the US and the Soviet Union had such different views about the world, its future trajectory and the best strategy for realizing strategic goals. This means that the purposes to which state institutions are put, and the way that the individuals who actually constitute states think about themselves and the social structure of which they are a part, may vary dramatically – and so might the goals and modus operandi of any great power.

The second point to emphasize, then, is that even the grandest of strategies from the most powerful of countries are not created in a historical, geographical, social or political vacuum. On the contrary, time, place, personalities and national identity make a big difference to the sorts of policies particular states adopt and the roles they see themselves as playing. Despite the disappearance of the Soviet Union, many policymakers in the US continue to see themselves as playing a special role in world history and fulfilling a sense of 'manifest destiny'.[4] The consequences for other, lesser lights in the international order might be problematic at any time when a nation suffers from such delusions of grandeur. But when both the US and China – its principal peer competitor – consider themselves to be 'exceptional' nations fulfilling a historical destiny,[5] then realists might be right to fret about the prospects for conflict. Whether they reach such conclusions for plausible reasons is another question, however.

This chapter examines why and how especially powerful states feel the need to develop grand strategies, and what makes them merit the moniker. Consequently, much of the discussion focuses on the current, albeit possibly declining, hegemonic power – the US – and its principal putative challenger – China. At the outset it's worth asking whether other, less-powerful states actually have the capacity to implement grand strategic objectives, even if they wanted to. Does it make sense to think of New Zealand having a grand strategy, for example? Some observers think that even the modestly credentialed Australian state ought to develop one.[6] And yet, even if it intuitively seems that only the most powerful of states can develop and implement them, it's worth asking what makes grand strategies grand, and what accounts for their particular and distinctive features.

It's also important to consider whether grand strategies can actually be realized or provide the basis for a coherent set of policies and goals that are appropriate for the early 21st century. It is not controversial to suggest that, as a result of the growing impact of global warming and other environmentally driven changes, the nature of security challenges and the best ways of achieving them have – in some ways, at least – changed significantly. If the COVID-19 crisis has done nothing else, it should have demonstrated to security analysts and policymakers around the world that some of the most immediate threats to human security do no emanate from other states and cannot be defeated by even the most sophisticated weapons systems.

Grand strategy: a short history

According to a recent review of grand strategy by Richard Betts, 'there is less in the idea of this voguish concept than meets the eye'. The reason for this scepticism is his belief that it is a 'grandiose' description of 'what actually drives government's actions'.[7] There is plainly something in this claim. But it's also true that the consequences and ambitions of some countries' strategic policies, and their theoretical ability to actually pursue them, set them apart from 'normal' states. It's not entirely surprising that the relative handful of states that fall into the great power category historically might generate policymakers who take themselves rather more seriously than their counterparts in, say, Vanuatu, Columbia, Kazakhstan, Tanzania or Poland, to take a fairly random assortment. We might never have had to wrestle with the horrors of Hitler if he'd stayed in Austria rather than becoming the head of one of the great powers of Europe, for example. While it's not surprising that policymakers are prone to fits of historical hubris when they have the requisite state capacity to enact their plans or fantasies, what is more surprising, perhaps, is that the populations that they claim to represent often support or even encourage them in their dreams and delusions.

Hitler is such an extreme example of the condition that it is not wise to extrapolate from such a unique and, we hope, extremely unlikely set of circumstances. But less virulent forms of the similar pathologies can be seen in other, more supposedly 'rational' leaders and enlightened countries. Victorian Britain was notorious for taking itself rather seriously as the leader of the 'civilized world', a quality that allowed it colonize and exploit vast tracts of the supposedly uncivilized parts. The presumed obligations that flowed from the 'White man's burden' even had their own theories of Darwinian racial and civilizational superiority in the form of Herbert Spencer's 'scientific' approach to human development.[8] The historian Arnold Toynbee's account of the rise and fall of civilizations also demonstrated how persistent such views could be while Britain remained hegemonic and influential – an illusion that even the calamity of the First World War and the economic traumas that followed it did not entirely erase.[9] Indeed, it is not too fanciful to argue that Boris Johnson's improbable goal of restoring British greatness owes much to a sense of national identity that has not come to terms with the reality that Britain is no longer a great power, nor is it capable of enacting grand strategic ambitions.[10]

But some countries are. The US is the principal example of this possibility in recent history, and much of the following discussion is taken up with the distinctive manner in which its collective sense of identity and the ambitions and beliefs of its policymakers have influenced its foreign policy and its pursuit of security. What is noteworthy about the present historical juncture is that American dominance is being actively challenged by another country whose people and leaders also take themselves and their history rather seriously. It's not hard to see why China's people and leaders might feel this way. After all, they have a longer continuing civilizational presence than anywhere else and they have dominated what we now think of as East Asia for hundreds of years.[11] Seen in the context of what Fernand Braudel described as the *longue durée*, the 'one hundred years of shame' that European imperialism precipitated in China looks like an aberrant interregnum.[12] For some observers in the US, China's approach is the quintessential example of a 'long game', in which a carefully thought-through and calculated strategy unfolds across time.[13] Before we try to assess how feasible such plans are for any country, it is important to say something about just what grand strategy is considered to be by the scholarly community. By this stage, the reader may be unsurprised to hear that there are a variety of opinions and theoretical positions on this most consequential of ideas.

Making strategic history

Historically, strategy has been primarily associated with the conduct of war and the direct application of coercive force. Given the notoriously unpredictable, chaotic and terrifying nature of war, it might seem slightly preposterous to think that anyone could impose order, let alone achieve long-term goals, through such means. Nevertheless, the sad reality is that down through the ages this has not stopped statesmen, madmen, strongmen, and even the occasional woman, from trying. As awful as the reality of war and conquest may be, there is no doubt that some individuals – Napoleon Bonaparte is the quintessential example[14] – have been rather good at it. And yet even Napoleon famously met his Waterloo; a suitably epochal reminder that nothing is certain about the outcome of conflicts – other than piles of corpses, of course, an increasing number of whom are civilians in the contemporary period.

If there is such a thing as a disinterested observer of an activity that has been such a regular and transformative feature of human existence, then they might reasonably be forgiven for asking: why do we continue to engage in wars when we know they invariably don't end well, and rarely achieve the sorts of things their architects hoped? The increased prominence of 'wars of choice', of a sort that the US undertook in Iraq, is perhaps the most instructive illustration of this possibility. But long before this we might reasonably have expected that the 'war to end all wars' might have given subsequent generations of military leaders pause for thought. And yet as we know, the First World War was merely the forerunner of an even more bloody and prolonged global conflagration. At the risk of being accused of an excess of what is sometimes known as *reductio ad Hitlerum*, however, it's important to acknowledge that the Second World War, unlike its predecessor, was arguably a 'good' and necessary conflict: it was the closest we have yet come to the cartoonish caricature of 'madman tries to take over the world'. If Hitler hadn't been stopped or had actually won the war, it is not too controversial to suggest that the world would look rather different today.[15]

One reason why states might feel that they need to take strategy and military security seriously, therefore, is because of the classic 'security dilemma' to which realists attach such importance. Even though Booth and Wheeler have usefully pointed out that the security dilemma is not a universal given, but highly dependent on processes of interpretation in which psychology and social context play an important part,[16] the reality is that policymakers have to decide how to respond to what may be seen as the potentially aggressive behaviour of neighbours or enemies. Indeed, the basic distinction between friends and enemies upon which thinkers as diverse as the Nazi intellectual Carl Schmitt and the contemporary IR theorist Alexander Wendt have placed such emphasis remains a decisive influence over strategic thinking, as we saw in the preceding chapter. The US and Canada famously have the longest undefended border in the world, because policymakers – and the populations of each country – have little cause for fear or concern about the potentially aggressive intentions of their neighbours. The difference from America's relations with the Soviet Union at the height of the Cold War could hardly be more different or instructive.

Before we consider the unique dynamics that distinguished that struggle and the impact it had on strategic thinking in the US in particular, it is important to try to define what grand strategy is in the contemporary era. John Lewis Gaddis, the pre-eminent historian of the Cold War, suggests that grand strategy is 'the alignment of potentially unlimited aspirations with necessarily limited capabilities'.[17] In other words, leaders from many countries might like to assert themselves and achieve lofty ambitions, but they will always be constrained by contingent circumstances, either their own or their prospective adversary's. There is, therefore, a sense that the 'grandness' of potential strategies is a direct function of their material power and ability to influence, by force or persuasion, the actions of other states. Many American observers argue that the US has no option other than to devise and implement a grand strategy that serves its own interests and simultaneously underpins the preservation of a stable world order. Indeed, some have gone so far as to argue that even China 'still favours a military presence in its region' as a stabilizing force.[18] To be fair, those words were written on 2003, and the world looks very different now. The reason we are all so interested – and, in many cases, worried – about China's strategic ambitions is simply because China now has the power to pursue them in a way that was impossible until very recently.[19]

Gaddis also makes the important point that even the best laid plans are always subject the whims of Fortuna and the personal qualities of leaders. As he wisely observes, 'the abstractions of strategy and the emotions of strategists can never be separated: they can only be balanced. The weight attached to each, however, will vary with circumstances. And the heat of emotion requires only an instant to melt abstractions drawn from years of cool reflections.'[20]

The most likely and compelling emotion for strategists to deal with is likely to be fear, something that can ultimately be 'institutionalized in the structures and processes of world politics'.[21] This is, of course, precisely what seems to have happened during the Cold War as the US policymakers fretted about the possibility of communist expansion and the Soviets became belatedly – and rightly, as it turned out – concerned with an existential crisis of state survival.[22] Even in this quintessential example of a 'structurally' determined great-power stand-off, therefore, fear, uncertainty, anxiety and different ideologies were embedded in the architecture of international security.

The fact that the Soviet Union and the US had very different ideas about the way the world worked, the possible course of history and their own potential roles in influencing its trajectory is significant here. As we saw in Chapter 2, America's revolutionary origins and the influence of liberal ideas derived from the European Enlightenment exerted a profound influence on the thinking both of the 'Founding Fathers' and about the country's historical role as the manifestation of those values. Tony Smith's seminal analysis of *America's Mission* carefully maps the way that liberalism, and a desire to create a world order of democratic states, has profoundly influenced the evolution of its foreign policy, a possibility that was especially evident in the ideological struggle with the Soviet Union.[23]

In the aftermath of the Second World War, when the US became the effective leader of the 'free world', the role that the perceptions – about themselves and their putative adversary – of key American leaders and thinkers had on subsequent American policy was very significant. Harry Truman's injunction that the American people should accept the 'great responsibilities' that history had placed upon them was both an expression of national identity and purpose, and a direct reflection of the thinking and influence of key policy advisors such as George Kennan, who drafted some of Truman's key speeches.[24] Kennan's so-called 'long telegram' from Moscow while ambassador, and the subsequent anonymously article in *Foreign Affairs*, published in 1947, both informed the subsequent 'Truman doctrine' and provided American officials with 'the intellectual framework they would employ in thinking about communism and Soviet foreign policy for the next two decades'.[25]

The key claim that animated Kennan's view of the Soviet Union was that it was 'neurotic' and profoundly insecure. The chances of cooperation were therefore minimal and the only feasible strategy from this perspective – which was nothing if not grand – was to 'contain' the Soviet Union's expansionist ambitions, especially in Europe, where it was creating a distinct sphere of influence and outright occupation.[26] The point to emphasize, though, is that, despite the fact that the Cold War is invariably seen as the quintessential example of a structurally determined balance of power between nuclear-armed rivals, its origins are to be found in the distinctive ideologies, historically generated national identities and specific strategic cultures that encouraged a pervasive sense of insecurity and existential angst. Even the grandest of strategies, in other words, are in large part derived from intersubjectively determined ideas about national identity and purpose.

The indeterminate and contingent nature of national policy is consequently important and potentially different for any nation. It also helps to explain the priority individual states attach to possible threats. It is especially important in the case of the US (and China, as we shall see) because American policy has been infused with a particular sense of its capacity and responsibility to improve the world.[27] The potential implications of such a dialectical interaction between contingency and identity were spelled out by Michael Hunt, who suggested that 'the American tendency to see the world as simple and pliable has been reinforced by geopolitics, with its conception of the globe as a chessboard, neatly demarcated and easily controlled by anyone with enough strong pieces and the proper strategy'.[28] The baleful consequences of such beliefs have been are all too evident in the presidencies of George W. Bush and Donald Trump.

Grand strategy and hegemony with American characteristics

Part of America's susceptibility to hubris and an inflated sense of its capabilities and responsibilities flows from its national identity and character, and is not a consequence of inevitable structural determinism. As Lipset famously pointed out, Americans think of themselves as 'exceptional' in part because they are 'utopian moralists who press hard to institutionalize virtue, to destroy evil people, and eliminate wicked institutions and practices'.[29] Even though more critically minded scholars might see America's subsequent foreign policies as being more about making 'the world safe for the system of transnational corporate capital accumulation',[30] the net effect has been the same. As Robert Kaplan suggests: 'since the end of World War II, and continuing into the second decade of the twenty-first century, [the US] was an empire in all but name'.[31] The effectiveness of the institutions associated with American hegemony or imperialism is currently being tested and challenged, and not just in the geopolitical sphere. Whatever else we may think about some of the organizations created under the auspices of American leadership, they generally haven't been very successful or even interested on addressing climate change. The Trump regime's scepticism about multilateralism in general and climate change in particular exacerbated all these problems. It merits spelling out what these institutions were, how they operated and why they are currently being undermined from without and within.

The story of the rise of the so-called Bretton Woods institutions has been told many times,[32] and there is no intention of exhaustively repeating that analysis here. However, given that they were a conscious creation and quintessential expression of 'American hegemony', it is important to say something about them, as they were such a distinctive and consequential part of the grand strategy of the US in the period following the Second World War. Two initial points are worth emphasizing: first, for all the talk of American isolationism before the Second World War, the US was already deeply engaged in the international system, even if the ambitions of leaders such as Woodrow Wilson were undermined by the actions of domestic opponents resistant to 'foreign entanglements'.[33] Indeed, notwithstanding the failure of initiatives such as the League of Nations, Walter McDougall completely rejects the isolationist label and claims that the US has always pursued a form of 'global meliorism', or the 'socio-economic and politico-cultural expression of the American mission to make the world a better place'.[34]

In the aftermath of the Second World War, this desire was given concrete expression as part of America's evolving grand strategy. The essence of this 'well defined' grand strategy was, according to one of the shrewder observers of American foreign policy, to

> preserve and, where possible and conducive to U.S. interests, to expand an American imperium. Central to this strategy is a commitment to global openness – removing barriers that inhibit the movement of goods, capital, ideas, and people. Its ultimate objective is the creation of an open and integrated international order based on principles of

democratic capitalism, the United States as the ultimate guarantor of order and enforcer of norms.[35]

Bacevich's point about the *enforcement* of norms is a telling one, and goes to the heart of contemporary debates about the efficacy, desirability and appropriateness of what has come to be known as the Washington consensus. This story is taken up in Chapter 6. At this stage it is important to emphasize that the US decided, unambiguously and forcefully, to assume the mantle of the international leadership of the 'free world' for two principal reasons. First, no sooner had the Second World War finished than the Cold War began. It is often forgotten how credible the Soviet threat seemed, not simply as an ideological competitor, but as the embodiment of an economic order that compared quite favourably to the discredited capitalist system that was associated with, if not blamed for, the economic catastrophe of the Great Depression. The second reason was in some ways much more straightforward: no other country had the capacity to provide the sort of leadership that was considered to be an essential part of creating a stable international economic, political and strategic order.

Given that the US accounted for something like 50% of global GDP at the end of the Second World War, it was uniquely placed to act in the international system in a way that was simply unavailable to any other power, including the Soviet Union. There were, however, a number of distinctive features of America's emerging grand strategy that merit emphasis, as they provide an important illustration of the *choices* available to the architects of the post-war order. If the only factor influencing American policy had been the structural pressures that flowed from the need to preserve a durable 'balance of power' with the Soviet Union, as realists would have us believe, then we might have expected the US and its internal political architecture to have been defined by external geopolitical pressures. In reality, however, the distinctive pattern of America's political development, values and national identity meant that it did not become a 'garrison state', predominantly focused on the more conventional military aspects of state power. As Aaron Friedberg suggests, 'the American people wanted a state that was strong enough to defend them against foreign enemies but not strong enough to threaten their domestic liberties'.[36]

This reluctance to rely exclusively or even primarily on the more coercive elements of the unfolding Cold War confrontation helps to explain the emphasis that the administration of Harry Truman placed on economic development. The reconstruction of the devastated economies of Western Europe and Japan was a key priority for

America's post-war planners and was part of a broader strategy predicated upon the idea that 'economic aid would produce greater benefit per dollar expended than would military build-up'.[37] It was a judgement that proved to be well founded and which continues to have important potential for policymakers to this day, even if it is China rather than the US that appears to be learning this. What was really distinctive about the approach taken by the US immediately after the war, however, was that grand strategy included not only direct economic assistance but an institutionalized order in which liberal values could be championed.[38]

.While the BWIs have become a familiar, influential but often controversial part of the international system, it is worth re-emphasizing just what a departure they were from what had gone before, and how much their role reflected a Western view of the world and the need for a particular form of leadership. To be sure, IOs of one sort or another had become a more prominent part of an increasingly interconnected international economy since the profoundly transformational 19th century, when technological changes, such as the telegraph, encouraged international collaboration and coordination.[39] It is no coincidence that the BWIs were primarily focused on economic cooperation, though. One of the seminal influences on the thinking of American policymakers in particular was that their predecessors in the interwar period had made 'mistakes' that unnecessarily deepened and prolonged the Great Depression.[40] Absence of leadership and of a state willing to keep the international economy functioning by providing necessary collective goods was seen as a major cause of the Depression.[41] The key idea animating the architects of the international order that emerged from the pivotal meeting at Bretton Woods was that the economic system needed to be actively *managed* and directed. Only the US was capable of providing this sort of leadership, if it chose to do so.

As we know, that is precisely what the Americans, with the support of significantly diminished European powers such as France and Britain, actually did. The result was the creation of a highly influential group of organizations charged with helping to manage the emerging global economy and encouraging economic development: the World Bank, the International Monetary Fund (IMF) and the General Agreement on Tariffs and Trade, which would subsequently become the World Trade Organization. The key points to emphasize about these developments in the context of the current discussion are that, first, the commitment to particular forms of economic policy was not a given, but the consequence of the preferences of the US's policymakers in particular.

The disagreement between the brilliant British economist Maynard Keynes and his American counterpart, Harry Dexter White, on the desirability of a world currency, for example, is indicative both of the ideationally fluid and technocratic environment that prevailed and of the decisive nature of American power.[42]

Despite the likes of Keynes claiming that unregulated finance was the cause of many of the Depression's pathologies, there was little enthusiasm for serious reform among the Americans, where 'Wall Street' was still highly influential. It still is, of course, which helps to explain the continuing crises and failures of adequate regulation. The second point to emphasize, therefore, is that although the attempt to create a new economic order predicated on liberalism and openness was a central goal, the options were circumscribed by, and reflective of, the preferences of the most powerful state. Representatives of what we might now call the 'Global South' were, of course, conspicuous by their absence, but even former great powers such as Britain and France were reduced to being rule takers rather than rule makers. French President Charles de Gaulle's resentment of what he famously described as America's 'exorbitant privilege' looked well founded when the administration of Richard Nixon unilaterally abandoned key elements of the very system that American power had effectively created.[43]

As we shall see in Chapter 6, there is still a good deal of debate about the long-term impact, efficacy and even morality of the BWIs. But one thing is clear: for the US and some of its closest strategic allies in Europe and Japan, the post-war international economic order was a huge success both economically and strategically, for not only were devastated economies successfully rebuilt, but in both Western Europe and Northeast Asia major strategic goals were realized as well.[44] In Europe former foes France and Germany became the cornerstones of what would eventually become the EU, in a stunning confirmation of both the strategic and developmental claims of liberal theorists. In East Asia, Japan became the foundation of an entirely unexpected and unprecedented economic 'miracle' that continues to this day.[45] In many ways, therefore, the post-war economic renaissance and the 'golden age' of capitalist development was a vindication of the potential efficacy of what we might now call geoeconomic policy.[46] At the very least this period and the policies that underpinned it are a demonstration of the possibility that there is more than one way of achieving security and broader grand strategic goals. Significantly, however, these undoubted success stories were not simply an inevitable function of American hegemony. On the contrary, they were achieved as a consequence of policy activism and choices, which continue to illustrate what a difference effective, goal-oriented strategy can make.

The rise of geoeconomics

This book has already had more than its fair share of theoretical discussion, and I am conscious that not all readers will be as enthusiastic about the topic as many of my more academically inclined colleagues. Indeed, the academic community is frequently castigated for its supposed self-absorption, insularity and failure to take 'the real world' seriously. Understandably enough, realists in particular take umbrage at such criticisms, even though they are not always without merit. Identifying the intellectual lineage of geoeconomic theory is worthwhile, however, if only to demonstrate how changes in state practice and policy can encourage a reassessment of the way we understand such processes; or they can for some scholars, at least. This discussion is especially important in the context of this book because it also provides another reminder of the possibility that policies are not given, but reflect a shifting calculus of both the 'national interest' and the optimal way of pursing security. It's even possible that 'good' geoeconomic policy could be employed to compel states to adopt more sustainable environmental policies if all else fails. As Drezner points out, if or 'when great powers act in concert, there will be effective policy harmonization through the exercise of both market power and coercive power'.[47] These days, unfortunately, there is precious little effective coordination, especially when it comes to 'non-traditional' security threats.

Be that as it may, there is a good case to be made that America's post-war policy was a quintessential example of geoeconomics, if we take that to mean 'applying economic instruments to advance geopolitical ends',[48] at least. This is far from a new phenomenon: many of the potential instruments of geoeconomics such as tariffs, embargoes, boycotts and the like have been described as 'economic statecraft' in earlier eras.[49] What sets geoeconomics apart is the sheer scale and ambition of some of the policies it includes. This is why it is not unreasonable to suggest that the Marshall Plan, which became such a fundamental, successful and transformative element of American foreign policy, is a quintessential example of geoeconomic thinking and strategy. Simply put, foreign aid and economic leverage became an integral part of a larger set of geopolitical goals. Such policies may still have been part of the pursuit of conventional security goals, but the rationale that underpinned them was new. As Hogan's study of their application makes clear, the Marshall Plan offered a way of reconciling otherwise potentially incompatible economic and security goals.[50] It is a grand strategic tradition with a long pedigree and major 'structural' consequences. Christopher Layne argues that since the 19th century the US's 'Open Door' of economic expansionism has underpinned American grand strategy and that this helps to explain its continuation even when the Cold War came to an abrupt end. Moreover, Layne suggests that 'even if the Soviet Union had not existed after World War II, America's Open Door aims on the Continent would have led to the establishment of US hegemony in Western Europe'.[51]

And yet, it is important to remember that the Europeans actively lobbied for greater strategic engagement on the part of the Americans. This was what Lundestad famously called an 'empire by invitation',[52] and suggests that even in the most economically and geopolitically fraught of circumstances less-powerful states have room for manoeuvre – if they have the capacity and will to exercise it. These efforts would culminate in the establishment of NATO, which remains an important element of Europe's security architecture, despite Donald Trump's best efforts to undermine it. The contrast with American policy in East Asia is instructive: the US created a system of bilateral, hub-and-spokes strategic relationships which revolved around Washington and which had the effect of thwarting any prospect of complete economic, let alone political, integration in the region. As Victor Cha's important study of American strategic policy in East Asia puts it, the US 'exercised near-total control over the foreign and domestic affairs of its allies, and it created an asymmetry of power that rendered inconceivable counterbalancing by these smaller countries, on their own or in concert with others'.[53]

The US had precisely the same instruments of geoeconomic influence available to it in Asia as it did in Europe, but it chose to exercise them in different ways because prominent American analysts had different ideas about, and culturally derived expectations of, their Asian counterparts. George Kennan, for example, 'believed that Southeast Asian nations were uncivilized, incapable of governing and developing themselves, and though susceptible to communism, they were not strategically valuable'.[54] Even when Southeast Asia eventually came to be seen as vital to containing the spread of communism, epic failures of strategy and judgement continued to plague American policy, leading to the final debacle of defeat at the hands on an impoverished Third World country. Indeed, while the direct impact of the Vietnam War on Americans was much less than it was for the Vietnamese, the long-term damage to America's sense of itself and its place in the world was immense, and not just for a generation of young people who were radicalized by the war's impact. On the contrary, American foreign policy was – for a while, at least – fundamentally recalibrated, and domestic politics were fractured in ways the prefigure some of today's conflicts.[55]

The Vietnam War was a visible, bloody and graphic failure that was famously beamed directly into the living rooms of middle America. While not all of the American population may have taken to the streets in opposition, it remains something of a benchmark for failed grand strategy and a striking contrast with what had gone before. In the minds of many Americans, at least, the Cold War had a moral clarity and Manichean quality that the Vietnam War lacked. While few Americans then or now may have heard of the US Objectives and Programs for National Security, more commonly known as NSC 68, or even its principal architect, Paul Nitze, it provided the intellectual rationale for the US's Cold War grand strategy and the massive increases in military spending that accompanied it. 'American preponderance' was – and for many strategic thinkers still is – the key objective and requirement of successful security policy. Importantly, however, as Michael Lind points out, 'the grand strategy of global hegemony was the strategy that dared not speak its name'. The popular conception of the US as a peace-loving force for good in international affairs, intent only on improving the world, was wildly at odds with reality:

> American policymakers could not openly say that the United States, out of fear of great power competitors, sought to keep China and Russia weak, Germany and Japan demilitarized, and the European Union incapable of acting as a coherent entity in foreign policy. A publicly acceptable rationale that could justify permanent U.S. military hegemony in Europe, Asia, and the Middle East was necessary.[56]

The paradoxes of American power

Despite the undoubted success of the geoeconomic component of American grand strategy in the immediate aftermath of the Second World War, 'diplomacy was imbued with an offensive spirit'.[57] As a consequence, both overt and covert conflict have been a feature of American foreign policy and strategy. Indeed, the US has been actively involved in fighting conflicts large and small for 93% of the time since its independence in 1776.[58] But one of the paradoxes of

American power is that, despite this overwhelming military pre-eminence, the US has not been able to utilize coercive power to realize its grand strategic aims.[59] Seen in this context, the policies of recent administrations in the US, especially the strategically disastrous policies of George W. Bush, are unusual only in the scale of their ambitions and the delusional, wishful thinking that shaped them. Indeed, seen in this light, the equally unlikely and notoriously erratic policies of the Trump administration looked measured and achievable. For some contemporary American observers,

> This realist worldview is not only legitimate but also resonates with American voters, who rightly recognize that the United States is no longer inhabiting the unipolar world it did since the end of the Cold War; instead, it is living in a more multipolar one, with greater competition. Trump is merely shedding shibboleths and seeing international politics for what it is and has always been: a highly competitive realm populated by self-interested states concerned with their own security and economic welfare. Trump's 'America first' agenda is radical only in the sense that it seeks to promote the interests of the United States above all.[60]

Whatever you may think of the Donald Trump and the policies he became associated with, Schweller's got a point: Trump's policies really did strike a chord with many voters in the US, and their appeal to selfish nationalism was entirely in keeping with realist predictions and assumptions about what drives domestic politics. As another prominent realist puts it in typically unvarnished fashion: 'No liberal state has ever shown serious interest in helping other states to gain economic advantages at its expense just to fight global injustice, and there is little reason to think it ever will'.[61] Again, it's not necessary endorse the world-weary cynicism that underpins such views in order to recognize that they have some merit: despite all the lofty rhetoric about freedom, human rights and liberalism, American grand strategy and the pursuit of primacy has been principally about the realization of American national interests; if that made the world a better, more peaceful and democratic place, so much the better.

The major points of difference in this context have been about the possible efficacy of American policy in pursuing such goals and the difficulty – even the necessity, perhaps – of maintaining the support of the American people. The administration of George W. Bush famously gave a masterclass in squandering blood (mainly Iraqi), treasure and 'soft power', both international *and* domestic. While the toppling of governments that the US disliked for one reason or another may be a long-standing part of American grand strategy, what set the invasion of Iraq apart was its entirely implausible justification and the suspicion that it was yet another expression of an ultimately futile and monstrously ill-conceived attempt to reshape the Middle East.

Much has already been written about this particular conflict and the miscalculations and hubris of the Bush regime, and there is no intention of trying to add to that literature here.[62] However, given its illustrative and enduring significance, it is worth making a few straightforward and relatively uncontroversial observations. First, and most tellingly, perhaps, the invasion of Iraq demonstrated yet again the limitations of conventional military power. To be sure, the US won an overwhelming and rapid military victory, but Americans proved incapable of imposing long-term 'regime change' on a country with no history of democracy and little love of the occupying forces. Yet, as Andrew Bacevich points out, 'American grand strategy since the era of Ronald Reagan, and especially throughout the era of George W. Bush, has been characterized by attempts to wish reality away'.[63]

The big lesson here, therefore, is that even arguably desirable changes – peace, democracy and a functioning economy – are not likely to be realized at the point of a gun. The second point to emphasize, therefore, is that geoeconomic influence, rather than the militarized geopolitical variety, is likely to prove more efficacious. To be sure, even that may not be sufficient; the remarkable successes of post-war Germany and Japan may be the exceptions that prove a rather dispiriting rule.[64] The experience of Iraq, by comparison, demonstrates that there are limits to coercion and that domestic culture, institutions and leadership matter. In this context, as we saw in the preceding chapter, the influence of 'the Blob' on American foreign policy options was decisive, as alternative policies were simply not taken seriously. As Porter notes, 'in the absence of a determined agent of change, the Blob's advantages persist. The Blob has a privileged position in presidential staffing and security expertise; it exerts dominance over the security discourse; and it is reinforced by the demands of allies'.[65] Biden's choice of Jake Sullivan – a quintessential Blobster – as national security advisor suggests there will indeed be a return to the conventional wisdom.

Whether this will allow the new administration to manage the growing competition with China, or to deal with the climate crisis any more effectively, remains to be seen. The renewed interest in geoeconomics and China's ability to utilize it as a tool of national strategy is indicative of just how much has changed, however, even if it is difficult for some observers and policymakers to recognize it.

The China challenge

Much of the recent interest in geoeconomics in particular has been sparked by the end of the Cold War and the 'rise of China'. Given that these are arguably the two most important events in the international system since the Second World War, this is both unsurprising and appropriate. The failure of realists to predict the former and the inability of just about everybody else to forecast China's unprecedented historical expansion, suggested that some serious rethinking about basic assumptions was in order, however.

One of the reasons why China's rise has attracted such attention in this context is that its remarkable economic expansion may shift the conventional balance of power and create the preconditions for hegemonic contestation – in precisely the way some theorists predict.[66] If such predictions are correct, of course, policy discussions about the environmental fate of the planet will cease to be of even academic interest, given the possible nightmarish implications of 'nuclear winters' and all the other horrors that war between the great powers would unleash. The fact that China is still notionally a 'communist' power and a non-Western state as well, adds an additional layer of complexity. But China's growing efforts to utilize geoeconomic leverage suggest that material factors may be more important than ideological or normative attraction when it comes to explaining influence in the international system. Because policymakers and analysts everywhere have never known anything other than an American-led international order it makes this a particularly unsettling possibility, especially for American scholars who insist that the US continues to provide a largely benign, essential and irreplaceable form of leadership.

Even those of us who believe that much of what we think of as the international system and the actors that populate it is socially constructed, time bound and contingent, would have to concede that, historically, states have tended to use whatever power and resources they may possess in order to pursue broadly conceived national interests. There is no reason to expect that China – even the People's Republic of – would be any different in this regard. On the contrary, even the communist revolutionaries who established the PRC recognized that nationalism was a more potent rallying force for illiterate peasants than the dialectics of historical materialism.[67] There has been a striking degree of pragmatism in much of China's development under the CCP, none more so than under the leadership of Deng Xiaoping. But, as has often been observed of late, the period of Chinese foreign policy that was shaped primarily by the strategy of 'hiding one's strength and biding one's time' is well and truly over.[68]

The key questions that China's rise and its growing ambitions pose, therefore, are what this will mean for the international system generally, and whether this is likely to have any implications for the environment in particular. The very fact that it is uncontroversial to even raise the question about China's environmental impact and possible responsibilities is a reminder of just how much has changed since the US assumed the mantle of hegemonic leadership. The policies of China, the world's largest emitter of greenhouse gases, assume a primacy and an immediate materiality that America's did not.[69] China's ability to become what Robert Zoellick famously described as a 'responsible stakeholder' is consequently a good deal more complicated in the context of a rapidly deteriorating natural environment.[70] That being said, few countries have more powerful or direct incentives to address environmental degradation than China, as its problems are already significant,[71] and it is one issue around which China's rapidly expanding middle class has shown a propensity to mobilize.[72]

What makes the PRC's environmental and foreign policies especially challenging is not simply that they are inextricably intertwined, but that they must also attempt to resolve a fundamental paradox: how can a state whose authority is in large part dependent on continuing to deliver growth, rising living standards and economic expansion also maintain a sustainable environment? It is not clear that any state has a solution to this problem, as I shall explain in more detail in Chapter 6, but, given that the CCP's continuing legitimacy is largely dependent on its ability to resolve this conundrum, it is an especially urgent problem. Indeed, as far as the realization of China's domestic and grand strategic ambitions are concerned, Ye Zicheng suggests that 'the greatest threat to China is not from the United States but, rather, from the accumulation of internal problems'.[73] Before considering the international dimensions of China's policies, therefore, it is important to make a few brief remarks about the domestic side of what Robert Putnam famously described as a 'two-level game'.[74]

Seen from a domestic perspective, things could be worse. While this will strike some readers as damning with faint praise, it's important to remember the sheer scale of China's developmental transformation and the inescapable impact this has had on the natural environment. The standard cliché about the PRC leadership lifting millions out of poverty is no less true *or* impressive for all its endless repetition. This remains a historically unprecedented achievement in terms of speed and scale and it would be remarkable if there were not problems as a consequence. Although many criticisms have been made of China's authoritarian regime, at one level they have made a significant contribution to addressing the world's principal security problem. Not only is China now the biggest investor in renewable energy,[75] but it's possible to argue that its much reviled one-child policy did more for the global environment than any other single initiative. Without it, China's population would be 400 million or so larger, and consequently its environmental footprint would be even larger than it already is.

In yet another paradox and equally clichéd observation, fears about overpopulation are – in some quarters, at least – being overtaken by concerns that China may grow old before it gets rich.[76] While there is plainly something in this when seen from the narrow perspective of economic development and the capacity of a diminished cohort of young productive workers to underpin social welfare, from a planetary perspective things are much less clear cut. The relationship between population expansion and the unsustainable demands that this places on a finite biosphere are, as we have seen, fairly uncontroversial. In this context it's important to recognize that, whatever the long-term implications of population decline may be, China's population will continue to increase in the immediate future and this is already having a major domestic and external impact. Given that the window of opportunity seems to be rapidly closing as far as environmental mitigation is concerned, the next ten years may determine the course of the next one hundred.[77]

The limits to the charm offensive

Seen in this sort of context, Xi Jinping's signature policy innovation, the Belt and Road Initiative (BRI) takes on a different appearance. At one level, the BRI looks like an extension of the 'charm offensive' that China launched more than a decade ago, and which was designed to reassure nervous neighbours about the implications of its rise.[78] In many ways the BRI can be seen as the quintessential expression of Chinese grand strategy and geoeconomic influence in action.[79] Indeed, its similarity to America's Marshall Plan discussed earlier is striking and not coincidental. On the contrary, the BRI is an important expression of China's growing ambitions and its capacity to export not just its vision of economic development and the best ways of achieving it, but some of its domestic problems, too. One of China's growing domestic challenges is productively utilizing the immense capacity it has developed in actually building infrastructure projects of a sort that are so central to the BRI. Outward investment would not only help to soak up some of this spare capacity, but it would also have the effect of quite literally cementing China's place at the centre of a global web of production networks. At another level, therefore, as Tom Miller points out, 'the goal of China's economic diplomacy is to create a modern tribute system, with all roads literally leading to Beijing'.[80]

Again, the most striking feature of this project is its scale, which will dwarf the Marshall Plan – if it is realized successfully.[81] Given that in addition to Central and Southeast Asia the BRI includes the likes of Pakistan and Sri Lanka, where there are growing concerns about security, state capacity and – especially in the latter's case – a less than enthusiastic popular response to Chinese investment, there must be real doubts about how easily such a potentially transformative project will be realized. There has also been a growing amount of resistance to some of China's initiatives in Southeast Asia, not least because the PRC is simultaneously developing an increasingly assertive approach to territorial disputes that directly impact on its regional neighbours.[82] That being said, China's geoeconomic power has not only muted potential opposition, but it has allowed it to buy the long-term support of states such as Cambodia, effectively nullifying ASEAN in the process.[83]

While some sceptics might say that undermining ASEAN's diplomatic impact was not that difficult, given its need for unanimity on any issue, or even that necessary, given its lacklustre record of tangible achievement, China's geoeconomic power has been highly effective nevertheless. The underlying material reality is that China's neighbours find it very hard to push back, as their respective economic relationships with the PRC are simply too important to jeopardize. Even when pivotally important issues such as water security are involved, there is little its weaker neighbours can do about China's impact or plans. It is unlikely that there will be a 'water war' between the states that share the Mekong River, for example, because there is very little other states can do about China's dam-building efforts, even though millions of people depend on continuing flows downstream. Significantly, China has shown little enthusiasm about taking part in meaningful multilateral negotiations on this issue, or on the more high-profile territorial disputes in the South China Sea, which impact on a number of ASEAN states. On the contrary, even on vital infrastructure development projects such as its signature connectivity agenda, 'ASEAN has been forced to engage with China on China's terms'.[84]

It is at neuralgic pressure points such as this, where national interests collide with the supposed obligations incumbent upon responsible stakeholders and good international citizens, that the importance of grand strategy becomes clear, and not just for traditional security reasons. As Wang Jisi, one of the more high-profile and influential commentators on China's foreign policy, observed, the evolution of a grand strategy to match China's new global status has involved the sort of 'comprehensive' approach to security that has been such a feature of Asian states: 'the Chinese government's adoption of a comprehensive understanding of security ... incorporates economic and non-traditional concerns with traditional military and political interests'.[85] It is important to recognize just how distinctive and different from some aspects of Western strategic thought this actually is, and how it might impact on security practice. In the sort of 'state capitalism' that has developed in China, in which the CCP continues to play a powerful interventionist role in the strategically important companies in the resource, technology and even finance sectors, 'the ultimate motive is not economic (maximizing growth) but *political* (maximizing the state's power and the leadership's chances of survival)' (emphasis in original).[86] The consequences are clear and nicely summarized by Qin Yaqing:

> security, sovereignty, and development are officially regarded as core national interests. Moreover, they are seen as a closely inter-related trinity, in which the security of the state and political system is the key link, and the other two constitute the enabling and indispensable factors. Accordingly, security, i.e. the security of the state and political system, is the most important consideration in designing China's international strategy.[87]

Despite the alarm that China's rise and the possible erosion or transformation of the existing order induces in some observers, especially in the US, most observers seem to be of the view that China is anything but a revolutionary power. At this stage, David Shambaugh suggests, 'China is more confident and active in international organizations but still exhibits a "defensive" posture in many negotiations. It is a nation that knows what it is against but not necessarily what it is for'.[88] And yet, the sorts of socialization processes discussed in the preceding chapter plainly have had some impact on China's ruling elites: not only are they more sophisticated and prominent participants in the international system now, but many of them, including Xi Jinping, recognize that it is a system from which China as a whole has benefited immensely.[89]

To be sure, the PRC's accession to the World Trade Organization may have been the quintessential expression of America's institutionalized hegemony, a vindication of its grand strategy and the effective end of ideological competition about the dominant economic mode of production, but it also provided a crucial catalyst for China's economic development.[90] Consequently, many think that 'the end-goal of China's grand strategy remains multipolarity'.[91]

Even if this interpretation is correct, however, there is more doubt about the possible implication of 'geoeconomics with Chinese characteristics', or even the development of a parallel set of China-sponsored institutions with which to rival and replicate the power of the American variety.[92] Given China's material and even ideational centrality in future economic development, the PRC's actions will be consequential, for better or worse. Much attention has been given to the BRI itself, and to associated initiatives such as the Asian Infrastructure Investment Bank (AIIB). The AIIB attracted particular attention because the US tried to dissuade key allies such as Britain and Australia from joining, as it was seen as a direct challenge to America's institutional dominance and influence. Significantly, this did not stop countries queuing up to be part of the AIIB, not least because the supposed threat it posed looked overblown. In practice, China's policymakers had to assure potential members that international regulatory best practice would be adopted, and that the PRC's influence would be constrained.[93]

Nevertheless, the AIIB is significant as an expression of both China's ambitions and its dissatisfaction with the status quo. As we shall see in more detail in Chapter 6, the actual utilization of geoeconomic influence is often easier said than done, but Friedberg's claim about the long-term transformation of Chinese policy looks accurate: 'With the passage of time, China has progressed from trying simply to bind others to it in order to deter them from applying pressure, to actively contemplating and beginning to experiment with the use of its own economic instruments for purposes of shaping the preferences and policies of some of its trading partners'.[94] Even though this may not always be successful and there are growing efforts to escape the possible dangers of 'debt diplomacy', as we shall see, the basic claim that rising powers will seek to assert themselves where they can looks uncontroversial. Like everything else about China, what makes its impact more significant is its sheer scale and growing importance to the global economy.

Comparative grand strategy

For some American observers, the distinctive – and most alarming – aspect of China's grand strategy is that it is explicitly designed to eventually replace the US as the world's dominant power.[95] Such thinking is entirely in keeping with a realist worldview that emphasizes the rise and fall of world powers and the endless quest for dominance and thus security. 'Hegemonic transition theory' has developed a substantial literature and gained new adherents as a consequence of China's rise and its growing assertiveness.[96] I shall consider some of the more practical aspects of these ideas later. The point to emphasize at this point is that – so far, at least – China remains relatively constrained by, and dependent on, an institutional order that was established under American hegemony and which still reflects its preferences. The principal general advantage of such an established system is that it significantly reduces the transaction costs associated with global dominance when other states buy into and actively support the hegemon's creation. The great paradox of the Trump administration was that it failed to realize what sorts of benefits accrued from America's earlier grand strategy and did everything it could to undermine it.

The principal reason why American hegemony has proved so durable is that it is embedded in and operates through the IFIs. The US is still the most powerful state in the world and part of this power stems from its indirect influence. True, the US has used direct coercive power more than any other country in recent history, but this has been only part of its ability to shape the behaviour of other actors in the international system, and a less effective one at that. Much of America's dominance results from the sort of soft power and attitudinal orientations discussed in Chapter 4. So, while part of China's grand strategy may be driven by an unhappiness with the institutional status quo and the fact that 'decision-making power in international institutions is held firmly by the developed world',[97] it is not clear how it will be able to replace the norms, practices and ideas about appropriate policy that currently hold sway.

The growing competition between the US and China is, therefore, significant for a number of reasons, all of which impinge directly or indirectly on environmental security, especially when that includes health crises. As we saw in Chapter 3, to have any hope at all of addressing global problems it is essential that our collective efforts have the support of the two most powerful countries in the world, not least, of course, because they are also the largest emitters of CO_2. The need for cooperation to deal with COVID-19 is especially acute, but has become a victim of the intensifying competition between China and the US.[98] The fact that the leaders *and* the populations of both the US and China believe that they are uniquely significant and the bearers of historically distinctive and desirable cultural values[99] makes the prospects for effective cooperation around complex issues such as climate change and pandemic control increasingly difficult. Different national perspectives on roles and goals inevitably spill over into grand strategic visions. The Trump administration appeared not to recognize just how well the transformative effect that its hegemonic dominance and long-term ambition of preserving capitalism actually worked.[100]

Whether the preservation of capitalism itself is a good thing from the perspective of the planet is another question, but there can be little doubt that China's elites and its people have largely bought into the idea that it is,[101] even if they have developed their own variation on the general capitalist theme. The net effect of China's variety of capitalism as far as the environment is concerned, however, is much the same as the Western variant: a huge impact on the global biosphere and unsustainable-looking patterns of economic expansion. In some ways China's leaders are just as constrained by economic imperatives as are their Western counterparts; perhaps more so, given the importance of 'performance legitimacy' in underpinning CCP rule.[102] In some ways, however, China remains what David Shambaugh describes as a 'partial power', one that it is '*in* the community of nations but is in many ways not really *part* of that community; it is formally involved, but it is not normatively integrated'.[103]

Unfortunately, from the perspective of those who would like to see major changes in the principles that influence economic activity at the domestic and international levels, such leadership is unlikely to come from China, but this is not the source of their unhappiness about the prevailing order. On the contrary, while China's leaders are as enthusiastic about boosting economic growth and trade as their counterparts in the West, they would like to have a bigger say in how it happens and see America's structural power relatively reduced.[104] Complaints about the dominance of the US dollar and the power of Wall Street, rather than the environmental impacts of relentless capitalist expansion, are some of the more prominent features of China's alternative discourse. Indeed, given that the BRI is the quintessential expression of China's state-directed form of capitalism, it is important to note that a growing number of observers have pointed out how this is contributing to environmental degradation and exploitation in regions where it is currently being rolled out.[105] It remains to be seen whether Xi's potentially important and welcome commitment to making China carbon neutral by 2060 can be realized or actually make a real difference.[106]

Whatever the environmental impact of the BRI may be, however, there is more agreement about the likely course of geopolitical development in the region, in which China has long exerted a powerful influence. The BRI is consolidating a network of trade and production links that revolve around Beijing and which are consolidating both its geoeconomic and geopolitical influence. As Feigenbaum notes, 'Asian economies are increasingly looking to one another, rather than the West, for investment and economic cooperation. The likely result is that by the 2030s, Asia will more closely resemble the integrated continent that existed before the US's arrival – more "Asia" than "Asia-Pacific" – than the one US policymakers have grown accustomed to since the end of World War II'.[107]

The old order is dying ...

One consequence of such developments is that it is becoming increasingly common to suggest that 'spheres of influence' are making an analytical and tangible comeback, as rising powers seek to consolidate their influence over their respective regions. Whether this will result in the re-emergence of a tribute system of the sort that existed between China and its neighbours for hundreds of years, as some believe, remains to be seen,[108] not least because China's more aggressive foreign policy is unsettling some of its perennially nervous neighbours.[109] One thing is clear, however: some of the key alliance relationships that once defined America's engagement with states in East Asia are coming under increasing stress as regional allies question America's commitment and competence. The case of the Philippines and its notoriously unpredictable and impulsive leader Rodrigo Duterte may be not be the most reliable indicator of wider trends, but its willingness to overturn long-standing ties to the US is significant, nevertheless. Significantly, China has demonstrated its willingness to use its geoeconomic leverage to indicate its unhappiness with, and try to influence the behaviour of, even more stalwart American allies such as South Korea and Australia. At the very least, such tactics on the part of the PRC have caused trade partners like Australia a good deal of angst as its policymakers struggle to strike a balance between economic dependence on China and strategic reliance on the US.[110] Ironically, the Biden administration may actually put pressure on climate recalcitrants such as Australia if it follows through on its planet-saving rhetoric.

Australia's pronounced economic interdependence with China notwithstanding, however, it is striking that alignment with America's evolving grand strategy has taken precedence over any parochial 'national interest', let alone one oriented toward addressing the greatest collective-action problem we have ever faced. The most important expression of this possibility at the moment is the development of the 'Indo-Pacific' as the basis for Australia's future strategic vision.[111] As we saw in Chapter 3, the fundamental distinction that states implicitly or explicitly make between friends and enemies helps to explain why smaller states such as Australia might choose to ally with the US rather than China, despite the fact that such an alignment is at odds with the logic of 'balancing' against the most powerful state in the system. More nuanced readings of alliance behaviour and the motivations of less-powerful states have made an important distinction between a balance of power and the potential threats posed by states that 'need not be the most powerful states in the system'.[112] While it may be possible to explain such enduring strategic ties as a function of common cultures, embedded security ties and institutionalized path-dependence, it is still remarkable that Australia's political elites chose to offer uncritical support to an ally whose leader denies climate change and who worked assiduously to undermine both mitigation efforts and the multilateral organizations that seek to address it.[113]

It is not simply that traditional realist security priorities continue to take precedence in a country such as Australia that is especially exposed to climate change that is noteworthy here. One might have expected that the major and prolonged bushfires that attracted global attention in the summer of 2019–20 would have brought home to security specialists just how immediate and direct the threat of national and individual security actually was. Revealingly, however, there was no significant change in the thinking of Australia's strategic elites about the relative importance of various security threats or the allocation of financial resources to combat them. As we saw in Chapter 4, distinctive national strategic cultures, especially when they are reinforced with deeply institutionalized ties, can impart a significant degree of path dependency and inertia to strategic ties that even someone as unpredictable and destabilizing as Donald Trump cannot unravel. Consequently, Australia remains committed to hugely expensive, high-profile investments in new submarines, fighter jets and the like because of the supposed threat posed by China and the desire to indicate to its principal ally that it is a serious and reliable partner when it comes to supporting America's grand strategic objectives.[114]

I have focused on Australia partly because that is where I live, but partly because Australia illustrates all of the paradoxes and inadequacies of conventional strategic thinking. Small or 'middle powers' may not be able to implement grand strategies, by definition. But this does not stop them from offering material and ideational support to those that can. The potential folly of such a policy was clearly evident in the Iraq war, in which Australia was an unlikely but enthusiastic participant. Australia's principal role in that conflict, as well as in the wars in Korea, Vietnam, Afghanistan and even Syria, has been as part of a supporting cast whose principal role was to offer a veneer of legitimacy to the strategic objectives of its alliance partner. And yet the misguided conflict in Iraq highlights that such a role was neither inevitable or necessary: other key allies from the 'Anglosphere', such as New Zealand and Canada, chose not to take part. Even less-powerful states can act independently if they choose to do so, and support causes and policies that are geared to broader collective and/or humanitarian goals, as Canada's championing of the outlawing of landmines demonstrates.

That being said, Canada is, like Australia, an example of a country that is constrained by its reliance on environmentally destructive resource industries.[115] These issues are taken up in more detail in the next chapter, but the general point about the *choices* that can be made about security and public policy priorities should be clear. New Zealand has virtually abandoned the effort to 'seriously' protect itself from traditional sorts of security threats, with absolutely no obvious impact on its status as an independent and secure state. Indeed, a record as a strategically independent and principled state has allowed other middle powers such as Norway to develop reputations for good international citizenship and as honest brokers in international disputes.[116] This is precisely the sort of role that Australia's policymakers give rhetorical support to, but which they invariably fail to honour in practice. Whatever the potential merits of 'creative middle power diplomacy' may be, in practice they require a potential independence of action and *thought* for them to be realized. Whatever the strategic merits of alliances may be, they inevitably restrict such possibilities.

Concluding remarks

If ever there was a need for a grand strategy that addresses the nature of threats that people actually face, now would seem to be the time. The emergence of the danger posed by the interconnected problems of environmental degradation, global warming and the increased prevalence and danger of pandemics would seem to be the quintessential threat to human security. And yet, as we saw in Chapter 3, not only have our efforts to combat climate change at either the national or the international level proved to be woefully inadequate, but the problems associated with environmental transformation are becoming more intense. For some readers such issues will no doubt seem far removed from the usual depictions of national grand strategies that are overwhelmingly geared to addressing traditional national security goals and possible threats from rival powers preoccupied with precisely the same problems. And yet there are some important lessons to be learned from the practice and theory of grand strategy, beyond the obvious one that current grand strategic objectives rather miss the point and are ill prepared to meet the challenges posed by environmental catastrophe.

The first lesson is that states, especially the most powerful ones, have the capacity to mobilize and utilize national resources in pursuit of national and international objectives. The fact that history suggests that these have been invariably directed at military threats or ideological rivals should not blind us to the possibility that such efforts *could* be directed toward other purposes and might even be predicated on the possibility of international cooperation as being integral to their pursuit. Once again, the EU demonstrates that such things are possible, at least. At some stage in the not very distant future, states will be faced with the prospect of either being compelled to cooperate to try to combat mutually destructive climate change, or trying to preserve their own national environmental spaces in something like working order for as long as possible. This looks like being the proverbial fool's errand, given that environmental problems and the consequences of mismanagement are plainly not respectful of national borders, as the COVID-19 pandemic has so vividly demonstrated.

I shall consider the implications of chronic climate insecurity in the final chapter, as well as the question of whether other actors can offer the sort of leadership and vision that the US and China are plainly failing to provide at present. I am not convinced that policymakers will have the capacity, will or imagination to make the sorts of changes in thinking that are required in order to address such unprecedented and complex challenges; but hope, as they say, springs eternal. The good news from this review of grand strategies is that policymakers can pursue and achieve remarkable things at times. For all the criticisms that have been routinely made of their operation and motivations, the BWIs, as well as other key organizations such as NATO and the UN, are illustrative of the sorts of innovations that are possible when deemed necessary by the most powerful actors in the international system. True, such states may have been primarily motivated by an expanded understanding of the best way of pursuing *national* interests in a more complex, interconnected world, but the record of achievement is impressive, nevertheless. Grand strategies may have been associated with rather restricted and impoverished worldviews at times, but they are indicative of what might be possible. The challenge is to encourage state-based policymakers to take a rather more far-sighted and even cosmopolitan view of the world than they have done hitherto.

6

Unequal Security

Even before COVID-19 plunged the world into the greatest economic downturn since the Great Depression, it was evident that economic security or, more precisely, its absence, was a major issue. Indeed, it is difficult to imagine a more fundamental or direct threat to human material and psychological security than extreme poverty. The links between unemployment and social unrest are long standing and widely understood.[1] Likewise, unhappiness about economic inequality, and a concomitant lack of social equality and justice, have driven some of the most important social movements in history, sometimes with catastrophically disruptive consequences.[2] Yet, despite the importance of economic issues, they are often noteworthy for their absence in conventional accounts of security, other than as the basis of national power and the capacity to acquire advanced military hardware.

Many accounts of material reality in the IR literature have, ironically enough, been rather impoverished as a result. Now, however, a failure to take economics seriously is, to use another suitably appropriate adjective, indefensible. Not only is economic inequality a source of insecurity in general, but there is an even more fundamental problem that flows from our collective attempts to realize our material wants: there are very real and enduring questions about the carrying capacity of the planet, especially when the economic system is based on continual expansion and the exploitation of finite resources.[3] As we have seen, these sorts of questions have been around for a long time, but they have assumed renewed importance as a consequence of our collective impact on the natural environment, as human beings transform the biosphere upon which we all ultimately depend. What makes these questions especially pertinent at this moment in history is, firstly, that capitalism looks to be part of the problem rather than the solution, and secondly, that the prospect of material plenitude looks unsustainable for the fortunate few, let alone the millions in the so-called developing world who are unlikely to ever experience it.[4]

Underlying structural inequality was a problem at the best of times, and one that ought to have attracted far more attention from mainstream security analysts as a result. After all, frustrated ambitions and resentment about the inequitable distribution of resources and the possible role of IOs in perpetuating such inequalities is potentially a recipe for social unrest, terrorism and destabilizing forms of radicalization.[5] And yet, the liberal account discussed in Chapter 2 is predicated upon the idea that globalization is a process that increases economic productivity by exploiting the logic of comparative advantage and eventually lifting all boats. Unfortunately, any boat-lifting currently looks more likely to occur as a result of rising sea levels than as a consequence of rising incomes.

This chapter looks at some of the consequences of economic development and non-development, as well as the possible implications of enduring sources of poverty and inequality that make the achievement of the most basic forms of security little more than a pipe-dream for a still large minority of the world's population. The idea that people have basic human rights that include economic security has been fundamentally undermined, Samuel Moyn argues, not least by the impact of neoliberal economic policies. The consequence, he suggests, 'is that local and global economic justice requires redesigning markets or at least redistributing from the rich to the rest, something that naming and shaming are never likely to achieve'.[6] In other words, the sorts of normative pressures that constructivists hope may influence the behaviour of policymakers and economic elites are unlikely to influence decision-making processes that are powerfully shaped by national or vested interests.

Despite the fact that many millions have been lifted out of absolute poverty, many others had little prospect of escape even before the foundations of the global economy were dramatically undermined by COVID-19.[7] The very idea of mutually enriching and beneficial economic interdependence has been dealt a mighty blow from which it may never recover. Significantly, this is not a phenomenon that is confined to the South or the supposedly developing world. On the contrary, the COVID-19 crisis has shone an unforgiving light on the startling levels of entrenched and institutionalized levels of inequality that exist in the US in particular. The economic order of the 21st century may look a lot more like that of the 18th than anyone may have imagined, and the ideas of Thomas Malthus may not be quite as anachronistic as most had assumed.

Structural constraints and their consequences

In most discussions of international relations, economic issues are generally not prominent. Where economic issues are mentioned, it is usually in conjunction with an individual state's capacity to acquire sophisticated weaponry, which is taken to be one of the preconditions for great-power status. And yet, as the rather anomalous but important case of Japan demonstrates, it is entirely possible to become a major power without fulfilling the standard expectations about the role of military prowess. On the contrary, not only have the Japanese people actively repudiated militarism and endorsed a state-led path of economic development, but this has not materially undermined their security.[8] To be sure, there are very distinctive circumstances that have allowed this, not the least of which has been the partial outsourcing of national security to another country, the US.[9] It is also the case that Japan's 'self-defence forces' represent a significant conventional capability, despite the mandated limit on defence spending. Nevertheless, the Japanese model of security is distinctive, notably at odds with much mainstream security thinking, and seems to confirm the idea that it is possible to carve out a successful and secure niche as a 'trading state' in the contemporary international political economy.[10]

However, Japan is also emblematic of a process of unequal ecological exchange in which more developed economies exploit the resources of poorer neighbours while maintaining or even improving their own domestic environments. This is another aspect of economic development that is an integral part of globalization, and one that Japan highlights; it ought to be fundamental to any discussion of contemporary capitalism and its impact on security and environmental issues as a consequence. One of the reasons why it isn't is because of the underlying asymmetries of power, interest and responsibility that even the most well-intentioned environmental movements in the West have thus far been unable to address. As Peter Dauvergne points out:

> Not only is environmentalism failing to produce sustainable patterns of global consumption, much of what policymakers in high-consuming economies are labeling as 'environmental progress' is in reality little more than the wealthy world deflecting the consequences and risks into ecosystems and onto people with less power – and thus less influence over global affairs.[11]

Economic and even environmental interdependency are also issues that were highlighted and given new emphasis as a result of COVID-19 as states increasingly came to question the possible security implications of increased exposure to cross-border vulnerabilities. And yet, the underlying reality is, as Stephen Brooks points out in one of the few books that directly addresses the links between economics and security, the entire nature of security and the logic of war have changed as a consequence global restructuring and the reorganization of production: 'The globalisation of production has significant ramifications for security affairs by virtue of the fact that is has altered the parameters of weapons development, the economic benefits of conquest, and the prospects for regional integration among security rivals'.[12]

The potentially increased theoretical and practical importance of the political economy of security reveals how aspects of globalization processes remain highly uneven and offer new competitive and *strategic* advantages to particular states. Unsurprisingly, perhaps, some states remain far more powerful than others even in a more interconnected and integrated global economy. What is more surprising, perhaps, is that the production networks that seem to be the hallmark and driver of greater economic interdependence actually seem to enhance the power and influence of some states that are home to critical 'hubs' in the global economy. The advantages that accrue to New York and London as key elements of the global financial sector have long been noted, for example.[13] Now it is becoming clear that playing a central role in the internet and the associated technologies that allow it to function is also a potentially critical source of geopolitical power and influence – a possibility that helps to explain the intense competition and strategic sensitivity about the roll-out of the 5G network.[14] As Farrell and Newman's pioneering analysis of global economic networks makes clear,

> network topography generates enduring power imbalances among states ... the tendency of complex systems to produce asymmetric network structures, in which some nodes are 'hubs,' and are far more connected than others ... states with political authority over the central nodes in the international networked structures through which money, goods, and information travel are uniquely positioned to impose costs on others.[15]

In short, the creation of such networks can generate path-dependent effects, allowing the state that controls them to 'weaponize' them to the strategic disadvantage of competitors. The ability of the US to utilize such possibilities was evident when it turned off Russia's access to the critically important SWIFT (Society for Worldwide Interbank Financial Telecommunication) messaging system in response to its aggressive policy toward Ukraine. We may, indeed, all be interconnected as the application of quantum theory to economics points out, but that does not make us all equal.

Two aspects of such recent developments in the way much trade, production and finance are now organized are especially noteworthy in the light of heightened concerns about our vulnerability to pandemics. First, the assumed benefits of economic interdependence that are so central to liberal arguments no longer look as compelling as they did. Concerns about economic vulnerability and reliance on potential rivals and adversaries are now seen as greater concerns than the possible benefits to be derived from specialization and comparative advantage. Economic nationalism and self-reliance, especially when it comes to 'strategically important' issues, be they military or medical, have suddenly assumed a heightened importance in the minds of policymakers. The second problem is more familiar but has not gone away simply because policy is starting to take on a neo-mercantilist appearance: capitalism is still an inherently expansionary system, even where a national logic is more prominent. It is, therefore, still a security threat as a consequence of its impact on the natural environment.[16]

At the most fundamental level, therefore, those Marxist scholars who have always emphasized the importance of the particular material circumstances that underpin and ultimately delimit economic activity look to have an increasingly salient point: there really *are* non-negotiable constraints when it comes to the way we collectively exploit the biosphere. As Karl Polanyi long ago pointed out, 'to allow the market mechanism to be the sole director of the fate of human beings and their natural environment … would result in the demolition of society'.[17] To be sure, the overall structure of economic activity at both the national and international levels may have been radically transformed over the last twenty or thirty years, and less resource-intensive service sector jobs may have become much more common, but this has not reduced the growing threat of climate change and global warming, as we saw in Chapter 3. Ironically, part of the problem has been the very success of the capitalist mode of production, which even Marx acknowledged was the most 'efficient' wealth-producing social system ever devised. And yet, even without the highly damaging and increasingly visible consequences of rapid, resource-intensive forms of economic development, as radical scholars have continually pointed out, there has always been another fundamental problem with capitalist development: economic inequality.[18]

Inequality as source of insecurity

'The poor will always be with you.' Even Christians might agree that this is one of the less encouraging quotes to be found in the Bible. Unfortunately, however, it looks as if it may have been remarkably prescient. Although it is always possible that some technological or even social transformation will change the way we live and 'save the planet', at this moment in history such an outcome looks as unlikely as ever. The rather grim reality would seem to be that, despite a remarkable, surprising and welcome decrease in inequality *between* nations, largely thanks to economic development in China and India, inequality is actually increasing *within* them.[19] Even the former somewhat encouraging development is rather overshadowed by the huge numbers of people who remain mired in poverty with very little chance of escaping it in the short term. Even more problematically, perhaps, it is doubtful whether large numbers of people will ever escape grinding poverty and immiseration, or even whether the gains that have been made will be sustainable.[20]

Indeed, sustainability is the key word in this context. As we have seen, economic development has exacted a fearful toll on the environment already, not least because of the sheer numbers of people who are trying to replicate the developmental successes of first, 'the West', and, more recently, China and (to a significantly lesser extent) India. Even these apparent success stories have to be treated with great caution and subjected to numerous caveats, however. India is now home to some of the most polluted cities on earth; so, too, is Pakistan, which does not even enjoy the benefit of significant improvements in living standards for at least some of its people. China remains the standard bearer in terms of both rapid economic development and the long-term impact it has had on the domestic environment. Air pollution, water shortages, soil contamination and desertification are among the most pressing problems the PRC faces.[21] This is more than an environmental question, however, as it threatens the implicit trade-off that seems to underpin 'successful' economic development among many 'late' developing states.

Two points are especially pertinent here that are central to this grand bargain between a rising (or aspiring) middle class and their governments, especially where they are non-democratic and/or authoritarian. First, as we saw in Chapter 3, the PRC has been able to manage the expectations of its increasingly well-educated and media-savvy urban populations so far, but there is no guarantee that this relationship will hold if people realize that their chances of achieving or continuing to enjoy the benefits of this tacit bargain may actually be diminishing. The fundamental cause of this political unravelling, and the second point to stress, is that environmental constraints appear to create insurmountable obstacles to the continuing viability of this trade-off. In China's case, there may be ways in which it can leverage its economic importance to its neighbours and the world so as to export some of its environmental problems in just the same way that other powerful states have in the past. Other less-developed economic actors have no such opportunities, however, which makes the impact of environmental threats to security that much greater.[22]

The possible significance of these sorts of developments becomes more apparent when they are seen in historical context. In the 19th century, when colonial expansion and exploitation was at its height, fewer people were concerned about the possible moral implications of the relationship between core and periphery, or what we might now describe as North and South. On the contrary, prominent Victorian intellectuals such as Herbert Spencer argued that there was a certain Darwinian inevitability about economic and social development in which more powerful and technologically advanced nations led the way, offering a model for more 'primitive' societies. To be fair, Spencer's ideas have been caricatured to some extent,[23] but they do capture something important about the way exploitation and inequality could be rationalized in a society in which Christian values were supposedly taken seriously. While such ideas may seem indefensible to many contemporary observers, there are a number of points about this period of imperial expansion that merit emphasis because they help to explain the ingrained nature of economic and even environmental inequality to this day.

First, the legacy of this period lives on. The consequences of uneven economic development are evident in the profoundly different levels of per capita income in different parts of the world. One of the consequences of colonialism and the exploitation of Africa, South America and large parts of Asia was to entrench patterns of uneven development in ways that help to account for seemingly ineradicable poverty in some parts of the world, and for the interlinked environmental pressures this generates.[24] Rather revealingly, IR scholars have not generally paid much attention to the underlying causes of asymmetries of power, or to the economic and environmental problems they generate. Fortunately, however, geographers have, and they have done more than most to highlight the implications and drivers of uneven development.[25]

The second point to emphasize in this context is that there is a certain 'logic' inherent to capitalism that necessitates continual expansion and the pursuit of profit, wherever it may lie. It is, of course, this irresistible internal dynamic that accounts for the outward expansion of the European powers from the 18th century onwards. To be sure, there was also a good deal of inter-imperial rivalry, and even a desire to play a 'civilizing' role among the 'less developed' nations of the world. But the expansion of Western powers, along with their distinctive mode of production and the Westphalian system of states, was driven in large part by capitalist dynamism, even if there were major differences in the impact of specific colonizers in the periphery. The search for new resources, markets and labour to exploit provided a powerful incentive for both industrialists and an increasingly important form of financial capital. Such forces remain important and distinctive, but one of the most important consequences of this period was to consolidate an emerging and increasingly transnational division of labour in which some parts of the world occupied decidedly more advantageous and lucrative positions.[26]

The paradoxes of development

The net effect of these changes was to compound the negative impact of uneven development, or the different rates of growth that were experienced in different sectors of capitalist economies.[27] The problem with this emerging transnational division of labour was not simply that some forms of economic activity were inherently more valuable than others, but that entire countries became locked into the lower rungs of the developmental ladder. This might have been a problem at any time, but when the ruling hegemon of the era was propounding the merits of free trade and economic liberalism, it was difficult for peripheral economies to overcome the disadvantages of 'late' development.[28] As Reinert points out, 'asymmetric free trade will lead to the poor nation specializing in being poor, while the rich nation will specialize in being rich'.[29] Adding political insult to economic injury was the hypocrisy of the advanced economies' attitude to development in the periphery. The doctrine of laissez-faire capitalism propounded by Britain effectively ensured that other countries would not be able to follow its path to economic development. As Ha-Joon Chang has pointed out, *all* countries that have successfully industrialized have done so with the support of states that employed various forms of assistance and protection; precisely the same sorts of policies they have subsequently discouraged other states from adopting.[30]

As if the challenges of post-colonial development were not enough of a problem, they were frequently compounded by their impact on the political systems of countries in the periphery when they eventually threw off the yoke of colonialism and established their own independent states. The path-dependent consequences of European imperialism are manifold and invariably negative, when seen from the immediate perspective of the South, at least.[31] It is no coincidence that one of the most important indigenous contributions to theories of economic development (and non-development) originated in Latin America. So-called 'dependency theory', which was developed initially by the Argentinian economist Raúl Prebisch, attempted to account for the failure of the major South American economies to 'take off' in the way predicted by proponents of the alternative doctrine of 'modernization'.[32]

There is no intention of attempting to provide a detailed critique of either of these alternative worldviews and theoretical positions. They are important to mention here because they illustrate that the very notion of development has always been highly contested, inescapably ideological and very dependent on context. The title of Walt Rostow's highly influential book, *The Stages of Economic Growth: A Non-Communist Manifesto*,[33] is indicative of just how ideologically contested the very idea development was in the Cold War context. In the minds of many strategic thinkers during the early phases of the struggle with the Soviet Union, nothing less than the survival of capitalism and the free market was at stake against what seemed like a formidable and attractive enemy to many people in what was then known as the Third World. It is not hard to see why: capitalism was often seen to be failing the poor and democracy was not the most important concern of people living in poverty with little chance of escape.[34]

It was because of Soviet-style communism's apparent success and attractiveness that other prominent intellectuals such as Samuel Huntington argued that what mattered most was the strength of political institutions, no matter what form they took. On page 1 of his magnum opus, Huntington states that 'the most important political distinction among countries concerns not their form of government but their degree of government'. In this context, Huntington argued, 'political modernisation involves the rationalisation of authority, the replacement of a large number of traditional, religious, familial, and ethnic political authorities by a single, secular, national political authority'.[35] In other words, if the US was to cultivate allies and client states in the unfolding bipolar contest, stability and development were more important than ideological purity.

The consequences of such a geopolitical calculus are well known but merit repetition, not least because they were dramatically at odds with the rhetoric of the US as the 'leader of the free world'. In reality, American policy during the Cold War was noteworthy for its direct support and assistance of a number of non-democratic, authoritarian regimes throughout the world, as well as a willingness to intervene overtly or covertly to prop up endangered allies.[36] It is not the narrowly strategic dimension of such policies that is of most interest here, however, but the inherent tension that existed between rhetoric and reality. Some will say it was ever thus, perhaps, but, given that the US was simultaneously empowering key IOs such as the IMF and the World Bank to promote capitalist development as part of its overall grand strategy, this is strikingly inconsistent, at the very least. The point to emphasize here is that in the first few decades of the American imperium, US strategic thinkers were willing to turn a blind eye to political and even economic practices of which they did not normatively approve.

Rather tellingly, those allies of the US that were best able to resist its policy recommendations and preferences tended to be the most successful and best placed to reap the potential benefits of 'late' development. It is important to stress that this is not simply an interesting historical episode and insight into the strategic calculations of great powers. On the contrary, the debate about the path to successful economic development has not gone away, and has gained renewed life as a consequence of the rise of China and the emergence of another apparently successful developmental model that is notably at odds with the liberal orthodoxy.[37] Indeed, the entire history of the 'Asian miracle', of which China is but the latest iteration, is testimony to the efficacy of the 'developmental state' pioneered by Japan and emulated widely across the region with various degrees of success.[38] Significantly, the rise of first Japan, and subsequently East Asia's other so-called 'tiger economies', was achieved in no small part by studiously ignoring the advice of the US and the BWIs over which it exerted such a powerful influence.[39] Indeed, as Joe Studwell has pointed out, one of the biggest lessons from the Asian experience for states pursuing rapid capitalist development was that 'governments must use their power – particularly their discretion over state-controlled assets, business licences, credit and scarce foreign exchange – to make private entrepreneurs do what industrial development requires'.[40]

For anyone who was paying attention and not blinded by ideological or theoretical assumptions, the idea that East Asia succeeded despite rather than because of the influence of liberal ideas, be they political or economic, may not come as a surprise. Even the World Bank eventually came to recognize this, not least because Japan encouraged it to do so.[41] This does not mean that the US did not influence the welcome transformation of an economic region that had largely been associated with underdevelopment hitherto. America's grand strategic goals and the creation of an environment in which greater economic interdependence was actively encouraged, often with direct aid and investment, did indeed allow the East Asian economies to take off, albeit by adhering to a decidedly East Asian flight plan.[42] Importantly, the East Asian experience demonstrated that there were 'paths from the periphery' and states weren't inevitably destined to permanent underdevelopment.[43] The question was why, if it was possible in Asia, it wasn't possible elsewhere. It was a question with the most profound security implications and it is noteworthy and rather unforgivable that is hasn't figured more prominently in the annals of IR analysis. This question is possibly even more relevant in a world in which recipes for successful economic development plainly exist, but they are based on a seemingly unsustainable model and exploitation that creates new forms of insecurity and unrealizable aspirations.

The geopolitics of development

One of the reasons for the limited discussion of economic issues in much IR theorizing is because the production of knowledge has a decidedly Eurocentric bias, as we have seen. More specifically, the dominance of American academics, journals and ideas gives an even narrower potential focus to the sorts of issues and places that are judged to be important. The quintessential expression of this idea and the implicit disdain it contains is captured in Henry Kissinger's famous observation that: 'Nothing important can come from the South. History has never been produced in the South. The axis of history starts in Moscow, goes to Bonn, crosses over to Washington, and then goes to Tokyo. What happens in the South is of no importance.'[44]

No doubt Kissinger would now add Beijing to his axis of power, but the general point remains: many American commentators judge the importance of other countries exclusively in terms of their possible relevance to the US and its global ambitions, role and security. What actually goes on within many of those countries, unless it is likely to have an impact on the prevailing balance of power, is of little interest.

As the other great American scholar–practitioner, Zbigniew Brzezinski, declared, 'the three grand imperatives of imperial geostrategy are to prevent collusion and maintain security dependence among the vassals, to keep tributaries pliant and protected, and to keep the barbarians from coming together'.[45]

While such views may explain why neo-realism proved to be such an attractive and influential paradigm with which to make sense of international relations, it is not simply startlingly cold-blooded about the fate of much of humanity: it is not even a terribly useful guide to world events. The failure to recognize the potential for what Chalmers Johnson presciently called 'blowback' from the periphery was dramatically illustrated by the events of 11 September 2001.[46] This sort of negligence on the part of policymakers and analysts no doubt owed much to the specific circumstances that obtained during America's 'unipolar moment', when – for what turned out to be a remarkably short and atypical interlude – the US dominated the international system. Not only did some observers think that such unipolarity was durable and unlikely to be seriously challenged,[47] but they actively urged policymakers to take advantage of the opportunity to reshape the international order in a manner that was compatible with American interests.[48] As we know, such hubris generated disastrously misconceived policies that directly undermined American dominance.

And yet, even before the egregious strategic errors of the administration of George W. Bush, there was a growing division between the economic and more narrowly conceived strategic elements of American foreign policy. As Michael Mastanduno perceptively pointed out, 'US statecraft became less integrated as foreign economic policy and national security proceeded on separate diplomatic and institutional tracks'.[49] In other words, the sort of multidimensional approach to grand strategy that distinguished the Marshall Plan was simply not feasible, not least because a more recent generation of policymakers had little comprehension of what was involved in nation building. The dearth of such expertise and absence of area specialists was revealed with painful clarity in the failed attempts to pacify, much less rebuild and genuinely democratize, Iraq. Winning a war against a minor Third World power is one thing; winning the peace and establishing 'good governance' is quite another.

The importance of the links between economics and the overall context within which governance of any sort occurs, whether in the 'advanced' or the 'emerging' economies, ought to have been evident long before the folly of Iraq, the global financial crisis or even the COVID-19 pandemic that currently threatens the world with a second

Great Depression. The unravelling of the post-war consensus about Keynesian-inspired social welfarism during the 1970s was a painful reminder of how susceptible even the best-managed economies could be to unexpected events and periodic crises of capitalism. It is also a reminder of the possibility that ideas, be they economic or more broadly security oriented, need champions with the capacity to place them on domestic and international agendas.[50]

The paradigmatic shift from Keynesianism to monetarism during the 1980s is the quintessential example of this possibility.[51] Ideas about the supposed efficiency of market forces and the desirability of 'small' states had been around for decades, if not hundreds of years. But it would take the powerful advocacy of one of Friedrich Hayek's most influential acolytes – British Prime Minster Margret Thatcher – to make such ideas a political reality, and the underlying rationale for economic policies in the so-called 'Anglo-American' economies in particular.[52] The impact and legacy of globalization and the 'neoliberal' policy revolution has long been in question,[53] but it is especially evident in the areas of health and environmental security, and not just in the developing world where a policy framework based on an equally contested notion of 'good governance' has been foisted upon countries with little capacity to implement such a framework even if they want to.[54]

Governing global capital

The BWIs discussed in Chapter 5 in many ways represented the apogee of institutionalized American hegemony. Whatever else may be said about them, there is little doubt that they have exerted a powerful influence over economic debates and practice for more than half a century.[55] It is important to note, however, that their mission has changed over time, and so have the dominant ideas about the sorts of policy that might be appropriate for economies in both the core and periphery. This is especially evident in the transformation of the IMF, which went from being an institution primarily concerned with managing problems in a system of fixed exchange rates to one in which it became a champion of deregulation and economic openness.

Significantly, for the first few decades of the Cold War, when geopolitical considerations were paramount and economic policy played a supportive role in grand strategic ambitions, the IMF was principally focused on helping individual states to manage balance-of-payments crises. As John Ruggie famously pointed out, individual states were part of an international order in which powerful IOs, such as the IMF, played a supportive role, but where states retained a good deal of autonomy in regard to domestic economic policy.[56] A form of 'embedded liberalism' underpinned the post-war accommodation between states, domestic industry and a working class that was seen as deserving of social welfarism and the 'good life' after the tribulations of the Depression and the Second World War. This sort of 'Fordist' approach to public policy marked an enduring and largely successful response to the inherent tensions between organized labour and capital, on the one hand, and the forces of supply and demand, on the other. It is no coincidence that the first few decades after the Second World War are now seen as the 'golden age' of capitalism – or they are in the Western core economies, at least.

Even if we put to one side for the moment the possibility that many parts of the world didn't derive the same sorts of benefits or developmental outcomes from this period as the advanced industrialized economies did, it still remains to be answered why such an apparently successful regime collapsed. The answer is instructive and another powerful reminder of the connections between 'economic' issues, broader security concerns and the unravelling of particular hegemonic orders.[57] Throughout the 1960s and into the 1970s, the US had been involved in a catastrophic conflict in Southeast Asia. Whatever the alleged merits of American intervention in Vietnam and the 'domino theory' that provided its strategic rationale, one thing is clear: the economic costs ultimately proved unsustainable and the US acted unilaterally to terminate the Bretton Woods regime.[58]

The central plank of the old order that the administration of Richard Nixon abandoned in 1971 was a system of fixed exchange rates in which the American dollar provided the foundation. In theory, anyone holding American dollars could exchange them for gold at a fixed price. But, as the Vietnam War dragged on, as the trade deficit grew and as foreign liabilities became unsustainable, the US became increasingly constrained by an overvalued dollar and an outflow of gold. When the US unilaterally decided to 'close the gold window' this effectively brought the old order to an end and created the conditions in which financial markets would determine the relative value of currencies and grow enormously, both in their sheer size and in the influence they wielded.[59]

One might expect these sorts of episodes to have a salutary effect on both the policy-making and academic communities. To be fair, at least some scholars have drawn important lessons from these sorts of events,[60] but many have remained resistant to recognizing both the economic and political significance of this period. George W. Bush is arguably the most consequential example of the failure of the policy-making elite in the US to learn from history, or to recognize the potentially devastating impact that wars of choice can have on the economy – to say nothing of half a million or so Iraqis who perished directly or indirectly because of the conflict. The point to emphasize, though, is that there is a powerful and enduring intersection between economic and strategic outcomes, and neither can be completely understood without taking cognizance of the other. What is most significant for the purposes of this chapter is that America's more narrowly conceived security policy was, paradoxically enough, instrumental in undermining the foundations of its overall hegemonic position.[61] Not only did this mark the beginning of America's long-run relative decline –in comparison first to Japan and the EU, and more recently and consequentially to China – but it effectively helped to usher in a form of neoliberalism that continues to exert a powerful and, some would say, pernicious influence in many parts of the world.[62]

The radical critique

Unsurprisingly, perhaps, scholars operating within the Marxist tradition have been especially scathing about the impact of, and rationale for, neoliberal policies. David Harvey, for example, argues that

> It has been part of the genius of neoliberal theory to provide a benevolent mask full of wonderful-sounding words like freedom, liberty, choice, and rights, to hide the grim realities of the restoration or reconstitution of naked class power, locally as well as transnationally, but most particularly in the main financial centres of global capitalism.[63]

Such criticisms assume particular importance in the context of debates about economic policy in a post–Cold War context. It is not too fanciful to suggest that during the Cold War, as far as the US was concerned, what mattered was not so much the *type* of broadly capitalist system that states adopted but the fact that they were in the capitalist camp at all. After the Cold War, however, two developments shifted the debate and raised questions about the durability of the broadly liberal project that underpinned American hegemony. First, stripped of its overarching geopolitical rationale, more attention was paid to the actual impact of the policies associated with 'good governance', which became the bland and unobjectionable way of describing the neoliberal agenda that was assiduously promoted by the World Bank in particular.[64] The World Bank's approach to encouraging development in the South was predicated upon the idea that the best way to emulate the success of the West was to replicate its theoretical path to development, even if this was rarely actually followed in practice. Adrian Leftwich described this as the 'technicist illusion' or the idea that 'there is always an administrative or managerial "fix" in the normally difficult affairs of human societies and organizations, and that this also applies to the field of development'.[65]

While some ways of organizing economic production plainly *are* better and more 'efficient' than others, actually implementing them successfully where there was inadequate state capacity,[66] or where the political process had already been captured by one elite group or another, meant that, no matter how well intentioned, there was little real prospect of peripheral states overcoming domestic or international obstacles to development. As Gandhi and Przeworski point out, 'authoritarian institutions are not just "window dressing": Because they are the result of strategic choices and have an impact on the survival of autocrats, they should also have effects on policy outcomes'.[67] The impacts of such institutionally embedded networks of patronage and power are especially evident where developing states face the additional problem of the 'resource curse', or the paradoxical 'advantage' of some valuable natural inheritance or other.[68] The development of countries such as Nigeria, which has a host of notional natural advantages, has been profoundly 'distorted' by the impact of a predatory elite who have benefited from their ability to capture the wealth of the country and distribute it among their supporters and cronies.[69] Nor is this a problem that is restricted to sub-Saharan Africa, or even Africa more generally for that matter. On the contrary, Saudi Arabia and Russia are geopolitically important examples of countries where political power has been used to consolidate the hold of frequently corrupt self-serving elites over the more valuable parts of the economy.[70]

It is not obligatory to think that there is something morally reprehensible about such developments, or to believe that this is a fundamental violation of the 'basic rights' of human beings – although these *are* powerful arguments that the 'international community' ought to take seriously. There is, in fact, a compelling moral argument that all human beings have a basic right to 'unpolluted air, unpolluted water, adequate food, adequate clothing, adequate shelter, and minimal preventative health care'.[71] The key point here is that kleptocratic, authoritarian regimes make the very idea of 'good governance' and a seamless transition to democracy almost comically at odds with the situation on the ground. Where such contradictions and inequities are the lived experience of people with little chance of enjoying the materially and psychologically consequential benefits that supposedly flow from development and the pursuit of good governance, it is hardly surprising that many individuals turn to other forms of self-realization.[72]

To be fair, the World Bank in particular has recognized the shortcomings of economic models that are plainly inappropriate or at odds with empirical reality. The emergence of a less doctrinaire 'post-Washington consensus', which places much greater emphasis on poverty reduction, social welfare, education, and democratic participation was one important, well-intentioned response to development failure and the widespread criticism of earlier policies.[73] Yet despite some progress toward the equally laudable 'millennium development goals',[74] many remain as elusive as ever,[75] and they have little correlation with notions of 'good governance'.[76] In the context of a discussion of the durability of an American-inspired development agenda and its continuing credibility as a role model for other countries this is plainly a problem, and not just one of Donald Trump's making. On the contrary, many of these problems have been around for decades. The intention – and hope – of many of the policy initiatives that sought to promote development within the context of an overarching American strategic order was not simply to promote a form of liberalism, but to 'change whole societies and the behaviour and values of the people within them. In attempting to promote direct social change, development has increasingly come to resemble a series of projects and strategies to change indigenous values and modes of organisation and replace them with liberal ones.'[77]

The logic underpinning such thinking was the belief that increased development and interdependence was not just beneficial in economic terms, but would ultimately have major strategic pay-offs as 'the rest' became more like 'the West': liberal and even democratic, in precisely the sort of way that Francis Fukuyama had predicted.[78] The 'capitalist peace' thesis was a sophisticated and superficially plausible articulation of this idea.[79] The reality on the ground, however, was rather different: the persistence of poverty and conflict, and the widespread failure of democracy to establish itself securely, if at all, across much of the 'developing world' has been a striking feature of the last few decades.[80] The rise of populist leaders even in the supposedly secure heartlands of liberal democracy is a dramatic reminder that the Western model is not secure even where it began.

Such developments ought to be a reminder to both the policy-making and scholarly communities about the challenges of governance in both the developing and the supposedly 'developed' world. Clearly, not even the West has definitively managed to secure the foundations of 'good' political institutions or economic practices. This raises important theoretical questions about the supposed link between rising living standards and a possible transition toward democratic rule, because it suggests that there are likely to be profound challenges to national and international security as a direct consequence of the failure to realize the liberal vision in the developing world. It has become increasingly common to note the limited and/or contradictory outcomes of globalization as a result. Not only has it had a very uneven effects, as we have seen, but in some parts of the world its impact has been fiercely resisted by defenders of 'traditional' values who regard modernity with great suspicion. Whatever we may personally make of the claims of cultural relativists and the rejection of any idea of universal values, the reality is that such ideas are embraced or imposed in some parts of the world; this is, of course, yet another fault line in the international order, and one with potentially violent and destabilizing consequences.[81]

One of the reasons that the so-called 'Washington consensus' has been so controversial is not simply because many of its recommendations about the need for fiscal discipline, financial and trade liberalization, openness to foreign direct investment, privatization and deregulation were difficult to implement, but because they simply didn't work. As noted, all countries that have successfully industrialized and become wealthy have done so with the support of the state, not by winding it back or diminishing its influence. In this context, it is important to recognize that, as Branko Milanovic points out, 'communist revolutions in the colonized Third World played the same functional role that the domestic bourgeoisie did in the West'.[82] Little surprise, therefore, that supposedly communist governments have remained such a feature of subsequent economic development in the PRC and the consolidation of 'political capitalism'.[83] Equally unsurprising is the possibility that other developing economies, especially those with a similar communist heritage, such as Vietnam, might find the highly interventionist 'China model' far more attractive than the notionally free market development model pioneered in Britain and the US.[84]

Even if such interventionist developmental strategies are likely to prove both more difficult to achieve and more destructive of the environment, in the short run, at least, they are likely to remain more attractive than the Anglo-America orthodoxy, and to be a continuing source of tension between their major exponents, the US and China.[85] In the long run, of course, as Keynes helpfully pointed out, 'we're all dead'. In the meantime, paradoxically enough, the 'success' of economic development is helping to give renewed poignancy to this famous aphorism.

The economic origins of environmental insecurity

Even before the sorts of environmental constraints and realities discussed in Chapter 3 became too great and tangible to ignore, many critical scholars argued that the developmental lodestar that underpinned the liberal model promoted by the US and the BWIs was an illusion.[86] The fundamental, structurally embedded economic inequalities that had been such an integral part of capitalist development across the world were an inescapable and seemingly necessary part of a system predicated on a hierarchical division of labour and exploitation. Now, however, as Gilbert Rist points out in his history of development as a theory and talismanic ideal, we have reached the end of that particular discursive narrative: 'the "development" celebrated in ultra-solemn declarations will never exist, because it presupposes infinite growth that is in reality impossible'.[87] For radical critics it is the direct link between the world's dominant economic system and the environment that is the underlying structural cause of the development impasse: 'Capitalism is not an economic system; it is not a social system; it is *a way of organizing nature*'(emphasis in original).[88]

As we have seen, there are simply geophysical limits to the amount of resources that can be exploited and utilized without a massive adverse impact on the complex natural cycles that determine our weather and the temperature of the planet. Replicating the sort of developmental techniques that allowed the original core economies to industrialize is simply not a feasible option, not least because many of the countries in the periphery remain locked in subordinate positions in the global economy, with little hope of escaping from desperate poverty, let alone moving up the value chain. As has been frequently pointed out, it would require more than this planet's resources if we were all to live in the same manner that the relatively fortunate few in the original core economies and the expanding middle classes of the rising powers aspire to do.[89] There is consequently a non-negotiable limit to the way human beings can live in an environmentally sustainable way. Not everyone can aspire to what Ulrich Brand and Markus Wissen describe as the 'imperial mode of living'. The crux of the problem, they argue, is as follows:

The current crisis of the regulation of society–nature relationships is first and foremost a crisis of the spread of the global North's patterns of production and consumption, which, from an ecological perspective, cannot be generalized. As long as the global North was able to externalize the socio-ecological costs of its development model, the 'environmental fix' of the latter was secured. Now that important countries of the global South are increasingly claiming their share of the global 'environmental space', this possibility of fixing an ecologically destructive and spatially exclusive mode of production diminishes. Capitalism needs a less-developed outside to manage not only its economic contradictions – this was the focus of the classical theory of imperialism – but also its ecological contradictions.[90]

The great irony of this situation is that not only do the populations of would-be wealthy nations find it difficult to ascend the developmental ladder en masse, but their domestic environments are being ravaged by their place in the global economic hierarchy. Indonesia is a classic example of a country that relies heavily on both its export of rainforest timber and its growing reliance on palm oil plantations. This process is literally cutting a swathe through Indonesia's original forest cover (and the habitats of the animals that lived there), while simultaneously helping to produce the notorious 'haze' problem that pollutes the region's atmosphere every year. The politics of the resource curse, and the networks of patronage and corruption that develop around it, help to explain the persistence of practices that are unsustainable in any sense of the word. Neither the Indonesian government nor regional groupings such as ASEAN have displayed any capacity to address this problem.[91] Only the not-too-distant prospect of a lack of available land to convert to plantation agriculture will 'solve' the problem, it seems.

Much the same story can be told about many other countries in the region and the world, which are dependent on the export of a limited number of finite resources that often have negative impacts on the local environment, not to mention social, political and economic structures. This story is well-enough known not to need exhaustive rehearsal here. However, the COVID-19 pandemic has thrown our collective impact on the natural environment into sharp relief, and the very real dangers of transforming and degrading nature have become unambiguously apparent.

Three aspects of the pandemic crisis are especially germane here. First, at the most fundamental level, population increase and the pursuit of higher living standards – and the maintenance of existing ones – have seen greater human encroachment into formerly 'natural', relatively pristine areas. Although much wildlife has been destroyed in the process, some animals have learned to cohabit with humans, dramatically raising the chances that viruses in animals will be transferred to human beings. Of the 335 new diseases that emerged between 1960 and 2004, it is estimated that 60% came from animals.[92] Second, the commodification of the natural environment, the rise of factory farming and the sale of wild animals in so-called 'wet markets' have all increased the chances of virus transmission. Third, blame shifting and attribution has further inflamed international tensions between the US and China in particular, making the chances of much-needed cooperation more difficult to achieve. Put simply, the impact we are collectively having on the environment is exacerbating underlying security problems and actually creating new ones.

Unsurprisingly, perhaps, the poorest, least-equipped countries are often the most badly affected by the newer security threats in particular. It is in this context that the illusion of universally rising living standards and sustainable development come into discordant juxtaposition. It is already evident that environmental problems are exacerbating or directly causing conflicts as tensions erupt over scarce resources in already impoverished and degraded parts of the planet.[93] While some of the examples of environmentally driven conflict remain contested, it hardly seems controversial to suggest that water shortages, declining crop yields and fish stocks, unpredictable and/or destructive 'weather events' and the like can only add to the desperation of people struggling to survive. Whether such people all make the connection between their fates and the consumer life-styles of the affluent North is another question, but there is little doubt that many would like to leave the South for the North, or that some will resort to violence in an effort to initiate change or simply to carve out a share of the spoils. The literature on 'greed and grievance' has detailed just how such forces can work to shape social, economic and political outcomes in the would-be developing world, and why this directly contributes to conflict.[94]

In a global era, however, it is no longer even possible to imagine dividing the world into discrete zones of peace and conflict, as some have suggested.[95] 'Lifeboat Earth' may indeed have very different classes of passenger, but the problems that are brewing in steerage are no longer possible to isolate or ignore. On the contrary, not only will politically and/or religiously motivated freedom fighters, terrorists or zealots export their grievances, but viruses are no respecters of borders either. While Homer-Dixon may be right to suggest that the 'ingenuity gap' will determine which countries can adapt to a rapidly changing environment and thus avoid turmoil,[96] it seems increasingly likely that they will not be able to do it for long. It is becoming increasingly apparent that the Anthropocene is the word for our times precisely because it captures something about the global, interdependent and potentially *inescapable* nature of our fate. To be sure, those on the upper decks of Lifeboat Earth will muddle through for longer, but if only some of the predictions about life in a 2-, 3- or even 4-degree warmer world prove correct,[97] it is difficult to see how anything resembling 'the good life' can even be contemplated, much less actually sustained.

Concluding remarks

One of the more unexpected and welcome consequences of the otherwise catastrophic COVID-19 crisis has been a dramatic improvement in pollution problems and an equally remarkable plunge in CO_2 emissions. Millions of people unable to travel, consume and generally affect the natural environment in harmful ways gave us a unique and possibly unrepeatable glimpse of what a more sustainable future might look like.[98] While many of these effects were widely welcomed – not least the surprising resilience of nature in some parts of the world – it was also a reminder of just how difficult achieving such outcomes on a continuing, crisis-free basis was likely to be. Even before the pandemic was under control, much less properly understood, business interests and their political supporters were agitating to end draconian social controls that had an enormous impact on the economy. The standard parallel was with the Great Depression, and for once the hyperbole was entirely justified.

To be fair, given the devastating impact the crisis has had on the poorest and most vulnerable members of society even in the wealthy parts of the planet, it is not hard to see why policymakers might be desperate to restart economic activity. The impact on the less economically developed parts of the world has been, as ever, even more appalling, as states with little capacity to deal with health and social welfare issues at the best of times have struggled to respond. The consequences of political failure promise to be more acute, too, even in those countries where social order has been maintained. One of the more ominous consequences of the crisis has been the reaction of authoritarian leaders who have frequently used it as an excuse to further erode civil liberties and constraints on their power.[99] Even in more 'progressive' social democracies, policymakers have struggled to strike a balance between personal security and the need to restart the capitalist growth engine upon which their societies are predicated.

And yet, the principal lesson of the crisis seems to be that if we really are serious about placing our collective relationship with the planet on a more sustainable footing, radical changes will be required, especially in the way we organize production and consumption. Even if the claim about the fundamental, seemingly irreconcilable nature of the tension between economic and environmental imperatives is actually accepted – and many still don't accept such ideas, of course – doing anything about it is yet another of the 'unprecedented' challenges that have been highlighted so dramatically by the COVID-19 pandemic. As we saw in Chapter 4, a pervasive sense of personal insecurity has become one of the more striking consequences of a deteriorating natural environment, despite all of the undoubted improvements in the living standards of those in the West, at least. But pandemics have no respect for national sovereignty or the arbitrary geopolitical demarcation of the biosphere. On the contrary, one of the most striking features of COVID-19 has been its ability to affect rich and poor, North and South, as well as the powerful and powerless – even if the world's plutocrats generally have a lot more agreeable options, of course.

One of the most complex and contentious questions as far as economic security and the impact of expansionary capitalist production structures and dynamics are concerned has been about who is primarily responsible for the destruction of nature. At one level, of course, we all are: the sheer numbers of people aspiring to the 'imperial mode of living' places an unsustainable burden on the natural environment. Even those who remain blithely unconcerned about the fate of our fellow creatures cannot insulate themselves from the effects of a degraded environment or the escalating impact of global warming. But even if we do accept that human beings are responsible for the situation we find ourselves in and the 'clear and present danger' environmental degradation poses, it is also clear that some human beings are much more culpable than others. Efforts to 'tax the rich' and enact progressive Green New Deal-style policies will be the quintessential challenge facing the development of progressive economic policies.[100]

Any discussion of the 'population problem' in such a context is fraught and contentious as a consequence. Even though it may seem uncontroversial to suggest that a population of seven billion people is going to have a bigger impact on the environment than one billion, it is also evident that most of the damage is being done by a comparatively small number of people in the wealthy North. It is for this reason that prominent commentators, such as George Monbiot, argue that demographic arguments are, so to speak, the last refuge of the environmental scoundrel: 'Population is where you go when you haven't thought your argument through. Population is where you go when you don't have the guts to face the structural, systemic causes of our predicament: inequality, oligarchic power, capitalism'.[101]

There is plainly something in such claims. Doing anything about them is quite another matter though, especially when some of the North's strategic thinkers consider that population decline in countries such as Japan, for example, is a major threat to security,[102] at least when viewed within a theoretical framework of 'methodological nationalism' that privileges the survival of the nation-state above that of individual members of the population. Even those policymakers who do feel obliged to at least pay lip-service to the idea of human security generally have only their own populations in mind, rather than the sort of planetary perspective that would seem necessary if we are actually to address the underlying structural causes of environmental degradation. The consequences of this sort of limited vision and its potential to exacerbate more conventional strategic problems and rivalries were also painfully evident in the way the COVID-19 pandemic was politicized and generally mishandled by the Trump administration. The implications of such short-sighted, parochial policies are taken up in the concluding chapter.

Conclusion

We live in surprisingly turbulent times. To be sure, plagues, conflicts, even cataclysmic environmental change, are not unknown in human history. On the contrary, they are the familiar accompaniment to the struggle for existence that continues to define life for so many on our overcrowded planet. It is hard to think of a period of human history when at least part of the world hasn't been subject to some sort of apocalyptic crisis or another, not least because of pandemics.[1] Whether it was 'natural', or the result of megalomania, miscalculation, or our collective mistreatment of the natural environment doesn't make a great deal of difference to those on the receiving end. Despite all the remarkable advances that have taken place in economic and broadly understood social development, for many people, life can still be 'nasty, brutish and short', as Thomas Hobbes cheerily observed. The good news is that there is nothing inevitable about anarchy, nor is it necessarily the best way of thinking about IR; the world is still surprisingly orderly and rule governed. The bad news is that actual anarchy or old-fashioned chaos and mayhem are real possibilities if we don't act collectively to address our common problems.

Realists might say that it was ever thus. And yet the remarkable thing about the times we inhabit is that, for a not inconsiderable number of people, something approaching 'the good life' is – or was – a reality. Significantly, in many parts of the world it is not only privileged elites who have benefited from the sorts of economic and technological developments that have underpinned truly astonishing increases in social welfare and standards of living. The fact that *any* society should have come to believe that this happy state of affairs is normal and likely to continue, and that it would be a major failure of public policy if it did not, is perhaps the most striking aspect of the recent interlocking crises that threaten to permanently upend our view of the future and our individual security.

Perhaps no country has taken the idea of progress and the betterment of humankind more seriously than the US. The belief that life is capable of being improved, not just domestically but internationally, has helped to define a national sense of identity and purpose that has exerted a powerful influence on the role the US has played in global affairs. Until very recently there was a widespread expectation that the living standards and opportunities of the young would eclipse those of their parents. Such observations may be commonplace, but they are worth repeating because they are currently a good deal less certain than they once were.[2] Joe Biden could hardly be less qualified or more inept than his predecessor, but he has to deal with a toxic legacy and faces enormous challenges in restoring America's domestic prospects and its reputation with its allies. It is far from certain that the fabled 'rules based international order' that the US helped to create can ever be restored – even if one accepts that it ever actually existed in quite the way many of its supporters claim in the first place.

Even without the outbreak of a truly global pandemic that has devastated economies and plunged millions into poverty – and not just in the impoverished hinterlands that usually don't impinge on our collective consciousness – there were good reasons for thinking that things could not go on as before. The most consequential and implacable of these, of course, was the rapidly deteriorating natural environment. It is not just the fact that forests are being rapidly felled, oceans are rising, entire species were rapidly dying off and the very basis of human security is being undermined that is so disconcerting. Nature itself seems to be more threatening. Whether it is increasingly deadly fires, floods and other 'weather events', or the outbreak of new diseases that directly threaten life everywhere, human existence has rarely seemed more *in*secure, especially for those of us who live in the privileged enclaves of 'the North'. True, great-power war is still unlikely, but this only highlights the difficulty policymakers have in assuring increasingly nervous, anxious and febrile populations that, to paraphrase Harold Macmillan, 'they've never had it so good'.

At the very least, such paradoxical and disconcerting developments ought to raise fundamental questions about the basis of security: if individuals living in countries that are routinely taken as emblematic of enviable standards of living and models of good public policy are struggling, what hope is there for the rest of the world where even more pressing problems and an absence of effective state capacity threaten catastrophe? What's the point of 'getting to Denmark' if it, too, is suffering from environmental degradation and social fragmentation when you arrive?[3] Getting to Denmark, or any other relative haven of peace and prosperity, is more than a metaphorical ambition for many, of course: voting with your feet is perhaps the most unequivocal indication of dashed hopes and unrealizable ambitions. Even if your journey to Utopia is likely to be perilous, your arrival unwelcome and the social reality often less beguiling than expected, this has not stopped millions from making the effort.[4]

Even some of the world's most widely admired social and political systems are creaking under the strain of novel crises and the unanticipated consequences of good intentions. The aftermath of Sweden's generous asylum-seeker policy and the bungled efforts to contain the coronavirus have dented the reputation of one of the world's model international citizens.[5] Likewise, despite the best efforts of the Trump regime to alienate even its most ardent friends and allies, it is important to remember that the US was considered to be a beacon of progress for good reason. There are still many enlightened and concerned individuals in America who would like to put right some of the damage inflicted by Trump and the polarization of American politics that allowed him to come to power.[6] These are not auspicious times to be attempting such a fundamental recalibration of national and international policy priorities, however, and it will be a major test of Biden's personal qualities and his willingness to confront America's increasingly evident political and economic pathologies.

Indeed, it is debateable whether *any* country has demonstrated the capacity to effectively respond to challenges posed by our collective impact on the deteriorating environment. Given that there is widespread agreement that unless radical action is taken to address climate change things are going to get worse – possibly much, much worse – the need for a rethink of the nature of security and even the possibility of attaining it would seem to be overwhelming. This Conclusion considers why thinking differently about security remains such a fundamental challenge, and what the prospects for a secure future actually are as a result.

The security experience

Let me say at the outset, that I am personally not confident that the sorts of massive changes in the way we organize social and, especially, economic activity that would seem to be required to secure the planet are actually likely to happen. I genuinely hope to be proven wrong, but for all of the reasons we have been considering in the earlier chapters of this book, the omens are not encouraging. More importantly, perhaps, nor is the historical record, which is the only guide we have for the likely behaviour of human beings in times of great stress. There are all too few examples of effective institutionalized cooperation, and the two most important recent examples – the EU and the American imperium – are seemingly unravelling, as we have seen. I make these observations not because I think they are startlingly original or necessarily any more persuasive than anyone else's; they are simply a reminder that the way we personally experience security is the ultimate measure of whether our leaders, policymakers and strategists are actually succeeding in their often well-intentioned efforts to make us feel safe and confident about the future. Even though my chances of being secure are significantly better than those of, say, a two-year-old girl in a Syrian refugee camp – to take but one random example from a panoply of appalling possibilities – I derive little comfort from this, much less an abiding sense of security.

This is not simply a subjective point or response to the contradictions, inequalities and sheer dumb luck that characterize the human experience, although it's that, too, of course. It is not necessary to suffer from an excess of sensitivity about the fate of strangers to recognize that in some ways our security and individual sense of safety is highly dependent on what happens to our invariably less fortunate counterparts elsewhere.[7] If pandemics are not controlled in less-affluent suburbs, let alone less-wealthy countries, we all remain susceptible to the ravages of plagues that famously have no respect for social position, wealth and power. To be sure, being in possession of valuable 'positional goods' – as the economists are wont to rather bloodlessly describe the accoutrements of civilized life – increases one's chances of insulation from harm and of receiving the best of care, if all else fails. But the lingering sense of unease and – for the more sensitive souls among us – the images of death and despair that punctuate the nightly news bulletins are unwelcome reminders of life's uncertainties.

Under such circumstances, one not unreasonable question to ask is whether our expectations of governments in particular and broadly defined processes of 'development' more generally are unrealistically inflated. Clearly, *who* we are, and *where* we are, will play a major role in determining the answer to that question. For those of us fortunate to live in the affluent and comparatively secure West, Isaiah Berlin's famous definition of 'negative liberty' might be the beginning rather than the end of our expectations about the role of political institutions and human rights.[8] For the more than ten million human beings who are incarcerated for one reason or another around the world, this might seem an unimaginable privilege, especially for those who are imprisoned for their political beliefs.

Significantly, the PRC is now home to the largest number of political prisoners in the world.[9] In the context of the developing competition for global leadership that has been a feature of strategic debates and policies throughout the book, this is another neuralgic flashpoint. Despite having the highest incarceration rate in the world, with a disproportionately high number of black men,[10] the US has been a prominent critic of what it sees as the CCP's mistreatment of its own people, especially if that is taken to include Xinjiang, Tibet and, most recently and controversially, Hong Kong. What much of the world sees as principled resistance to tyranny on the part of young Hong Kong people, the government – and the majority of the population, it seems – on the mainland sees as a threat to security by an over-privileged and disloyal group of malcontents.[11]

Whatever we may think of the respective policies and hypocrisy of either China or the US when it comes to issues of human rights and equality, the point to stress is that it is ultimately state leaders who define what is deemed to be a threat to the security of the nation. In China's case even more than in the US's, this essentially means the security of the nation-state or, more particularly, the CCP. As we have seen, it is for precisely this reason that so many social theorists – and citizen-activists, for that matter – have drawn attention to the self-serving, ideationally constructed nature of security threats. Domestic security in particular is inevitably a central determinant of social stability and the continuity of particular regimes. This is most evident historically in the abrupt collapse of authoritarian regimes if and when 'personality cults' unravel or popular revolts overthrow tyrants of one stripe or another. In such circumstances, the role of the military can be decisive in deciding who rules and on what basis, as well as in maintaining domestic peace.

Consequently, civil–military relations remain one of the defining 'variables' that shape the practice and ideational vindication of the possible application of coercive force. As has been frequently pointed out, in many countries the military is the greatest threat to domestic populations, not some notional external foe.[12] In China's case the military's role in brutally suppressing ethnically based opposition movements in Tibet and, especially, Xinjiang has become another growing focus of international criticism as the extent of the crackdown on the Uyghur people has become more apparent.[13] Any definition of national security that includes herding particular ethnic groups into concentration camps and forcibly sterilizing them looks to have more in common with the 'Final Solution' than it does with any sustainable or morally defensible notion of safety.

Many observers have drawn attention to the extent of China's surveillance state and its ability to monitor every citizen and threaten those deemed to be flouting laws or undermining domestic security[14]. For those of us who value freedom of speech and the ability to act with relative independence, there is much to be concerned about in this context, and not just in the case of China. On the contrary, the existence of culturally and strategically significant relationships such as the 'Five Eyes' intelligence-sharing partnership between the Anglosphere nations is also an increasing threat to civil liberties, to say nothing of its role in solidifying the alliance against a rising China. If India joins this network, it may have the welcome effect of diluting the grouping's rather unfortunate racial/cultural profile, but it is unlikely to further the cause of normative and ideational transformation in China. On the contrary, it is hard to see how such action wouldn't increase paranoia in China and help to fulfil the predictions of those who claim we are entering a new Cold War.[15]

And yet, no matter how repellent and alarming we may find China's social control and surveillance, it is hard to see it disappearing – especially if it can be justified as a vital component of social stability and even a weapon against environmental threats. Serious environmentalists would presumably not object to surveillance techniques that monitored polluting companies or that even detected individuals selfishly flouting agreed standards of environmentally responsible behaviour. It is even possible that environmentally minded authoritarian governments might actually be better placed to enact the sorts of very demanding, inherently unpopular measures that seem likely to be needed to either ward off or cope with the impacts of abrupt climate change and its consequences.[16]

In this context, it is rather ironic that 'real' Marxists have some of the most compelling explanations of the situation we collectively find ourselves in, even if their solutions generally seem improbable at best.[17] Whether establishing a socialist Utopia with an ecologically sustainable economic basis is any less likely than the development of some new technological wonder or other that will enable us all to go on consuming forever is a moot point. Both look implausible to me, especially if the 'us' in question includes the growing number of poor people who make up an increasing part of the population globally and locally. The US may be the richest country in the world, but it is riven by growing inequalities of opportunity, wealth and even health.

It is hard to see such a system surviving unscathed from the even more searching examination that will be provided by climate change. The one thing we do know with some certainty is that if any country in the world is serious about trying to actually do something about climate change, it will not be able to do it on its own. International cooperation is the *sine qua non* of any attempt to rebalance our collective relationship with nature. Things don't look too promising in that arena, either.

Transnational security: sounds like a good idea

To many of the more traditionally minded strategic analysts who dominate policy making and scholarship around the world, the idea of transnational security sounds like something of an oxymoron. After all, the reason why the nation-state has become the universal default option for organizing the security of distinct 'communities of fate' against outsiders is because it is highly effective – especially against other similarly organized groups. As realists never tire of arguing, if we don't provide for our own security, nobody else is going to do it for us. Historically, at least, they have a point. Plainly, one of the why reasons powerful European states were able to colonize and exploit other parts of the world is because 'the rest' lacked the capacity to resist effectively. Little wonder that the first generation of post-colonial leaders wanted to create states of their own, even if they were primarily concerned with domestic security rather than fear of invasion.

The dramatic decline in the number of interstate wars is one of the most remarkable and rather optimism-inducing features of international history over the last half century or so. One oft-cited reason for this happy state of affairs, as we have seen, is that weapons have become too dangerous to use; or they have become so with any confidence about 'winning' a war that involves nuclear weapons, at least. The other striking paradox about nuclear weapons in particular, therefore, is that relative peace is dependent on avoiding an apocalypse of our own making. Even if this equation proves durable – about which there is absolutely no guarantee, of course[18] – it is not exactly a reassuring reality hovering constantly in the back of our collective consciousness. Even more problematically, of course, trying to keep up with the latest developments in military technology is ruinously expensive. And yet even in this seemingly most unforgiving of issue areas, compromise, coordination and agreement have been possible.[19] The arms agreements that were negotiated between the US and the Soviet Union are illustrative of what is possible if national leaders adjust their beliefs about their counterparts.[20] Such agreements also held out the possibility of an enduring 'peace dividend' as nations could concentrate on economic development (and competition), rather than on the military variety. The underlying logic of international relations seemed – albeit for an all too fleeting moment, perhaps – to have changed. It's not impossible that a more 'realistic' recognition of the relative threats posed by unmitigated climate change versus traditional war could *still* provide the basis for a grand bargain between the US and China, especially if the money saved on buying military hardware were to be redeployed to subsidizing renewable energy, for example.[21]

The fact that negotiated paths to enhanced security are possible in practice as well as theory is something, at least. Leadership and contingent historical circumstances plainly go some way to explaining such remarkable and counter-intuitive outcomes. Trump's withdrawal from painstakingly negotiated arms control agreements was unhelpful, but Biden's commitment to revisiting the deal with Iran,[22] for example, provides yet another reminder that it makes a difference who is in charge of a country. Even in a country as famously protective of constitutional freedoms as the US, individual leadership failure rather than broader cultural values is seen by many as the cause of America's appallingly inept response to the coronavirus pandemic.[23] In this regard, the growing number of commentators drawing attention to the psychological problems and insecurities of former President Trump is yet another reminder that we ignore the personal fallibilities of leaders at our collective peril.[24]

At least other countries can attempt to isolate themselves from the consequences of America's domestic failings – and those of other incompetent populists, for that matter. Unfortunately, the same logic and policy options do not apply to climate change: destructive nationally based decisions by individual governments will inevitably contribute to a common problem that only collective action can address – even in theory. I shall not repeat the well-known problems that prevent effective collaborative action to mitigate climate change, some of which were outlined earlier. In this context, however, I have become something of a reluctant realist. Although I don't believe that anything is inevitable or teleological, or that the actions of states flow deterministically from the nature of the system of which they are a part, material circumstances plainly make a difference. At the very least, the size of the planet we inhabit and our collective impact upon the biosphere is clearly an inescapable problem we all face. Whether we describe this as a 'contradiction', a market failure, an inevitable consequence of unbridled human nature, the result of powerful vested interests or simply dumb luck, the simple reality is that growing insecurity is going to be a feature of our collective future. The best we can hope for, according the growing number of scientifically credible estimates of the environmental transformation we are wittingly causing, is to make our prospects – and those of future generations, of course – less awful and challenging than they might be otherwise.[25]

No doubt this will strike many readers as excessively alarmist, bleak and even irresponsible, but that is, I'm afraid, the way I feel about our prospects. I hope to be proven wrong and that 'something will turn up', as Mr Micawber might say, but in the meantime I feel anything but secure, safe or confident about my future – which is going to be a lot shorter than that of most other people on the planet. This is another 'inconvenient truth' that most policymakers and strategic analysts refuse to take seriously: despite claims about the growth in human population beginning to level off, it is still increasing, especially in those parts of the world with an inability to secure the lives of their existing populations, let alone the growing numbers that are predicted in the future. Nigeria's population, for example, is still growing at over 3% a year and is expected to double by 2050 and could reach over 700 million by the end of the century.[26]

The idea that countries such as Nigeria or even India will enjoy the economic benefits of a population bulge in such circumstances look almost comically detached from the underlying environmental reality. On the contrary, 'youth bulges' are overwhelmingly associated with social upheaval and even violence.[27] The chances of providing adequate food and water, let alone jobs and productive lives, in a rapidly deteriorating environment for even a fraction of such gargantuan populations look remote indeed. The possibility that millions and millions of people will vote with their feet, not just in search of the 'good life' but to reach somewhere where life of any sort is feasible and sustainable, looks certain to be the defining experiential and strategic reality of the current century.[28] Steadily rising temperatures alone will make some parts of the world uninhabitable, without even factoring in the all-too-real possibility of runaway, uncontrollable climate change and the likely cascade of catastrophes that will almost certainly follow in its wake. At least some strategic thinkers have recognized the enormity of the possible security challenges that such developments may pose to even the most prosperous, well-organized and comparatively secure states.[29] Predictably enough, many think that the way to maintain this fortunate position – in the very short term, at least – is to increase defence spending and ensure that the nation and its existing inhabitants are secured.[30]

Confessions of a reluctant realist

If there is one thing that I hope readers will take away from this book, it is the inherent futility of this position. To be sure, some parts of the world will be able to survive in better shape for longer than others. Rather depressingly, strategic thinkers in some countries, Russia being the most egregious example, see actual opportunities opening up as the world gets warmer: access to the Arctic and new agricultural opportunities in Siberia.[31] Unfortunately, as Siberia defrosts it will release huge amounts of methane gas which will dramatically add to greenhouse gases, while the disappearance of the ice sheet from the Artic will raise sea levels and rob the world of one of its giant solar reflectors, further speeding the warming process. But, given the parlous state of the Russian economy and the decline in Vladimir Putin's popularity, it is all too likely that national interests and short-term thinking will prevail.

My aim is not to make the reader as despondent and despairing about our prospects as I am, but to draw attention to the fact that even the most over-privileged citizens of the North cannot possibly feel secure if they pay attention to the predictions of the specialist scientific community – or to the evidence of their own eyes, for that matter. The great potential benefit of the 'psychological turn' in IR theory is not just that we may get a little more insight into the factors that shape the thinking and decisions of leaders, or which stop new ideas and realities having any impact on institutionalized strategic cultures, but that psychology pays some attention to how people actually feel. Surely it is not too controversial to suggest that if a growing proportion of the world's population is endlessly fretting about the reality or possibility of economic, environmental and even health security, then the pursuit of security is failing in the most profound way? Even for older generations less likely to be as directly impacted by climate change as their children and grandchildren, a growing sense of what Glenn Albrecht calls 'solastalgia', or 'the sense of desolation connected to the present state of one's home and territory',[32] is becoming increasingly commonplace.

Unsurprisingly, perhaps, the way that we experience security (or its absence) will influence the way we think about security policy, and even the very possibility of realizing a more secure, stable and just world. At this stage I should also confess that, as we say in IR circles, some of my best friends are cosmopolitans or 'world savers' of one sort or another. Indeed, Australian-based scholars have made some of the most important contributions to the literature on the pursuit of peace, global governance and environmental security and theory.[33] I should also say that they are often some of the smartest, morally upright and well-intentioned people you could ever hope to meet. Unfortunately, this does not make their understanding of reality any better than mine. On the contrary, the historical record and current state of international affairs offer no compelling evidence to support the idea that deliberative democracy, effective global governance or even world government are ever likely to happen, no matter how clever and well-intentioned some of the arguments made in its support may be.[34] In fact, we seem to be heading in precisely the opposite direction as a new generation of authoritarian nationalists come to power as a direct consequence of some of the seemingly implacable forces that are reshaping the world and contributing to a heightened sense of disorder.[35]

The reason I have become a reluctant realist is because I recognize that, no matter how much I may personally dislike it, powerful figures and forces are reconfiguring international politics and the material and psychological circumstances in which we experience and strive for security. The fact that I live in Australia makes my experience of, and expectations about, security rather different from those of someone living in Haiti, the Democratic Republic of Congo or North Korea, to take a few random examples. One of the principal reasons why Australia is so fortunate is sheer geographical and historical good luck. Even if many members of the indigenous community who were often brutally shunted aside in the development of the country might not agree with this characterization, by world standards Australians don't have too much to complain about. Or they didn't, at least. One of the key reasons for this happy state of affairs is that, by world standards, Australia generally has competent, uncorrupted governments and lots of state capacity.

Now, however, it is becoming painfully apparent that climate change is destroying the natural environment of the world's driest continent and threatening to make much of the country uninhabitable – an unthinkable reality that the leaders of both major political parties are struggling to come to terms with.[36] Despite the dramatic, unambiguous and highly visible impact of global warming on Australia, policymakers remain preoccupied with very traditional threats to national security, especially those that possibly emanate from China. This is not the place for a detailed analysis of Australia's woefully inept response to the challenge of climate change, but its experience does highlight the difficulties that confront all of us who believe that existing ways of thinking about security priorities – and the spending decisions they inform – are simply inappropriate and misguided. The threat posed by climate change is immediate and possibly implacable; it certainly will be without action.

Being a reluctant realist also means acknowledging that I am part of a shared community of fate with particular characteristics and limits. In an ideal world, this community would mirror planetary rather than political boundaries, as it must if we are ever to achieve the laudable but increasingly unlikely aspirations of cosmopolitans. These are certainly not going to be realized in my lifetime. In the meantime, we can only do what we can as individual members of one nation-state or another. I have developed this argument in more detail elsewhere,[37] but one reason for my reluctant realism is that I recognize that the only way of trying to change the security environment I inhabit is by trying to influence the policies of the state in which I live. While there is absolutely no discernible evidence of my having any success in this endeavour, the process is mildly therapeutic. We must all try to find ways to reconcile our own lived experiences with the realities of profound economic, political and environmental change. Little wonder, though, that there is an opioid epidemic in the US,[38] which is, paradoxically, one of the richest, most unequal and crisis-prone countries in the world at present. The prospects for 'achieving a good life for all within planetary boundaries', which requires that 'rich nations begin to gradually downscale their aggregate economic activity, embarking on a trajectory of planned de-growth' looks improbable in such circumstances, to say the least.[39]

The implications of such deflating claims are especially acute for parents, of course: they have a profoundly important stake in the future and an understandable unwillingness to confront the possibility that their offspring may witness 'the end of civilisation as we know it'. Unfortunately, this phrase is no longer the stuff of journalistic cliché.[40] On the contrary, the consensus within the relevant scientific community is increasingly that the very foundations of human existence – highlighted most dramatically in our dependence on, and destruction of, the natural environment – are unravelling before our eyes.[41] Under such circumstances, national and personal identities predicated on the notions of progress, self-improvement, personal development and enrichment will turn into mocking reminders of a bygone era and the failure of the present generation of leaders to respond to the challenge of climate change. They can hardly say they weren't warned or that the consequences of our collective actions haven't been spelled out in sufficient detail. Like me, though, the likes of Trump, Xi and, especially, Joe Biden won't be around to answer for the consequences of their misplaced priorities and futile attempts to make America and China great again.

Not only is it difficult to imagine a future in which *any* country is going to look especially great – even in the unlikely event that a new era of global cooperation breaks out – but climate change also highlights the ambiguous role of nation-states, especially those that look best placed to actually take actions that might make a difference. Whatever the great powers do, it will make a difference, just not one that is likely to benefit the rest of us, unfortunately. Even China, which arguably has a more impressive record than the US in making the transition to more economically sustainable practices, is simultaneously continuing to expand its use of coal.[42] The chances of other rising powers such as India abandoning coal in the short term – which is the only time frame that matters now, of course – look even more remote. Likewise, the chances of the leaders of my own country curbing coal exports for the benefit and security of the rest of the planet look even less likely than the arrival of global government.[43]

Although I have great normative sympathy with the arguments that are made about sustainable environmental governance by some of the more thoughtful, less doctrinaire, Marxist-oriented scholars, I have no expectation that some of their ideas about 'de-growth', much less the abolition of capitalism, are likely to come to pass. Even in the unlikely event that a worldwide revolution of some sort is triggered by the growing recognition that our current economic structures, political relations and (especially) strategic thinking are inappropriate and incapable of providing anything remotely like a secure environment, there is always the difficult question: and then what? Even with the best political will, not to mention an army of informed experts whose views about energy, social welfare, economic redistribution and (of course) climate mitigation are taken seriously, it is hard to see quite how we can make the sorts of changes that are necessary. Not only are the fortunate few unlikely to give up their privileges easily, but it is far from clear that 'the rest' would be willing to abandon their goal of sharing them.

At this point many a PhD thesis solemnly informs the reader that 'this is an important area for future research'. Indeed it is, and interesting work is already being done.[44] Whether it's likely to help us answer practical or even theoretical questions is another matter. One thing we can say with confidence, though: the most influential models of IR – realism and, to a lesser extent, liberalism – have got us to where we are now, and not just in the way we think about international politics.

Many of the assumptions about the best ways of achieving strategic and economic security are conscious or unconscious reflections of *ideas* about the best way to organize complex social activities. The fact that they may be ill-informed, self-serving or leading us to collective disaster doesn't make them any the less influential. On the contrary, not only do we face the real prospect of – utterly pointless and unwinnable – old-fashioned interstate war, but we have also created a natural environment that may not even be able to support human life by the end of the century. If this is where the conventional wisdom and 'serious' strategic analysis has got us, it's plainly not a flawless guide, to put it kindly.

Twenty years ago I wrote my first rather naive and somewhat incredulous 'security paper'.[45] The paper may not have been terribly good, but the question it raised seems as relevant as ever – to me at least: is this finally the time for a paradigm shift and a change in our collective thinking about the best ways of pursuing security? At least some realists have recognized that, as Anatol Lieven puts it, 'barring a full-scale nuclear exchange between the great powers, no security threat comes anywhere near to matching the threat posed by climate change to existing states'.[46] The environment is simply no longer a niche interest that is of little concern to those who take responsibility for keeping us safe. It hasn't been for decades. The wonder is that it has taken this long for the policy-making and analytical communities to wake up to its unambiguous, literally world-changing implications. Even this belated, often grudging, recognition is neither universal nor necessarily endorsed by many security experts who remain convinced that the real concern of grand strategists and 'serious' analysts is the relative strength of military forces.

Absent an unprecedented and highly improbable global change in collective consciousness about life's most fundamental questions – consumption, production, reproduction, the make-up and extent of our truly global community of fate – borders, barriers and beliefs look likely to trump noble intentions. And yet (some) hope springs in the unlikeliest of places. Quantum theory may be dauntingly difficult to understand, but one of its attractions – for me, at least – is that it seems to tell us something profoundly important about human consciousness and its relationship to material reality. As Wendt puts it, 'all intentional phenomena are quantum mechanical. That goes for the private thoughts inside our heads and for the public or collective intentions like norms, culture, and language, which we might generally call institutions'.[47] The possibility that all human consciousness is a function of our individual and *collective* interaction with nature and the biosphere – not to mention the cosmos – is an astounding idea and one with potentially profound implications, not least for the way we think about ourselves and the natural environment. True, human beings have been wrestling with these sorts of questions for several thousand years, and the likes of Hegel and Spinoza made them into something of an art form. But what sets the current generation of philosophers and theorists apart from their predecessors is that we have a much better understanding of our literal place in the universe than they did, even if some of the greatest questions about the possible origins and even purpose of existence remain as unanswered and deeply mysterious as ever.

Quite what we make of all this is, at one level, still deeply personal, solipsistic and anything but universal. At another level, though, the great promise of quantum theory is to make a recognition of our interconnectedness with each other and with nature a more widely recognized phenomenon, and one that might actually lead to different sorts of behaviours and priorities about what might make us more secure on a planet that is plainly not in the best of shape. In this context, I hope Bohm and Hiley are correct when they argue that 'life is eternally enfolded in matter and more deeply in the underlying ground of a generalized holomovement as is mind and consciousness. Under suitable conditions, all of these unfold and evolve to become manifest in ever higher stages of organisation'.[48] If ever there was a moment for a 'higher stage of organisation' this must be it, as we wrestle with the implications of possible environmental and even civilizational collapse. Perhaps it will take collapse of a different sort – a collective, broadly based wave function – to bring about a recognition of the reality of our situation and make action feasible. A *scientifically informed* ontological realism may prove an unlikely saviour.

But then again, it may not. My reluctant *political* realism flows from the fact that there are no historical precedents for such an outcome. To be sure, we undoubtedly know more than we did, and have a more accurate and *true* understanding of material reality and even our connection to it, but this doesn't necessarily lay the groundwork for what looks like a necessary change in collective consciousness. In the absence of such a – frankly unimaginable – transformation, however, conventional thinking about security and much else will likely prove too difficult to change, and become self-fulfilling as a consequence. As global warming intensifies – as it surely will – and some parts of the world become literally unliveable, forced migration and a contest for the shrinking space within which human life of any sort – let alone the proverbial good life – can occur will indeed produce real threats to national security. Ironically enough, they are not likely to be the sort that military planners and strategic analysts have spent their lives and our taxes preparing for. Perhaps it is not yet too late to avoid some of the more apocalyptic scenarios that have been predicted, but the quality of international leadership and the absence of urgent and effective change in policy and thinking does not inspire confidence. Perhaps we shouldn't be too surprised at this outcome. After all, the challenges are global, unprecedented, fiendishly complex and impossible to address without real international cooperation. As realists never tire of claiming, such cooperation is inherently unlikely, as a consequence of both the nature of the international system and the nature of human beings. We must hope we live long enough to prove them wrong.

Notes

Chapter 1

1   Wight, C. (2006) *Agents, Structures and International Relations: Politics as Ontology*, Cambridge: Cambridge University Press, p 2.
2   The literature is vast but two of the more useful and influential contributions are: Booth, K. (2007) *Theory of World Security*, Cambridge: Cambridge University Press; Buzan, B., Waever, O. and de Wilde, J. (1998) *Security: A New Framework for Analysis*, Boulder: Lynne Rienner.
3   The relationship between consciousness, perception and reality is extremely complex and well beyond the scope of this book and, I fear, the competence of this author. For a taste of some of the more interesting and/or provocative contributions, especially in the context of contemporary social theory, however, see: Feyerabend, P. (1965) *Problems of Empiricism*, Cambridge: Cambridge University Press; Baudrillard, J. (1995) *The Gulf War Did Not Take Place*, Indiana: Indiana University Press; Best, S. and Kellner, D. (1991) *Postmodern Theory: Critical Interrogations*, New York: Guilford Press.
4   Polkinghorne, J. (2002) *Quantum Theory: A Very Short Introduction*, Oxford: Oxford University Press, p 40.
5   Wendt, A. (1999) *Social Theory of International Politics*, Cambridge: Cambridge University Press.
6   Wendt, A. (2015) *Quantum Mind and Social Science: Unifying Physical and Social Ontology*, Cambridge: Cambridge University Press, p 4.
7   The nearest thing in the social sciences, perhaps, are events such as the shift from Keynesian to monetarism and/or 'neoliberalism', something discussed in greater detail in Chapter 5.
8   Gribbin, J. (2011) *In Search of Schrodinger's Cat: Quantum Physics and Reality*, New York: Bantam.
9   Capra, F. and Luisi, P.L. (2014) *The Systems View of Life: A Unifying Vision*, Cambridge: Cambridge University Press, p 72.
10 Lovelock, J. (2006) *The Revenge of Gaia: Why the Earth is Fighting Back – And How We Can Still Save Humanity*, London: Allen Lane.
11 Woolaston, K. and Fisher, J.L. (2020) 'UN report says up to 850,000 animal viruses could be caught by humans, unless we protect nature', *The Conversation*, 30 October.
12 Castells, M. (1996) *The Rise of the Network Society*, Oxford: Blackwell.
13 Jervis, R. (1998) *System Effects: Complexity in Political and Social Life*, Ithaca: Princeton University Press.

[14] Barad, K. (2007) *Meeting the Universe Halfway: Quantum Physics and the Entanglement of Matter and Meaning*, Durham: Duke University Press, p 141.

[15] Barad (2007), p 181.

[16] Wendt (2015), p 3.

[17] Wendt (2015), p 265.

[18] Wendt (2015), p 267.

[19] Chalmers, D.J. (1996) *The Conscious Mind: In Search of a Fundamental Theory*, Oxford: Oxford University Press, p 120. Interestingly and controversially, Roger Penrose has attempted to provide a detailed, biologically and neurologically based explanation of quantum effects in the brain. See Penrose, R. (2017) *Fashion, Faith, and Fantasy in the new Physics of the Universe*, Princeton: Princeton University Press.

[20] Arfi, B. (2018) 'Challenges to a quantum-theoretic social theory', *Millennium: Journal of International Studies*, 47(1): 99–113.

[21] Pan, C. (2018) 'Toward a new relational ontology in global politics: China's rise as holographic transition', *International Relations of the Asia-Pacific*, 18 (June): 339–67; Der Derian, J. and Wendt, A. (forthcoming) ' "Quantizing international relations": the case for quantum approaches to international theory and security practice', *Security Dialogue*; Höne, K.E. (2017) *Quantum Social Science*, Oxford: Oxford University Press; Allan, B.B. (2018) 'Social action in quantum social science', *Millennium*, 47(1): 87–98; Pan, C. (2020) 'Enfolding wholes in parts: quantum holography and international relations', *European Journal of International Relations*, 26: 14–38.

[22] Bohm, D. (2002) *Wholeness and the Implicate Order*, London: Routledge, p 2 and p 194.

[23] Stapp, H.P. (2007) 'Quantum approaches to consciousness', in P.D. Zelazo, M. Moscovitch and E. Thompson (eds), *The Cambridge Handbook of Consciousness*, Cambridge: Cambridge University Press, p 882.

[24] Klein, N. (2014) *This Changes Everything: Capitalism vs the Climate*, London: Penguin.

[25] Booth, K. (ed) 2011) *Realism and World Politics*, London: Routledge.

[26] Keynes's famous observation about economists applies equally well to mainstream strategic thinkers: 'The ideas of economists and political philosophers, both when they are right and when they are wrong are more powerful than is commonly understood. Indeed, the world is ruled by little else. Practical men, who believe themselves to be quite exempt from any intellectual influences, are usually slaves of some defunct economist.' Keynes, J.M. (2018) *The General Theory of Employment, Interest and Money*, Cham: Springer Nature.

[27] Kissinger, H. (2014) *World Order*, New York: Penguin; Brzezinski, Z. (1997) *The Grand Chess Board: American Primacy and Its Geostrategic Imperatives*, New York: Basic Books.

[28] See Connor, W.R. (1984) *Thucydides*, Princeton: Princeton University Press.

[29] Ayoob, M. (2005) 'Security in the age of globalization: separating appearance from reality', in E. Aydinli and J.N. Rosenau (eds), *Globalization, Security, and the Nation State: Paradigms in Transition*, New York: State University of New York Press, p 15.

[30] Hobbes was a complex and sometimes caricatured thinker about whom much has been written. A good starting point is Sorell, T. (ed) (1996) *The Cambridge Companion to Hobbes*, Cambridge: Cambridge University Press.

[31] Machiavelli, N. (2008) *The Prince*, Indianapolis: Hackett Publishing.

[32] Bull, H. (1977) *The Anarchical Society: A Study of Order in World Politics*, New York: Columbia University Press, pp 46–51.

[33] Wendt, A. (1992) 'Anarchy is what states make of it: the social construction of power politics', *International Organization*, 46(2): 394.

[34] Carr, E.H. (1939) *The Twenty Years' Crisis, 1919–1939*, New York: Harper and Row.

[35] Dunne, T. (2000) 'Theories as weapons: E.H. Carr and international relations', in M. Cox (ed), *E.H. Carr*, London: Palgrave Macmillan, pp 217–33.

[36] Morgenthau, H.J. (1972 [1948]) *Politics Among Nations: The Struggle for Power and Peace* (5th edn), New York: Knopf.

[37] Lebow, R.N. (1994) 'The long peace, the end of the cold war, and the failure of realism', *International Organization*, 48(2): 249–77.

[38] Waltz, K.N. (1979) *Theory of International Politics*, New York: McGraw-Hill, p 80.

[39] Kaufman, S.J., Little, R. and Wohlforth, W.C. (2007) *The Balance of Power in World History*, Berlin: Springer.

[40] Layne, C. (2018) 'The US–Chinese power shift and the end of Pax Americana', *International Affairs*, 94(1): 89–111; Pei, M. (2018) 'A play for global leadership', *Journal of Democracy*, 29(2): 37–51.

[41] Gilpin, R. (1981) *War and Change in World Politics*, Cambridge: Cambridge University Press, 9. Also see Organski, A.F.K. (1968) *World Politics*, New York: Knopf.

[42] Allison, G. (2017) *Destined for War: Can America and China Escape Thucydides's Trap?* Boston: Houghton Mifflin Harcourt, p 184.

[43] Rose, G. (1998) 'Neoclassical realism and theories of foreign policy', *World Politics*, 51(01): 144–72.

[44] Pinker, S. (2012) *The Better Angels of Our Nature: Why Violence Has Declined*, New York: Viking.

[45] Lieven, A. (2020) *Climate Change and the Nation State: The Case for Nationalism in a Warming World*, Oxford: Oxford University Press, p xii.

[46] Wainwright, J. and Mann, G. (2018) *Climate Leviathan: A Political Theory of Our Planetary Future*, London: Verso Books, pp 125–6.

[47] Mearsheimer, J.J. (2018) *The Great Delusion: Liberal Dreams and International Realities*, New Haven: Yale University Press, p 220.

[48] Mearsheimer, J.J. (1994/95) 'The false promise of institutions', *International Security*, 19(3): 5–49.

[49] Bhaskar, R. (2010) *Reclaiming Reality: A Critical Introduction to Contemporary Philosophy*, London: Routledge, p 151.

[50] Elliott, R. (2018) 'The sociology of climate change as a sociology of loss', *European Journal of Sociology*, 59(3): 301–37.

[51] Joseph, J. (2002) *Hegemony: A Realist Analysis*, London: Routledge.

[52] Marx, K. (1978) *The Eighteenth Brumaire of Louis Bonaparte*, Peking: Foreign Languages Press.

[53] Moore, J.W. (2011) 'Ecology, capital, and the nature of our times: accumulation and crisis in the capitalist world-ecology', *Journal of World-Systems Research*, 17(1): 107–46.

[54] Marx, K. and Engels, F. (2002 [1848]) *The Communist Manifesto*, London: Penguin.

[55] Eagleton, T. (2014) *Ideology*, London: Routledge.

[56] Marx, K. and Engels, F. (1970 [1846]) *The German Ideology*, New York: International Publishers Co.

[57] Eyerman, R. (1981) 'False consciousness and ideology in Marxist theory', *Acta Sociologica*, 24(1–2): 43–56.

[58] Gamble, A. (1995) 'The new political economy', *Political Studies*, 43(3): 516–30.

[59] Cox, R.W. (1986) 'Social forces, states and world orders: beyond international relations theory', in R.O. Keohane (ed), *Neorealism and Its Critics*, New York: Columbia

University Press, pp 204–54; Gill, S.R. and Law, D. (1989) 'Global hegemony and the structural power of capital', *International Studies Quarterly*, 33(4): 475–99.

[60] Hindess, B. (1987) *Politics and Class Analysis*, Oxford: Basil Blackwell.

[61] Younger, R. and Partnoy, F. (2018) 'What would Karl Marx write today?', *Financial Times*, 9 March; Varghese, R. (2018) 'Marxist world: what did you expect from capitalism', *Foreign Affairs*, 97(July/August): 34–42.

[62] Piketty, T. (2014) *Capital in the Twenty-first Century*, Cambridge, MA: Belknap Press.

[63] Peet, R. (2003) *Unholy Trinity: The IMF, World Bank and WTO*, London: Zed Books.

[64] Wallerstein, I. (1979) *The Capitalist World-Economy*, vol. 2, Cambridge: Cambridge University Press; Frank, A.G. and Gills, B.K. (1996) *The World System: Five Hundred Years or Five Thousand?* London: Routledge.

[65] Robinson, W.I. (2004) *A Theory of Global Capitalism: Production, Class, and State in a Transnational World*, Baltimore: Johns Hopkins University Press, p 87.

[66] Cox, R.W. (1987) *Production, Power, and World Order: Social Forces in the Making of History*, New York: Columbia University Press.

[67] Harvey, D. (1988) *The Condition of Postmodernity: An Enquiry into the Origins of Cultural Change*, Oxford: Blackwell; Offe, C. (1984) *Contradictions of the Welfare State*, London: Hutchinson.

[68] Harvey, D. (2007) *A Brief History of Neoliberalism*, Oxford: Oxford University Press, p 119.

[69] Whitley, R. (2009) 'US capitalism: a tarnished model?', *Academy of Management Perspectives*, 23(2): 11–22.

[70] Mearsheimer, J.J. (2019) 'Bound to fail: the rise and fall of the liberal international order', *International Security*, 43(4): 7–50.

[71] Wallerstein (1979).

[72] Anievas, A. and Nisancioglu, K. (2015) *How the West Came to Rule: The Geopolitical Origins of Capitalism*, London: Pluto Press; Chacko, P. and Jayasuriya, K. (2017) 'A capitalising foreign policy: regulatory geographies and transnationalised state projects', *European Journal of International Relations*, 24(1): 82–105.

[73] Rosenberg, J. (2010) 'Basic problems in the theory of uneven and combined development. Part II: Unevenness and political multiplicity', *Cambridge Review of International Affairs*, 23(1): 168.

[74] Jackson, R. (1990) *Quasi-states: Sovereignty, International Relations and the Third World*, Cambridge: Cambridge University Press.

[75] Anievas, A. and Nisancioglu, K. (2015) *How the West Came to Rule: The Geopolitical Origins of Capitalism*, London: Pluto Press.

[76] Hardt, M. and Negri, A. (2000) *Empire*, Cambridge, MA: Harvard University Press.

[77] Bonneuil, C. and Fressoz, J.-B. (2016) *The Shock of the Anthropocene: The Earth, History and Us*, London: Verso Books.

[78] Foster, J.B., Clark, B. and York, R. (2010) *The Ecological Rift: Capitalism's War on the Earth*, New York: Monthly Review Press.

[79] Malm, A. (2016) *Fossil Capital: The Rise of Steam Power and the Roots of Global Warming*, London: Verso Books.

[80] O'Connor, J.R. (1998) *Natural Causes: Essays in Ecological Marxism*, New York: Guilford Press.

[81] Ziegler, C.E. (1990) *Environmental Policy in the USSR*, Amherst: University of Massachusetts Press; Shapiro, J. (2001) *Mao's War against Nature: Politics and the Environment in Revolutionary China*, Cambridge: Cambridge University Press.

[82] But see Burkett, P. (2006) *Marxism and Ecological Economics: Toward a Red and Green Political Economy*, Chicago: Haymarket Books; O'Connor, J.R. (1998) *Natural Causes: Essays in Ecological Marxism*, New York: Guilford Press.

[83] Ponting, C. (1991) *A Green History of the World: The Environment and the Collapse of Great Civilizations*, New York: Penguin.

[84] Dauvergne, P. (2010) *The Shadows of Consumption: Consequences for the Global Environment*, Cambridge, MA: MIT Press, p 214.

[85] Hornborg, A. (1998) 'Towards an ecological theory of unequal exchange: articulating world system theory and ecological economics', *Ecological Economics*, 25(1): 128.

[86] Adeola, F.O. (2001) 'Environmental injustice and human rights abuse: the states, MNCs, and repression of minority groups in the world system', *Human Ecology Review*, 8(1): 39–59.

[87] Gowdy, J.M. and McDaniel, C.N. (1999) 'The physical destruction of Nauru: an example of weak sustainability', *Land Economics*, 75(2): 333–8; Doherty, B. (2016) 'A short history of Nauru, Australia's dumping ground for refugees', *The Guardian*, 10 August.

[88] Dauvergne, P. (1997) *Shadows in the Forest: Japan and the Politics of Timber in Southeast Asia*, Cambridge, MA: MIT Press.

[89] Peng, S., Zhang, W. and Sun, C. (2016) ' "Environmental load displacement" from the North to the South: a consumption-based perspective with a focus on China', *Ecological Economics*, 128: 147–58.

[90] Givens, J.E., Huang, X. and Jorgenson, A.K. (2019) 'Ecologically unequal exchange: a theory of global environmental injustice', *Sociology Compass*, 13(5): 2.

[91] Peck, J. (2008) ' Remaking laissez-faire', *Progress in Human Geography*, 32(1): 3–43.

[92] Harvey, D. (2003) *The New Imperialism*, Oxford: Oxford University Press.

[93] Kovel, J. (2007) *The Enemy of Nature: The End of Capitalism or the End of the World?* (2nd edn), London: Zed Books.

[94] Foster, J.B., Clark, B. and York, R. (2010) *The Ecological Rift: Capitalism's War on the Earth*, New York: Monthly Review Press, pp 397–8.

[95] Cohen, J.E. (1995) *How Many People Can the Earth Support?* New York: W.W. Norton; Coole, D. (2013) 'Too many bodies? The return and disavowal of the population question', *Environmental Politics*, 22(2): 195–215.

[96] Kaplan, R.D. (1994) 'The coming anarchy', *The Atlantic Monthly* 273(2): 5–15.

[97] Hickel, J. (2020) *Less Is More: How Degrowth Will Save the World*, London: Penguin, p 29.

Chapter 2

[1] Buzan, B. (2004) *From International Society to World Society? English School Theory and the Social Structure of Globalisation*, Cambridge: Cambridge University Press.

[2] Acharya, A. and Buzan, B. (2019) *The Making of Global International Relations*, Cambridge: Cambridge University Press.

[3] For example, Buzan, B. and Hansen, L. (2009) *The Evolution of International Security Studies*, Cambridge: Cambridge University Press; Collins, A. (ed) (2016) *Contemporary Security Studies*, Oxford: Oxford University Press.

[4] Hobson, C. (2012) 'Addressing climate change and promoting democracy abroad: compatible agendas?', *Democratization*, 19(5): 987.

[5] Gray, J. (2000) *The Two Faces of Liberalism*, Cambridge: Polity Press, p 70.

6   Legro, J.W. (2005) *Rethinking the World: Great Power Strategies and International Order*, Ithaca: Cornell University Press, p 21.

7   Vernon, R. (ed) (2010) *Locke on Toleration*, Cambridge: Cambridge University Press.

8   Vaughn, K.I. (2012) *John Locke: Economist and Social Scientist*, Chicago: University of Chicago Press.

9   Aage, H. (2008) 'Economic ideology about the environment: from Adam Smith to Bjørn Lomborg', *Global Environment*, 1(2): 8–45.

10   Otteson, J.R. (2002) *Adam Smith's Marketplace of Life*, Cambridge: Cambridge University Press.

11   O'Neill, O. (1989) *Constructions of Reason: Explorations of Kant's Practical Philosophy*, Cambridge: Cambridge University Press.

12   Kant, I. (2015) *On Perpetual Peace*, Peterborough: Broadview Press.

13   Mousseau, M. (2019) 'The end of war: how a robust marketplace and liberal hegemony are leading to perpetual world peace', *International Security*, 44(1): 160.

14   Cerny, P.G. (1995) 'Globalization and the changing logic of collective action', *International Organization*, 49(4): 595–625.

15   Beeson, M. (2019) *Rethinking Global Governance*, Basingstoke: Palgrave Macmillan.

16   Vernon, R. (1971) *Sovereignty at Bay: The Multinational Spread of US Enterprises*, New York: Basic Books; Barnet, R.J. and Cavanagh, J. (1995) *Global Dreams: Imperial Corporations and the New World Order*, New York: Simon & Schuster.

17   Strange, S. (1970) 'International economics and international relations: a case of mutual neglect', *International Affairs*, 46(2): 304–15.

18   Angell, N. (2012 [1909]) *The Great Illusion*, New York: Bottom of the Hill, p 245.

19   Keohane, R.O. and Nye, J.S. (1977) *Power and Interdependence: World Politics in Transition*, Boston: Little, Brown & Co.

20   Keohane, R.O. (1982) 'The demand for international regimes', *International Organization*, 36(25): 325–55; Keohane, R.O. (1989) 'Neoliberal institutionalism: a perspective on world politics', *International Institutions and State Power: Essays in International Relations Theory*, Boulder: Westview Press, pp 1–20.

21   Ikenberry, G.J. (2001) *After Victory: Institutions, Strategic Restraint, and the Rebuilding of Order after Major Wars*, Princeton: Princeton University Press.

22   Ikenberry, G.J. (1998) 'Institutions, strategic restraint, and the persistence of the American postwar order', *International Security*, 23(3): 43–78.

23   Beeson, M. and Zeng, J. (2018) 'The BRICS and global governance: China's contradictory role', *Third World Quarterly*, 39(10): 1962–78.

24   Ikenberry, G.J. (2011) 'The future of the liberal world order', *Foreign Affairs*, 90(3): 57–8.

25   Ruggie, J.G. (1992) 'Multilateralism: the anatomy of an institution', *International Organization*, 46(3): 561–98.

26   Hall, P.A. and Soskice, D. (eds) (2001) *Varieties of Capitalism: The Institutional Foundations of Comparative Advantage*, Oxford: Oxford University Press.

27   Gilley, B. (2009) *The Right to Rule: How States Win and Lose Legitimacy*, New York: Columbia University Press.

28   Herrmann, R.K., Tetlock, P.E. and Diascro, M.N. (2001) 'How Americans think about trade: reconciling conflicts among money, power, and principles', *International Studies Quarterly*, 45(2): 191–218.

29   Gartzke, E. (2007) 'The capitalist peace', *American Journal of Political Science*, 51(1): 166.

30   The *New York Times*'s columnist Thomas Friedman is probably the most influential exponent of this rather discredited view. Friedman, T.L. (2006) *The World is Flat: A Brief History of the Twenty-first Century*, New York: Macmillan.

31   Brooks, S.G. (2005) *Producing Security: Multinational Corporations, Globalization, and the Changing Calculus of Conflict*, Princeton: Princeton University Press, p 10.

32   Russett, B.M. (1995) *Grasping the Democratic Peace: Principles for a post-Cold War World*, Princeton: Princeton University Press.

33   Rosecrance, R. (1986) *The Rise of the Trading State: Commerce and Conquest in the Modern World*, New York: Basic Books; Arrighi, G. (1994) *The Long Twentieth Century: Money, Power, and the Origins of Our Times*, London: Verso.

34   Not all, though. Critical realists are very alert to the role of ideas and values in constituting particular forms of hegemony. See Joseph, J. (2002) *Hegemony: A Realist Analysis*, London: Routledge.

35   For an excellent introduction, see McDonald, M. (2018) 'Constructivisms', in P.D. Williams and M. McDonald (eds), *Security Studies*, London: Routledge, pp 48–59.

36   Finnemore, M. and Sikkink, K. (1998) 'International norm dynamics and political change', *International Organization*, 52(04): 891.

37   Wendt, A. (1999) *Social Theory of International Politics*, Cambridge: Cambridge University Press, p 20.

38   Berger, P. and Luckmann, T. (1967) *The Social Construction of Reality: A Treatise in the Sociology Knowledge*, London: Penguin.

39   Searle, J.R. (1995) *The Construction of Social Reality*, New York: Free Press.

40   Postone, M., LiPuma, E. and Calhoun, C.J. (1993) 'Introduction: Bourdieu and social theory', in M. Postone, E. LiPuma and C.J. Calhoun (eds), *Bourdieu: Critical Perspectives*, Cambridge: Polity Press, pp 1–14.

41   McDonald, M. (2008) 'Securitization and the construction of security', *European Journal of International Relations*, 14(4): 563–87.

42   See Weber, M. (1946) 'Politics as a vocation', in H.H. Gerthand and C. Wright-Mills (eds), *From Max Weber: Essays in Sociology*, New York: Oxford University Press, pp 77–128.

43   Weber, M. (1978) *Economy and Society: An Outline of Interpretive Sociology*, vol. 1, Berkeley: University of California Press, p 315.

44   Migdal, J.S. (1988) *Strong States and Weak Societies: State–Society Relations and State Capabilities in the Third World*, Princeton: Princeton University Press.

45   Jackson, R. (1990) *Quasi-states: Sovereignty, International Relations and the Third World*, Cambridge: Cambridge University Press.

46   Drezner, D.W. (2007) *All Politics is Global: Explaining International Regulatory Regimes*, Princeton: Princeton University Press.

47   Onuf, N.G. (1989) *World of Our Making: Rules and Rule in Social Theory and International Relations*, Columbia: University of South Carolina Press, p 238.

48   Pu, X. (2012) 'Socialisation as a two-way process: emerging powers and the diffusion of international norms', *Chinese Journal of International Politics*, 5(4): 341–67; Risse-Kappen, T. (1994) 'Ideas do not float freely: transnational coalitions, domestic structures, and the end of the cold war', *International Organization*, 48(2): 185–214.

49   Giddens, A. (1985) *The Nation State and Violence*, Cambridge: Polity Press, p 33.

50   Huntington, S.P. (1996) *The Clash of Civilizations and the Remaking of World Order*, New York: Simon & Schuster.

51 Katzenstein, P.J. (2009) 'A world of plural and pluralist civilizations: multiple actors, traditions, and practices', in P.J. Katzenstein, *Civilizations in World Politics: Plural and Pluralist Perspectives*, London: Routledge, p 37.

52 Reus-Smit, C. (1999) *The Moral Purpose of the State*, Princeton: Princeton University Press, p 30.

53 Gong, G.W. (1984) *The Standard of 'Civilisation' in International Society*, Oxford: Clarendon Press.

54 Morris-Suzuki, T. (1996) *The Technological Transformation of Japan: From the Seventeenth to the Twenty-first Century*, vol. 24, London: Routledge.

55 Beeson, M. (2009) 'Geopolitics and the making of regions: the fall and rise of East Asia', *Political Studies*, 57(4): 98–516.

56 Zarakol, A. (2010) *After Defeat: How the East Learned to Live with the West*, Cambridge: Cambridge University Press.

57 Ruggie, J.G. (1998) 'What makes the world hang together? Neo-utilitarianism and the social constructivist challenge', *International Organization*, 52(4): 871.

58 Risse, T. and Sikkink, K. (1999) 'The socialization of international human rights norms into domestic practices: introduction', in T. Risse-Kappen, S.C. Ropp and K. Sikkink (eds), *The Power of Human Rights: International Norms and Domestic Change*, Cambridge: Cambridge University Press, p 5.

59 Beeson, M. and Li, F. (2016) 'China's place in regional and global governance: a new world comes into view', *Global Policy*, 7(4): 491–9.

60 Cashore, B. (2002) 'Legitimacy and the privatization of environmental governance: how non-state market-driven (NSMD) governance systems gain rule-making authority', *Governance*, 15(4): 503–29; Falkner, R. and Buzan, B. (2019) 'The emergence of environmental stewardship as a primary institution of global international society', *European Journal of International Relations*, 25(1): 131–55.

61 Cameron, M.A., Lawson, R.J. and Tomlin, B.W. (1998) *To Walk without Fear: The Global Movement to Ban Landmines*, Toronto: Oxford University Press.

62 Johnston, A.I. (2001) 'Treating international institutions as social environments', *International Studies Quarterly*, 45: 496.

63 Cockett, R. (1994) *Thinking the Unthinkable: Think-Tanks and the Economic Counter-Revolution 1931–1983*, New York: Harper Collins; Culpepper, P.D. and Reinke, R. (2014) 'Structural power and bank bailouts in the United Kingdom and the United States', *Politics & Society*, 42(4): 427–54.

64 Hall, P.A. (1993) 'Policy paradigms, social learning, and the state: the case of economic policymaking in Britain', *Comparative Politics*, 25(3): 275–96.

65 March, J.G. and Olsen, J.P. (1998) 'The institutional dynamics of international political orders', *International Organization*, 52(4): 943–69.

66 Sil, R. and Katzenstein, P.J. (2010) *Beyond Paradigms: Analytic Eclecticism in the Study of World Politics*, London: Palgrave Macmillan.

67 Berenskötter, F. (2018) 'Deep theorizing in International Relations', *European Journal of International Relations*, 24(4): 825.

Chapter 3

1   Bardhan, P. (1997) 'Corruption and development: a review of issues', *Journal of Economic Literature*, 35(3): 1320–46; Hopkin, J. and Rodríguez-Pose, A. (2007) ' "Grabbing hand" or "helping hand"? Corruption and the economic role of the state', *Governance*, 20(2): 187–208.

2   Beeson, M. (2020) 'The lucky country's lacklustre leadership', *Australian Journal of International Affairs*, 72(2): 109–15.

3   Kassam, N. (2020) Lowy Institute Poll 2020, Sydney: Lowy Institute, p 16.

4   Deudney, D. (1990) 'The case against linking environmental degradation and national security', *Millennium – Journal of International Studies*, 19(3): 461–76.

5   Villarreal, A. (2020) 'Meet the doomers: why some young US voters have given up hope on climate', *The Guardian*, 21 September.

6   Malthus, T.R. (2007 [1798]) *An Essay on the Principle of Population*, New York: Cosimo Classics.

7   Goldstone, J.A. (2001) 'Demography, environment, and security', in P.F. Diehl and N.P. Gleditsch (eds), *Environmental Conflict*, Boulder: Westview Press, pp 84–108.

8   Fischer, F. (2019) 'Knowledge politics and post-truth in climate denial: on the social construction of alternative facts', *Critical Policy Studies*, 13(2): 1–19.

9   Carstensen, M.B. (2011) 'Ideas are not as stable as political scientists want them to be: a theory of incremental ideational change', *Political Studies*, 59(3): 596–615.

10 Dalby, S. (2009) *Security and Environmental Change*, Oxford: Polity, p 161.

11 Green, M. (2019) 'Extinction Rebellion: inside the new climate resistance', *Financial Times*, 11 April.

12 Barad, K. (2007) *Meeting the Universe Halfway: Quantum Physics and the Entanglement of Matter and Meaning*, Durham: Duke University Press, p 150.

13 Dinda, S. (2004) 'Environmental Kuznets Curve hypothesis: a survey', *Ecological Economics*, 49(4): 431–55.

14 Oreskes, N. and Conway, E.M. (2010) *Merchants of Doubt: How a Handful of Scientists Obscured the Truth on Issues from Tobacco Smoke to Global Warming*, New York: Bloomsbury Press.

15 Goldmacher, S. (2019) 'How David Koch and his brother shaped American politics', *New York Times*, 23 August; Waton, K. (2020) 'How "Murdochracy" controls the climate debate in Australia', *Al Jazeera*, 24 January.

16 Fischer, F. (2019) 'Knowledge politics and post-truth in climate denial: on the social construction of alternative facts', *Critical Policy Studies*, 13(2): 142.

17 Jacques, P.J. (2012) 'A general theory of climate denial', *Global Environmental Politics*, 12(2): 11.

18 Kuhn, T.S. (2012 [1962]) *The Structure of Scientific Revolutions*, Chicago: University of Chicago Press.

19 Jackson, P.T. (2016) *The Conduct of Inquiry in International Relations: Philosophy of Science and Its Implications for the Study of World Politics*, London: Routledge.

20 Dunlap, R.E. and Mertig, A.G. (2014) 'Trends in public opinion toward environmental issues: 1965–1990', in R.E. Dunlap and A.G. Mertig, *American Environmentalism: The US Environmental Movement, 1970–1990*, New York: Taylor & Francis, pp 101–28.

21 Carson, R. (2002) *Silent Spring*, New York: Houghton Mifflin Harcourt.

22 Eyerman, R. and Jamison, A. (1989) 'Environmental knowledge as an organizational weapon: the case of Greenpeace', *Information (International Social Science Council)*, 28(1): 99–119.

23 Walker, R.B.J. (1993) *Inside/Outside*, Cambridge: Cambridge University Press.

24 Lipschutz, R.D. (1992) 'Reconstructing world politics: the emergence of global civil society', *Millennium*, 21(3): 389–420; Keane, J. (2003) *Global Civil Society?* Cambridge: Cambridge University Press.

25 Hardin, G. (1968) 'The tragedy of the commons', *Science*, 162: 1243–8.

26 Beeson, M. (2019) *Rethinking Global Governance*, Basingstoke: Palgrave Macmillan.

27 Kaplan, R.D. (2002) *The Coming Anarchy: Shattering the Dreams of the Post-Cold War*, New York: Vintage.

28 Krause, D. (1993) 'Environmental consciousness: an empirical study', *Environment and Behavior*, 25(1): 126–42.

29 Bonneuil, C. and Fressoz, J.-B. (2016) *The Shock of the Anthropocene: The Earth, History and Us*, London: Verso Books; Burke, A. and Fishel, S. (2019) 'Power, world politics, and thing-systems in the Anthropocene', in F. Biermann and E. Lovbrand (eds) *Anthropocene Encounters: New Directions in Green Political Thinking*, Cambridge: Cambridge University Press, pp 87–107.

30 Zalasiewicz, J., Williams, M., Steffen, W. and Crutzen, P. (2010) 'The new world of the Anthropocene', *Environmental Science & Technology*, 44(7): 2231.

31 Bonneuil, C. and Fressoz, J.-B. (2016) *The Shock of the Anthropocene: The Earth, History and Us*, London: Verso Books, p 22.

32 IPCC (2007) *Climate Change 2007: The Physical Science Basis*, Geneva: IPCC WGI Fourth Assessment Report, p 2.

33 Lynas, M. (2008) *Six Degrees: Our Future on a Hotter Planet*, London: Harper.

34 Steffen, W., Broadgate, W., Deutsch, L., Gaffney, O. and Ludwig, C. (2015) 'The trajectory of the anthropocene: the great acceleration', *Anthropocene Review*, 2(1): 82.

35 McKibben, B. (2019) *Falter: Has the Human Game Begun to Play Itself Out?*, London: Wildfire.

36 Times Editorial Board (2019) 'Editorial: Wealthy countries are responsible for climate change, but it's the poor who will suffer most', *Los Angeles Times*, 15 September.

37 Anyadike, O. (2019) 'Drought in Africa leaves 45 million in need across 14 countries', *The New Humanitarian*, 10 June.

38 Homer-Dixon, T. (1991) 'On the threshold: environmental changes as causes of conflict', *International Security*, 16(2): 76–116.

39 Vaughan, A. (2020) 'Sea levels in Bangladesh could rise twice as much as predicted', *New Scientist*, 6 January.

40 Xie, E. (2019) 'Climate change is causing Himalayan glaciers to melt twice as fast, research shows', *South China Morning Post*, 20 June.

41 Heijden, K. and Stinson, C. (2019) 'Water is a growing source of global conflict: here's what we need to do', *World Economic Forum*, 18 March.

42 Bernstein, R. (2017) 'China's Mekong plans threaten disaster for countries downstream', *Foreign Policy*, 27 September.

43 Harb, I.K. (2019) 'River of the dammed', *Foreign Policy*, 15 November.

44 Sabbagh, D. (2020) 'UK to strengthen sea patrols to ward off post-Brexit fishing wars', *The Guardian*, 6 February.

45 Clover, C. (2005) *The End of the Line: How Overfishing is Changing the World and What We Eat*, London: Ebury Press.

46 Montaigne, F. (2019) 'Will deforestation and warming push the Amazon to a tipping point?' *YaleEnvironment360*, 4 September. Available at: https://e360.yale.edu/features/will-deforestation-and-warming-push-the-amazon-to-a-tipping-point

47 Anderson, T. and Leal, D. (eds) (2015) *Free Market Environmentalism for the Next Generation*, Basingstoke: Palgrave Macmillan.

48 Lipton, E., Sanger, D.E., Haberman, M., Shear, M.D., Mazzetti, M. and Barnes, J.E. (2020) 'He could have seen what was coming: behind Trump's failure on the virus', *New York Times*, 11 April.

49 Fukuyama, F. (2020) 'The thing that determines a country's resistance to the Coronavirus', *The Atlantic*, 30 March.

[50] Gabuev, A. (2020) 'The pandemic could tighten China's grip on Eurasia', *Foreign Policy*, 23 April.

[51] Lustgarten, A. (2020) 'How climate change is contributing to skyrocketing rates of infectious disease', *ProPublica*, 7 May.

[52] Shah, S. (2016) *Pandemic: Tracking Contagions, from Cholera to Ebola and Beyond*, London: Macmillan, p 98.

[53] Milman, O. (2020) 'Pandemic side-effects offer glimpse of alternative future on Earth Day 2020', *The Guardian*, 22 April.

[54] Carrington, D. (2020) 'Sixth mass extinction of wildlife accelerating, scientists warn', *The Guardian*, 2 June; Harvey, F. (2020) 'Coronavirus pandemic "will cause famine of biblical proportions"', *The Guardian*, 22 April.

[55] Jamieson, D. (2014) *Reason in a Dark Time: Why the Struggle against Climate Change Failed – and What It Means for Our Future*, Oxford: Oxford University Press.

[56] Krasner, S.D. (1982) 'Structural causes and regime consequences: regimes as intervening variables', *International Organization*, 36(2): 186.

[57] Ohmae, K. (1990) *The Borderless World: Power and Strategy in the Interlinked Economy*, New York: Harper Business.

[58] Konings, M. (2008) 'The institutional foundations of US structural power in international finance: from the re-emergence of global finance to the monetarist turn', *Review of International Political Economy*, 15(1): 38.

[59] Zenko, M. and Friedman Lissner, R. (2017) 'Trump is going to regret not having a grand strategy', *Foreign Policy*, 13 January.

[60] Layne, C. (2012) 'This time it's real: the end of unipolarity and the Pax Americana', *International Studies Quarterly*, 56(1): 203–13.

[61] Kagan, R. (2018) *The Jungle Grows Back: American and Our Imperiled World*, New York: Knopf.

[62] Fedor, L. and Manson, K. (2020) 'Trump suspends funding to World Health Organization', *Financial Times*, 15 April.

[63] Townsend, B. (2020) 'COVID-19 fuels global health tensions', *East Asia Forum*, 10 May.

[64] Beeson, M. and Watson, N. (2019) 'Is international leadership changing hands or disappearing? China and the USA in comparative perspective', *Asian Perspective*, 43(2): 389–417.

[65] Keohane, R.O. (1984) *After Hegemony: Cooperation and Discord in the World Political Economy*, Princeton: Princeton University Press, p 50.

[66] Howland, D. (2015) 'An alternative mode of international order: the international administrative union in the nineteenth century', *Review of International Studies*, 41(1): 161–83.

[67] Mitzen, J. (2013) *Power in Concert: The Nineteenth-century Origins of Global Governance*, Chicago: University of Chicago Press, p 31.

[68] Braithwaite, J. and Drahos, P. (2000) *Global Business Regulation*, Cambridge: Cambridge University Press; Helleiner, E. (1994) *States and the Reemergence of Global Finance*, Ithaca: Cornell University Press.

[69] Pieterse, J.N. (2004) *Globalization or Empire?* London: Routledge.

[70] Mazower, M. (2012) *Governing the World: The History of an Idea*, London: Allen Lane, p 215.

[71] Harvey, F. (2020) 'Humanity is waging war on nature, says UN secretary general', *The Guardian*, 3 December.

72 Weiss, T.G., Forsythe, D.P., Coate, R.A. and Pease, K. (eds) (2018) *The United Nations and Changing World Politics*, London: Routledge; Menon, A. (2008) *Europe: The State of the Union*, London: Atlantic Books.

73 Mearsheimer, J.J. (1994–95) 'The false promise of institutions', *International Security*, 19(3): 5–49.

74 Mazower, M. (2013) *No Enchanted Palace: The End of Empire and the Ideological Origins of the United Nations*, Princeton: Princeton University Press.

75 Malone, D. (2004) *The UN Security Council: From the Cold War to the 21st century*, Boulder: Lynne Rienner Publishers.

76 Mingst, K. and Karns, M.P. (2019) *The United Nations in the Post-Cold War Era*, London: Routledge.

77 Reinicke, W.H., Deng, F., Witte, J.M., Benner, T. and Whitaker, B. (2000) *Critical Choices: The United Nations, Networks, and the Future of Global Governance*, Ottawa: IDRC.

78 Panke, D. (2013) *Unequal Actors in Equalising Institutions: Negotiations in the United Nations General Assembly*, Basingstoke: Palgrave Macmillan.

79 Adams, V., Novotny, T.E. and Leslie, H. (2008) 'Global health diplomacy', *Medical Anthropology*, 27(4): 315–23.

80 Ivanova, M. (2007) 'Designing the United Nations Environment Programme: a story of compromise and confrontation', *International Environmental Agreements: Politics, Law and Economics*, 7(4): 337–61.

81 Pachauri, R.K. (2004) 'Climate change and its implications for development: the role of IPCC assessments', *IDS Bulletin*, 35(3): 11–14.

82 Grundmann, R. (2007) 'Climate change and knowledge politics', *Environmental Politics*, 16(3): 414–32.

83 Vanhala, L. and Hestbaek, C. (2016) 'Framing climate change loss and damage in UNFCCC negotiations', *Global Environmental Politics*, 16(4): 111–29.

84 Christoff, P. (2006) 'Post-Kyoto? Post-Bush? Towards an effective "climate coalition of the willing"', *International Affairs*, 82(5): 831–60; Crowley, K. (2007) 'Is Australia faking it? The Kyoto Protocol and the greenhouse policy challenge', *Global Environmental Politics*, 7(4): 118–39.

85 Roberts, J.T. and Parks, B.C. (2007) *A Climate of Injustice: Global Inequality, North-South Politics, and Climate Policy*, Cambridge, MA: MIT Press, p 48.

86 Dryzek, J.S. and Stevenson, H. (2011) 'Global democracy and earth system governance', *Ecological Economics*, 70(11): 1871.

87 Falkner, R., Stephan, H. and Vogler, J. (2010) 'International climate policy after Copenhagen: towards a "building blocks" approach', *Global Policy*, 1(3): 256.

88 Conrad, B. (2012) 'China in Copenhagen: reconciling the "Beijing climate revolution" and the "Copenhagen climate obstinacy"', *The China Quarterly*, 210: 435–55.

89 Shambaugh, D. (2013) *China Goes Global: The Partial Power*, Oxford: Oxford University Press, p 7.

90 Conrad (2012), p 443.

91 Li, S., Abbott, B. and Wang, J. (2020) 'Coronavirus outbreak a major test of China's system, says Xi Jinping', *New York Times*, 3 February.

92 Falkner, R. and Buzan, B. (2017) 'The emergence of environmental stewardship as a primary institution of global international society', *European Journal of International Relations*, 25(1): 146.

[93] Scientific knowledge and expertise were taken seriously by policymakers in devising feasible policies for a specific problem. See Parson, E.A. (2012) *Protecting the Ozone Layer: Science and Strategy*, Oxford: Oxford University Press.

[94] Dimitrov, R.S. (2016) 'The Paris agreement on climate change: behind closed doors', *Global Environmental Politics*, 16(3): 1–11.

[95] Daly, T. and Xu, M. (2019) 'China's 2018 coal usage rises 1 percent, but share of energy mix falls', *Reuters*, 28 February.

[96] Zhong, Y. and Hwang, W. (2015) 'Pollution, institutions and street protests in urban China', *Journal of Contemporary China*, 25(98): 216–32.

[97] Gross, S. (2019) 'Coal is king in India – and will likely remain so', *Brookings*, 8 March.

[98] Casado, L. and Londoño, E. (2019) 'Under Brazil's far right leader, Amazon protections slashed and forests fall', *New York Times*, 28 July.

[99] Apergis, N. and Ozturk, I. (2015) 'Testing environmental Kuznets curve hypothesis in Asian countries', *Ecological Indicators*, 52: 16–22.

[100] Diamond, L. (2008) *The Spirit of Democracy: The Struggle to Build Free Societies Throughout the World*, New York: Holt; Przeworski, A., Alvarez, M.E., Cheibub, J.A. and Limongi, F. (2000) *Democracy and Development: Political Institutions and Well-Being in the World, 1950–1990*, Cambridge: Cambridge University Press.

[101] Sen, A. (1999) 'Democracy as a universal value', *Journal of Democracy*, 10(3): 3–17.

[102] Fukuyama, F. (1992) *The End of History and the Last Man*, New York: Free Press.

[103] Holzinger, K., Knill, C. and Sommerer, T. (2008) 'Environmental policy convergence: the impact of international harmonization, transnational communication, and regulatory competition', *International Organization*, 62(04): 553–87.

[104] Teets, J.C. (2014) *Civil Society Under Authoritarianism: The China Model*, Cambridge: Cambridge University Press, p 176.

[105] Galston, W.A. (2018) *Anti-Pluralism: The Real Populist Threat to Liberal Democracy*, New Haven: Yale University Press; Levitsky, S. and Ziblatt, D. (2018) *How Democracies Die: What History Reveals about Our Future*, London: Viking.

[106] Biermann, F. and Pattberg, P. (2008) 'Global environmental governance: taking stock, moving forward', *Annual Review of Environment and Resources*, 33(1): 280.

[107] Fischer, F. (2019) 'Knowledge politics and post-truth in climate denial: on the social construction of alternative facts', *Critical Policy Studies*, 13(2): 1–19.

[108] Mounk, Y. (2018) *The People vs. Democracy: Why Our Freedom is in Danger and How to Save it*, Cambridge, MA: Harvard University Press; Sunstein, C.R. (ed) (2018) *Can It Happen Here? Authoritarianism in America*. New York: HarperCollins.

[109] Smith, D. (2019) ' "He has faults, but don't we all?": Trump supporters say he will defeat impeachment', *The Guardian*, 12 October.

[110] Sevastopulo, D. (2020) ' "This is a guy who is a thug": how US elite became hawks on Xi's China', *Financial Times*, 8 October.

[111] Beeson, M. (2018) 'Institutionalizing the Indo-Pacific: the challenges of regional cooperation', *East Asia*, 35: 1–14.

[112] Campbell, K.M., Gulledge, J., McNeill, J.R., Podesta, J., Ogden, P., Fuerth, L., Woolsey, R.J., Lennon, A.T., Smith, J. and Weitz, R. (2007) *The Age of Consequences: The Foreign Policy and National Security Implications of Global Climate Change*, DTIC Document, p 77.

[113] Beeson, M. and Chako, P. (2020) 'Covid-19 in China, the US, India: comparative crisis management 101', *The Interpreter*, 11 March.

[114] Hobson (2012).

[115] Meckling, J. (2018) 'The developmental state in global regulation: economic change and climate policy', *European Journal of International Relations*, 24(1): 58–81.

[116] Beeson, M. (2017) 'What does China's rise mean for the developmental state paradigm?', in T. Carroll and D. Jarvis (eds), *Asia after the Developmental State: Disembedding Autonomy*, Cambridge: Cambridge University Press, pp 174–97.

[117] Luce, E. (2012) *Time to Start Thinking: America in the Age of Descent*, New York: Atlantic Monthly Press.

[118] Kindleberger, C.P. (1973) *The World in Depression, 1929–1939*, Berkeley: University of California Press.

[119] Jervis, R. (2013) 'Do leaders matter and how would we know?', *Security Studies*, 22(2): 153–79; Jones, B.F. and Olken, B.A. (2005) 'Do leaders matter? National leadership and growth since World War II', *The Quarterly Journal of Economics*, 120(1): 835–64; Ahlquist, J.S. and Levi, M. (2011) 'Leadership: what it means, what it does, and what we want to know about it', *Annual Review of Political Science*, 14(1): 1–24.

[120] Tooze, A. (2020) 'Biden will have the presidency. But Republicans still have the power', *The Guardian*, 25 November.

[121] Roberts, J.T. (2011) 'Multipolarity and the new world (dis)order: US hegemonic decline and the fragmentation of the global climate regime', *Global Environmental Change-Human and Policy Dimensions*, 21(3): 776–84.

[122] Singer, A. and Wildavsky, M. (1993) *The Real World Order: Zones of Peace/Zones of Turmoil*, New Jersey: Chatham House Publishers.

[123] Kelemen, R.D. and Vogel, D. (2010) 'Trading places: the role of the United States and the European Union in international environmental politics', *Comparative Political Studies*, 43(4): 427–56.

[124] Zito, A.R., Burns, C. and Lenschow, A. (2019) 'Is the trajectory of European Union environmental policy less certain?' *Environmental Politics*, 28(2): 187–207.

[125] Manners, I. (2002) 'Normative power Europe: a contradiction in terms?', *JCMS: Journal of Common Market Studies*, 40(2): 235–58.

[126] Held, D. (2016) 'Climate change, migration and the cosmopolitan dilemma', *Global Policy*, 7(2): 240.

[127] Barber, T. (2018) 'Europe risks failure on migration', *Financial Times*, 20 August.

[128] Kojm, C. (2012) *Global Trends 2030: Alternative Worlds Alternative Worlds*, Washington: National Intelligence Council, p 20.

[129] Norris, P. and Inglehart, R. (2019) *Cultural Backlash: Trump, Brexit, and Authoritarian Populism*, Cambridge: Cambridge University Press.

[130] Kreuder-Sonnen, C. (2018) 'An authoritarian turn in Europe and European Studies?', *Journal of European Public Policy*, 25(3): 452–64.

[131] Burns, C., Eckersley, P. and Tobin, P. (2020) 'EU environmental policy in times of crisis', *Journal of European Public Policy*, 27(1): 15.

[132] Green, J.F. and Colgan, J. (2013) 'Protecting sovereignty, protecting the planet: state delegation to international organizations and private actors in environmental politics', *Governance*, 26(3): 473–97.

[133] Holzinger, K., Knill, C. and Sommerer, T. (2008) 'Environmental policy convergence: the impact of international harmonization, transnational communication, and regulatory competition', *International Organization*, 62 (04): 553–87.

[134] Koppel, J.G.S. (2010) *World Rule: Accountability, Legitimacy, and the Design of Global Governance*, Chicago: University of Chicago Press.

[135] Agnew, J. (2018) *Globalization and Sovereignty: Beyond the Territorial Trap* (2nd edn), Lanham: Rowman & Littlefield Publishers.

136 Hall, P.A. (2012) 'The economics and politics of the euro crisis', *German Politics*, 21(4): 367.

137 Avishai, B. (2020) 'The pandemic isn't a black swan but a portent of a more fragile global system', *New Yorker*, 21 April.

138 Harvey, D. (2009) *Cosmopolitanism and the Geographies of Freedom*, New York: Columbia University Press; Cabrera, L. (2006) *Political Theory of Global Justice: A Cosmopolitan Case for the World State*, London: Routledge; Linklater, A. (2010) 'Global civilizing processes and the ambiguities of human interconnectedness', *European Journal of International Relations*, 16(2): 155–78.

139 Schweller, R.L. (2014) *Maxwell's Demon and the Golden Apple: Global Discord in the New Millennium*, Baltimore: Johns Hopkins University Press.

140 Broome, A., Clegg, L. and Rethel, L. (eds) (2015) *Global Governance in Crisis*, London: Routledge.

141 Wilke, R., Fetterolf, J. and Fagan, M. (2019) 'Europeans credit EU with promoting peace and prosperity, but say Brussels is out of touch with its citizens', *Pew Research Centre*, 19 March.

142 Ekengren, M. (2008) 'From a European security community to a secure European community: tracing the new security identity of the EU', in H.G. Brauch (ed), *Globalization and Environmental Challenges*, Berlin: Springer, pp 695–704.

143 Webber, D. (2014) 'How likely is it that the European Union will disintegrate? A critical analysis of competing theoretical perspectives', *European Journal of International Relations*, 20(2): 341–65.

Chapter 4

1 CIA (2020) *The World Factbook*, available at: https://www.cia.gov/library/publications/the-world-factbook/rankorder/2102rank.html

2 Urdal, H. (2006) 'A clash of generations? Youth bulges and political violence', *International Studies Quarterly*, 50(3): 607–29.

3 For an influential example see Jervis, R. (1976) *Perception and Misperception in International Politics*, Princeton: Princeton University Press.

4 Morgenthau, H. J. (1978 [1948]) *Politics Among Nations: The Struggle for Power and Peace* (5th edn), New York: Knopf, p 266.

5 May, E.T. (2008) *Homeward Bound: American Families in the Cold War Era*, London: Hachette UK.

6 Busemeyer, J.R. and Bruza, P.D. (2012) *Quantum Models of Cognition and Decision*, Cambridge: Cambridge University Press.

7 Seybert, L.A. and Katzenstein, P.J. (2018) 'Protean power and control power: conceptual analysis', in L.A. Seybert and P.J. Katzenstein, *Protean Power: Exploring the Uncertain and Unexpected in World Politics*, Cambridge: Cambridge University Press, p 4.

8 Bell, S. (2012) 'The power of ideas: the ideational shaping of the structural power of business', *International Studies Quarterly*, 56(4): 663.

9 Bloom, W. (1993) *Personal Identity, National Identity and International Relations*, Cambridge: Cambridge University Press.

10 Hafner-Burton, E.M., Haggard, S., Lake, D.A. and Victor, D.G. (2017) 'The behavioural revolution and international relations', *International Organization* 71(S1): S1–S31.

11 Allison, G.T. (1971) *Essence of Decision: Explaining the Cuban Missile Crisis*, New York: Little, Brown and Company.

12 Lebow, R.N. (1984) *Between Peace and War: The Nature of International Crisis*, Baltimore: Johns Hopkins University Press, p 105.

13 Drezner, D.W. (2020) *The Toddler in Chief: What Donald Trump Teaches Us about the Modern Presidency*, Chicago: University of Chicago Press, p 205.

14 Woodward, B. (2004) *Plan of Attack*, New York: Simon & Schuster.

15 Wright, T. and Campbell, K. (2020) 'The coronavirus is exposing the limits of populism', *Brookings*, 5 March.

16 Eckersley, R. (2020) 'Rethinking leadership: understanding the roles of the US and China in the negotiation of the Paris Agreement', *European Journal of International Relations*, 26(4): 1178–202.

17 Mann, J. (2004) *Rise of the Vulcans: The History of Bush's War Cabinet*, New York: Viking.

18 Horowitz, M.C. and Stam, A.C. (2014) 'How prior military experience influences the future militarized behavior of leaders', *International Organization*, 68(3): 527–59.

19 Kahneman, D. (2011) *Thinking, Fast and Slow*, London: Macmillan.

20 Rosati, J.A. (2000) 'The power of human cognition in the study of world politics', *International Studies Review*, 2(3): 53.

21 Economy, E.C. (2014) 'China's imperial president: Xi Jinping tightens his grip', *Foreign Affairs*, 93(6): 80–9.

22 Mounk, Y. and Foa, R.S. (2018) 'The end of the democratic century: autocracy's global ascendance', *Foreign Affairs*, 97(3): 31.

23 Smith, D. (2020) '"It eats him alive inside": Trump's latest attack shows endless obsession with Obama', *The Guardian*, 16 May.

24 Drezner (2020), p 106.

25 Funk, C., Heffron, M., Kennedy, B. and Johnson, C. (2019) 'Trust and mistrust in Americans' views of scientific experts', *Pew Research Centre*, 2 August. Available at: https://www.pewresearch.org/science/2019/08/02/trust-and-mistrust-in-americans-views-of-scientific-experts/

26 Taggart, P. (2000) *Populism*, Buckingham: Open University Press.

27 Mudde, C. and Kaltwasser, C.R. (2017) *Populism: A Very Short Introduction*, Oxford: Oxford University Press, pp 47–8.

28 McGreal, C. (2020) 'Where Christian evangelicals worship Trump more than Jesus – key voters stay loyal to president', *The Guardian*, 15 January.

29 Kazin, M. (1998) *The Populist Persuasion: An American History*, Ithaca: Cornell University Press.

30 Rehman, I. (2017) 'Rise of the reactionaries: the American far right and U.S. foreign policy', *The Washington Quarterly*, 40(4): 40.

31 Sandel, M.J. (2018) 'Populism, liberalism, and democracy', *Philosophy and Social Criticism*, 44(4): 354.

32 Tilly, C. (2015) *Social Movements 1768–2012* (3rd edn), London: Routledge.

33 Levitsky, S. and Ziblatt, D. (2018) *How Democracies Die: What History Reveals about Our Future*, London: Viking, p 146.

34 Krugman, P. (2020) '"A terrifying performance": Donald Trump is close to inciting civil war', *Sydney Morning Herald*, 3 June.

35 Kaufmann, E. (2018) *Whiteshift: Populism, Immigration and the Future of White Majorities*, London: Allen Lane, p 515.

36 Barber, B.R. (2001) *Jihad vs. McWorld*, New York: Ballantine Books.

37 O'Toole, F. (2018) *Heroic Failure: Brexit and the Politics of Pain*, London: Head of Zeus.

38 Ascherson, N. (2019) 'The long Brexit ordeal will finish off the break-up of Britain', *The Guardian*, 28 October.

39 Vaughan, A. (2020) 'UK sets ambitious climate goal of 68 per cent emissions cut by 2030', *New Scientist*, 3 December.

40 Beeson, M. (2020) *'The Decline of the West': What Is It, and Why Might It Matter?* Hong Kong: Asia Global Institute.

41 Tyson, A. and Kennedy, B. (2020) 'Two-thirds of Americans think government should do more on climate', *Pew Research Centre*, 23 June; Murphy, K. (2020) 'Three-quarters of Australians back target of net zero by 2030, Guardian Essential poll shows', *The Guardian*, 1 December.

42 Buckley, F.H. (2020) *American Secession: The Looming Threat of a National Breakup*, New York: Encounter Books.

43 Fukuyama, F. (2018) *Identity: Contemporary Identity Politics and the Struggle for Recognition*, London: Profile, p 90.

44 Reich, R. (2020) 'Trump's use of the military backfired – but will it back him if he refuses to go?', *The Guardian*, 8 June.

45 Brooks, R. (2017) *How Everything Became War and the Military Became Everything: Tales from the Pentagon*, New York: Simon & Schuster, p 299.

46 Allen, J. (2020) 'A moment of national shame and peril – and hope', *Foreign Policy*, 3 June.

47 Acemoglu, D. (2020) 'The coronavirus exposed America's authoritarian turn', *Foreign Affairs*, 23 March.

48 Zhang, S. (2020) 'We don't even have a COVID-19 vaccine, and yet the conspiracies are here', *The Atlantic*, 24 May.

49 Putnam, R. (1995) 'Bowling alone: America's declining social capital', *Journal of Democracy*, 6(1): 65–78.

50 Higgott, R. (2019) *Civlizations, States, and World Order: Where Are We? Where Are We Heading?* Berlin: DOC Research Institute, p 17.

51 Goldstone, J.A. (1991) *Revolution and Rebellion in the Early Modern World*, Berkeley: University of California Press, p 458.

52 Geertz, C. (1973) *The Interpretation of Cultures*, New York: Basic Books, p 89.

53 Wolf, E.R. (1997) *Europe and the People Without History*, Berkeley: University of California Press.

54 Acharya, A. (2009) *Whose Ideas Matter? Agency and Power in Asian Regionalism*, Ithaca: Cornell University Press.

55 Callahan, W.A. (2010) *China: The Pessoptimist Nation*, Oxford: Oxford University Press.

56 Deng, Y. (2008) *China's Struggle for Status: The Realignment of International Relations*, Cambridge: Cambridge University Press.

57 Watts, G. (2020) 'China stokes the furnace of nationalism', *Asia Times*, 11 May.

58 Johnson, C.A. (1962) *Peasant Nationalism and Communist Power: The Emergence of Revolutionary China, 1937–1945*, Stanford: Stanford University Press.

59 Lebow, R.N. (2008) *A Cultural Theory of International Relations*, Cambridge: Cambridge University Press.

60 Armstrong, C.K. (2009) *Juche and North Korea's Global Aspirations*, Washington: Woodrow Wilson Center.

61 Strategy Division, Directorate for Strategic Plans and Policy (J-5), Joint Staff (2020) *Joint Vision 2020: America's Military – Preparing for Tomorrow*, Washington.

62 Schrader, S. (2020) 'Yes, American police act like occupying armies. They literally studied their tactics', *The Guardian*, 8 June.

63 Kennan, G. (1946) 'The long telegram', available at: http://memoriapoliticademexico. org/Textos/6Revolucion/IM/1946-feb-22-the_kennan_telegram.pdf. Also see Harper, J.L. (1994) *American Visions of Europe: Franklin D. Roosevelt, George F. Kennan, and Dean G. Acheson*, Cambridge: Cambridge University Press.

64 Nugent, E.R. (2020) 'The psychology of repression and polarization', *World Politics*, 72(2): 295–6.

65 Jervis, R. (1985) 'Perceiving and coping with threat', in *Psychology and Deterrence*, Baltimore: Johns Hopkins University Press, p 33.

66 Jepporson, R.L., Wendt, A. and Katzenstein, P. (1996) 'Norms, identity, and culture in national security', in P. Katzenstein (ed), *The Culture of National Security: Norms and Ideology in World Politics*, New York: Columbia University Press, p 33.

67 Thelen, K. (1999) 'Historical institutionalism in comparative politics', *Annual Review of Political Science*, 2(1): 369–404.

68 Vucetic, S. (2011) *The Anglosphere: A Genealogy of a Racialized Identity in International Relations*, Stanford: Stanford University Press, p 141.

69 Adler, E. and Barnett, M. (1998) 'A framework for the study of security communities', in E. Adler and M. Barnett, *Security Communities*, Cambridge: Cambridge University Press, p 30.

70 My own country of residence illustrates these tensions with depressing clarity: Morton, A. (2020) 'Australia's climate record labelled "simply embarrassing" and among worst of G20 nations', *The Guardian*, 18 November.

71 Allison (1971), p 71.

72 Gray, C.S. (1981) 'National style in strategy: the American example', *International Security*, 6(2): 21–47.

73 Glenn, J. (2009) 'Realism versus strategic culture: competition and collaboration?', *International Studies Review*, 11(3): 530.

74 Bloomfield, A. and Nossal, K.R. (2007) 'Towards an explicative understanding of strategic culture: the cases of Australia and Canada', *Contemporary Security Policy*, 28(2): 286–307.

75 Pearlman, J. (2020) 'Australia unnecessarily exposed itself to Beijing's fury, but relying on the US now is risky', *The Guardian*, 25 May.

76 Johnston, A.I. (1995) *Cultural Realism: Strategic Culture and Grand Strategy in Chinese History*, Princeton: Princeton University Press.

77 Klein, B.S. (1988) 'Hegemony and strategic culture: American power projection and alliance defence politics', *Review of International Studies*, 14(2): 136.

78 Checkel, J.T. (1997) *Ideas and International Political Change: Soviet/Russian Behavior and the End of the Cold War*, New Haven: Yale University Press.

79 Domber, G.F. (2014) *Empowering Revolution: America, Poland, and the End of the Cold War*, Chapel Hill: University of North Carolina Press.

80 Rosenau, J.N. (1990) *Turbulence in World Politics: A Theory of Change and Continuity*, Princeton: Princeton University Press, p 88.

81 Harvey, D. (1988) *The Condition of Postmodernity: An Enquiry into the Origins of Cultural Change*, Oxford: Blackwell, p 298.

82 Jameson, F. (1991) *Postmodernism, or, the Cultural Logic of Late Capitalism*, London: Verso, p 4.

83 Nicholson, R. (2016) '"Poor little snowflake" – the defining insult of 2016', *The Guardian*, 29 November.

[84] Gerbaudo, P. (2017) *The Mask and the Flag: Populism, Citizenism, and Global Protest*, London: Hurst.

[85] Appadurai, A. (1996) *Modernity at Large: Cultural Dimensions of Globalization*, Minneapolis: University of Minnesota Press, p 15.

[86] Goldgeier, J.M. (1997) 'Psychology and security', *Security Studies*, 6(4): 156.

[87] Bleiker, R. and Hutchison, E. (2008) 'Fear no more: emotions and world politics', *Review of International Studies*, 34(S1): 115–35.

[88] Duffield, J.S. (1999) 'Political culture and state behavior: Why Germany confounds neorealism', *International Organization*, 53(04): 765–803.

[89] Rosecrance, R. (1986) *The Rise of the Trading State: Commerce and Conquest in the Modern World*, New York: Basic Books; Katzenstein, P.J. (1996) *Cultural Norms and National Security: Police and Military in Postwar Japan*, Ithaca: Cornell University Press.

[90] Crawford, N.C. (2000) 'The passion of world politics: propositions on emotion and emotional relationships', *International Security*, 24(4): 119.

[91] Wood, E.A. (2011) 'Performing memory: Vladimir Putin and the celebration of World War II in Russia', *The Soviet and Post-Soviet Review*, 38(2): 172–200.

[92] Coble, P.M. (2007) 'China's "new remembering" of the Anti-Japanese War of Resistance, 1937–1945', *The China Quarterly*, 190: 394–410.

[93] Mercer, J. and Martin, L. (2013) 'Rationality and psychology in international politics', *International Organization*, 59(1): 77–106.

[94] Sartori, G. (1989) 'The essence of the political in Carl Schmitt', *Journal of Theoretical Politics*, 1(1): 63–75.

[95] Wendt, A. (1999) *Social Theory of International Politics*, Cambridge: Cambridge University Press, p 197.

[96] Newman, E. (2009) 'Failed states and international order: constructing a post-Westphalian world', *Contemporary Security Policy*, 30(3): 421–43.

[97] Gray, J. (2020) 'Why this crisis is a turning point in history', *New Statesman*, 1 April.

[98] Coyne, C.J. and Hall, A.R. (2018) *Tyranny Comes Home: The Domestic Fate of US Militarism*, Stanford: Stanford University Press.

[99] UNDP (1994) *Human Development Report 1994: New Dimensions of Human Security*, New York: Oxford University Press.

[100] Newman, E. (2010) 'Critical human security studies', *Review of International Studies*, 36(01): 79.

[101] Thomas, C. (2000) *Global Governance, Development and Human Security*, London: Pluto Press, p 4.

[102] Preble, C.A. (2020) 'Comparing military spending and COVID-19 related medical costs', *Cato At Liberty*, 7 April. Available at: https://www.cato.org/blog/comparing-military-spending-covid-19-related-medical-costs

[103] Adams, V., Novotny, T.E. and Leslie, H. (2008) 'Global health diplomacy', *Medical Anthropology*, 27(4): 321.

[104] Beeson, M. (2019) *Rethinking Global Governance*, Basingstoke: Palgrave Macmillan.

[105] Savage, M. (2020) 'Once we have a vaccine, how will it be shared fairly around the world?' *The Guardian*, 26 April.

[106] Konyndyk, J. (2020) 'Exceptionalism is killing Americans: an insular political culture failed the test of the pandemic', *Foreign Affairs*, 8 June.

[107] Strauss, V. (2018) 'How are America's public schools really doing?' *Washington Post*, 16 October.

[108] Kliff, S. (2020) 'Most coronavirus tests cost about $100. Why did one cost $2,315?', *New York Times*, 16 June; Lerner, S. (2020) 'Big pharma prepares to profit from the coronavirus', *The Intercept*, 14 March.

[109] Rothkopf, D. (2012) *Power, Inc: The Epic Rivalry between Big Business and Government – and the Reckoning that Lies Ahead*, New York: Farrar, Straus and Giroux, p 13.

[110] Reich, R.B. (2016) *Saving Capitalism: For the Many, Not the Few*, New York: Vintage, p 157.

[111] Brown, M.B. (2014) 'Climate science, populism, and the democracy of rejection', in D.A. Crow and M.T. Boykoff (eds), *Culture, Politics and Climate Change: How Information Shapes Our Common Future*, London: Routledge, pp 129–45.

[112] Gross, M. and McGoey, L. (eds) (2015) *Routledge International Handbook of Ignorance Studies*, London: Routledge.

[113] Keane, J. (2018) *Power and Humility: The Future of Monitory Democracy*, Cambridge: Cambridge University Press.

[114] Nichols, T. (2017) *The Death of Expertise: The Campaign Against Established Knowledge and Why It Matters*, Oxford: Oxford University Press, p xix.

[115] AFP (2020) 'Only half of Americans would get a COVID-19 vaccine: poll', *Australian Financial Review*, 28 May.

[116] Nichols (2017), p 99.

[117] Brennan, J. (2017) *Against Democracy*, Princeton: Princeton University Press.

[118] Achen, C.H. and Bartels, L.M. (2017) *Democracy for Realists: Why Elections Do not Produce Responsive Government*, Princeton: Princeton University Press, p 4.

[119] Greenhill, B. (2008) 'Recognition and collective identity formation in international politics', *European Journal of International Relations*, 14(2): 361.

[120] Robin, C. (2004) *Fear: The History of a Political Idea*, Oxford: Oxford University Press, p 141.

[121] Krastev, I. and Holmes, S. (2019) *The Light that Failed: A Reckoning*, London: Allen Lane, p 12.

[122] Packer, G. (2020) 'We are living in a failed state', *The Atlantic*, 15 June.

[123] Pearce, N. (2019) 'What are the roots of Britain's identity crisis? From Enoch Powell to Brexit', *Financial Times*, 4 October.

[124] Brands, H., Feaver, P. and Inboden, W. (2020) 'In defense of the Blob: America's foreign policy establishment is the solution, not the problem', *Foreign Affairs*, 29 April.

[125] Ashford, E. (2020) 'Build a better Blob: foreign policy is not a binary choice between Trumpism and discredited elites', *Foreign Affairs*, 29 May.

[126] Frum, D. (2020) 'This is Trump's fault: the president is failing, and Americans are paying for his failures', *The Atlantic*, 7 April; Wong, E. and Crowley, M. (2020) 'The biggest obstacle to China policy: President Trump', *New York Times*, 18 June.

[127] Hopf, T. (2010) 'The logic of habit in international relations', *European Journal of International Relations*, 16(4): 548.

[128] Ringmar, E. (2018) What are public moods? *European Journal of Social Theory*, 21(4): 453–69.

[129] Zhang, F. (2013) 'The rise of Chinese exceptionalism in international relations', *European Journal of International Relations*, 19(2): 305–28.

[130] Gries, P.H. (2005) 'Social psychology and the identity-conflict debate: is a "China threat" inevitable?', *European Journal of International Relations*, 11(2): 257.

[131] Mounk, Y. and Foa, R.S. (2018) 'The end of the democratic century: autocracy's global ascendance', *Foreign Affairs*, 97(3): 31.

Chapter 5

[1] Acharya, A. (2014) *The End of the American World Order*, Cambridge: Polity Press; Beeson, M. (2019) *Rethinking Global Governance*, Basingstoke: Palgrave Macmillan; Ikenberry, G.J. (2018) 'The end of liberal international order?', *International Affairs*, 94(1): 7–23; Stokes, D. (2018) 'Trump, American hegemony and the future of the liberal international order', *International Affairs*, 94(1): 133–50.

[2] Layne, C. (2017) 'The US foreign policy establishment and grand strategy: how American elites obstruct strategic adjustment', *International Politics*, 54(3): 261.

[3] Ruggiero, J. (2015) *Hitler's Enabler: Neville Chamberlain and the Origins of the Second World War*, Santa Barbara: Praeger.

[4] Merk, F. and Merk, L.B. (1995) *Manifest Destiny and Mission in American History: A Reinterpretation*, Cambridge, MA: Harvard University Press.

[5] Zhang, F. (2013) 'The rise of Chinese exceptionalism in international relations', *European Journal of International Relations*, 19(2): 305–28.

[6] Layton, P. (2020) 'Designing an Australian grand strategy for China', *The Strategist*, 23 June.

[7] Betts, R.K. (2019) 'The grandiosity of grand strategy', *The Washington Quarterly*, 42(4): 7.

[8] Cain, P.J. and Hopkins, A.G. (2014) *British Imperialism: 1688–2000*, London: Routledge.

[9] Toynbee, A.J. (1987) *A Study of History*, vol. 1, Oxford: Oxford Paperbacks.

[10] O'Toole, F. (2018) *Heroic Failure: Brexit and the Politics of Pain*, London: Head of Zeus; Stokes, D. and Whitman, R.G. (2013) 'Transatlantic triage? European and UK "grand strategy" after the US rebalance to Asia', *International Affairs*, 89(5): 1087–107.

[11] Kang, D.C. (2010) *East Asia before the West: Five Centuries of Trade and Tribute*, New York: Columbia University Press.

[12] Braudel, F. (1995) *A History of Civilizations*, New York: Penguin Books; Callahan, W.A. (2010) *China: The Pessoptimist Nation*, Oxford: Oxford University Press.

[13] Pillsbury, M. (2015) *The Hundred-year Marathon: China's Secret Strategy to Replace America as the Global Superpower*, New York: Henry Holt.

[14] Esdaile, C. (2008) *Napoleon's Wars: An International History, 1803–1815*, London: Penguin.

[15] Rosenfeld, G.D. (2005) *The World Hitler Never Made: Alternate History and the Memory of Nazism*, Cambridge: Cambridge University Press. Also see Phillip Roth's (2004) novel *The Plot against America: A Novel*, New York: Houghton Mifflin Harcourt.

[16] Booth, K. and Wheeler, N.J. (2008) *The Security Dilemma: Fear, Cooperation, and Trust in World Politics*, Basingstoke: Palgrave Macmillan, pp 4–5.

[17] Gaddis, J.L. (2018) *On Grand Strategy*, New York: Penguin, p 21.

[18] Art, R.J. (2003) *A Grand Strategy for America*, Ithaca: Cornell University Press, p 143. It is also worth noting that Art was equally sanguine about the United States' relative invulnerability to environmental threats (p 32) – another idea that looks to have rapidly dated.

[19] Cordesman, A.H. and Colley, S. (2016) *Chinese Strategy and Military Modernization in 2015: A Comparative Analysis*, Lanham: Rowman & Littlefield.

[20] Gaddis (2018), p 55.

[21] Crawford, N.C. (2000) 'The passion of world politics: propositions on emotion and emotional relationships', *International Security*, 24(4): 119.

22 Blum, D.W. (1993) 'The Soviet foreign policy belief system: beliefs, politics, and foreign policy outcomes', *International Studies Quarterly*, 37(4): 373–94.

23 Smith, T. (1994) *America's Mission: The United States and the Worldwide Struggle for Democracy in the Twentieth Century*, Princeton: Princeton University Press.

24 Hogan, M.J. (1998) *A Cross of Iron: Harry S. Truman and the Origins of the National Security State 1945–1954*, Cambridge: Cambridge University Press.

25 Gaddis, J.L. (1972) *The United States and the Origins of the Cold War, 1941–1947*, New York: Columbia University Press, p 304.

26 Gaddis, J.L. (1982) *Strategies of Containment: A Critical Appraisal of Postwar American Security Policy*, Oxford: Oxford University Press.

27 McDougall, W.A. (1997) *Promised Land, Crusader State: The American Encounter with the World Since 1776*, Boston: Mariner Books.

28 Hunt, M.H. (1987) *Ideology and US Foreign Policy*, New Haven: Yale University Press, p 176.

29 Lipset, S.M. (1996) *American Exceptionalism: A Double-edged Sword*, New York: W.W. Norton, p 63.

30 Parenti, M. (2013) 'The logic of US intervention', in C. Boggs (ed), *Masters of War: Militarism and Blowback in the Era of American Empire*, London: Routledge, p 34.

31 Kaplan, R. (2020) 'Confronting China', *The National Interest* (July–August), p 11.

32 Steil, B. (2013) *The Battle of Bretton Woods*, Princeton: Princeton University Press; Corbridge, S. (1994) 'Bretton-Woods revisited – hegemony, stability, and territory', *Environment and Planning A*, 26(12): 1829–59; Strange, S. (1994) 'From Bretton Woods to the casino economy', in S. Corbridge, R. Martin and N. Thrift (eds), *Money, Power and Space*, Oxford: Blackwell, pp 49–62; Eichengreen, B. and Kenen, P. (1994) 'Managing the world economy under the Bretton Woods system: an overview', in P. Kenen *Managing the World Economy: Fifty Years After Bretton Woods*, Washington: Institute for International Economics, pp 3–57.

33 The phrase was coined by George Washington in his farewell address when he warned of the dangers of becoming caught up in other people's conflicts, especially in Europe.

34 McDougall, W.A. (1997) *Promised Land, Crusader State: The American Encounter with the World Since 1776*, Boston: Mariner Books, p 173.

35 Bacevich, A.J. (2002) *American Empire: The Realities and Consequences of US Diplomacy*, Cambridge, MA: Harvard University Press, p 3.

36 Friedberg, A. (2000) *In the Shadow of the Garrison State: America's Anti-Statism and Its Cold War Strategy*, Princeton: Princeton University Press, p 61.

37 Gaddis, J.L. (1982) *Strategies of Containment: A Critical Appraisal of Postwar American Security Policy*, Oxford: Oxford University Press, p 62.

38 Latham, R. (1997) *The Liberal Moment: Modernity, Security, and the Making of Postwar International Order*, New York: Columbia University Press.

39 The International Telegraph Union was created as early as 1865, and was an indicator of the growing need for inter-state cooperation if technological advances were to be exploited. See Mazower, M. (2012) *Governing the World: The History of an Idea*, London: Allen Lane.

40 The dismantling of regulations intended to guard against future crisis significantly contributed to the global financial crisis of 2008. See, Acharya, V.A., Cooley, T., Richardson, M., Sylla, R. and Walter, I. (2011) 'A bird's eye view: the Dodd-Frank Wall Street Reform and Consumer Protection Act', in V.A. Acharya, T. Cooley,

M. Richardson and I. Walter (eds), *Regulating Wall Street: The Dodd Frank Act and the New Architecture of Global Finance*, New York: Wiley, pp 1–32.

[41] Charles Kindleberger's highly influential analysis of the Great Depression gave a theoretically informed account of this process and spawned a major discussion about the nature and importance of hegemony. See Kindleberger, C.P. (1973) *The World in Depression 1929–1939*, Berkeley: University of California Press.

[42] Ikenberry, G.J. (1992) 'A world-economy restored – expert consensus and the Anglo-American postwar settlement', *International Organization*, 46(1): 289–321.

[43] Eichengreen, B. (2011) *Exorbitant Privilege: The Rise and Fall of the Dollar and the Future of the International Monetary System*, Oxford: Oxford University Press.

[44] Stubbs, R. (2005) *Rethinking Asia's Economic Miracle*, Basingstoke: Palgrave Macmillan; Milward, A.S. (2003) *The Reconstruction of Western Europe, 1945–51*, London: Routledge.

[45] Stubbs, R. (2005) *Rethinking Asia's Economic Miracle*, Basingstoke: Palgrave Macmillan; Beeson, M. (2014) *Regionalism and Globalization in East Asia: Politics, Security and Economic Development* (2nd edn), Basingstoke: Palgrave Macmillan.

[46] Marglin, S. (1990) 'Lessons of the Golden Age: an overview', in S. Marglin and J. Schor (eds), *The Golden Age of Capitalism: Reinterpreting the Postwar Experience*, Oxford: Clarendon Press, pp 1–38.

[47] Drezner, D.W. (2005) 'Globalization, harmonization, and competition: the different pathways to policy convergence', *Journal of European Public Policy*, 12(5): 842.

[48] Blackwill, R.D. and Harris, J.M. (2016) *War by Other Means: Geoeconomics and Statecraft*, Cambridge, MA: Harvard University Press, p 8.

[49] Baldwin, D.A. (1985) *Economic Statecraft*, Princeton: Princeton University Press.

[50] Hogan, M.J. (1987) *The Marshall Plan: America, Britain, and the Reconstruction of Western Europe, 1947–1952*, Cambridge: Cambridge University Press.

[51] Layne, C. (2006) *The Peace of Illusions: American Grand Strategy from 1940 to the Present*, New York: Cambridge University Press, p 70.

[52] Lundestad, G. (1986) 'Empire by invitation? The United States and Western Europe, 1945–1952', *Journal of Peace Research*, 23(3): 263–77.

[53] Cha, V.D. (2016) *Powerplay: The Origins of the American Alliance System*, Princeton: Princeton University Press, p 4.

[54] Cha (2016), p 51.

[55] Appy, C.G. (2015) *American Reckoning: The Vietnam War and Our National Identity*, New York: Penguin Books.

[56] Lind, M. (2006) *The American Way of Strategy: US Foreign Policy and the American Way of Life*, Oxford: Oxford University Press, p 130.

[57] Leffler (1992), p 357.

[58] Washington's Blog (2019) 'America has been at war 93% of the time – 222 out of 239 years – since 1776', *Global Research*, 20 February. Available at: https://www.globalresearch.ca/america-has-been-at-war-93-of-the-time-222-out-of-239-years-since-1776/5565946

[59] Nye, J.S. (2002) *The Paradox of American Power*, Oxford: Oxford University Press.

[60] Schweller, R. (2018) 'Three cheers for Trump's foreign policy', *Foreign Affairs*, 97(5): 135.

[61] Mearsheimer, J.J. (2018) *The Great Delusion: Liberal Dreams and International Realities*, New Haven: Yale University Press, pp 128–9.

[62] See Packer, G. (2005) *The Assassin's Gate: America in Iraq*, New York: Farrar, Strauss and Giroux; Stiglitz, J.E. and Bilmes, L.J. (2008) *The Three Trillion Dollar War: The True Cost of the Iraq Conflict*, New York: W.W. Norton.

63 Bacevich, A.J. (2008) *The Limits of Power: The End of American Exceptionalism*, New York: Metropolitan Books, p 66.

64 Weber, K. and Kowert, P.A. (2012) *Cultures of Order: Leadership, Language, and Social Reconstruction in Germany and Japan*, New York: SUNY Press.

65 Porter, P. (2018) 'Why America's grand strategy has not changed: power, habit, and the US foreign policy establishment', *International Security*, 42(4): 43.

66 Allison, G. (2017) *Destined for War: Can America and China Escape Thucydides's Trap?* Boston: Houghton Mifflin Harcourt; Mearsheimer, J.J. (2010) 'The gathering storm: China 's challenge to US power in Asia', *The Chinese Journal of International Politics*, 3(4): 381–96. For a useful discussion of the general issues, see H. Feng and K. He (eds) (2020) *China's Challenges and International Order Transition: Beyond the 'Thucydides Trap'*, Ann Arbor: University of Michigan Press.

67 Johnson, C.A. (1962) *Peasant Nationalism and Communist Power: The Emergence of Revolutionary China, 1937–1945*, Stanford: Stanford University Press.

68 Clover, C. (2017) 'Xi Jinping signals departure from low-profile policy', *Financial Times*, 20 October.

69 *The Economist* (2019) 'China is surprisingly carbon-efficient – but still the world's biggest emitter', 25 May.

70 Zoellick, R.B. (2005) *Whither China: From Membership to Responsibility?* New York. Available at: http://2001–2009.state.gov/s/d/former/zoellick/rem/53682.htm.

71 Economy, E.C. (2004) *The River Runs Black: The Environmental Challenge to China's Future*, Ithaca: Cornell University Press.

72 Steinhardt, H.C. and Wu, F. (2016) 'In the name of the public: environmental protest and the changing landscape of popular contention in China', *The China Journal* (75): 61–82.

73 Ye, Z. (2011) *Inside China's Grand Strategy: The Perspective from the People's Republic*, Lexington: University Press of Kentucky, p 125.

74 Putnam, R.D. (1988) 'Diplomacy and domestic politics: the logic of two-level games', *International Organization*, 42(3): 427–60.

75 Chen, G.C. and Lees, C. (2016) 'Growing China's renewables sector: a developmental state approach', *New Political Economy*, 21(6): 574–86.

76 Hu, N. and Yang, Y. (2012) 'The real old-age dependency ratio and the inadequacy of public pension finance in China', *Journal of Population Ageing*, 5(3): 193–209.

77 Dryzek, J.S. and Pickering, J. (2019) *The Politics of the Anthropocene*, Oxford: Oxford University Press.

78 Kurlantzick, J. (2007) *Charm Offensive: How China's Soft Power Is Transforming the World*, New Haven: Yale University Press.

79 Winter, T. (2019) *Geocultural Power: China's Quest to Revive the Silk Roads for the Twenty-First Century*, Chicago: University of Chicago Press.

80 Miller, T. (2017) *China's Asian Dream: Empire Building along the New Silk Road*, London: Zed Books, p 18.

81 Shen, S. (2016) 'How China's "Belt and Road" compares to the Marshall Plan', *The Diplomat*, 6 February.

82 Bradsher, K. (2019) 'China proceeds with Belt and Road push, but does it more quietly', *New York Times*, 22 January.

83 Beeson, M. (2015) 'Can ASEAN cope with China?', *Journal of Current Southeast Asian Affairs*, 35(1): 5–28.

84 Mueller, L.M. (forthcoming) 'Challenges to ASEAN centrality and hedging in connectivity governance – regional and national pressure points and national pressure points', *The Pacific Review*.

[85] Wang, J. (2011) 'China's search for a grand strategy', *Foreign Affairs*, 90(2): 74. For discussions of strategic thinking in Asia, see Alagappa, M. (1998) 'Asian practice of security: key features and explanations', in M. Alagappa, *Asian Security Practice: Material and Ideational Influences*, Stanford: Stanford University Press, pp 611–76; Beeson, M. (2014) 'Security in Asia: what's different, what's not?', *Journal of Asian Security and International Affairs*, 1(1): 1–23.

[86] Bremmer, I. (2010) *The End of the Free Market: Who Wins the War between States and Corporations?* New York: Penguin, p 5.

[87] Qin, Y. (2014) ' Continuity through change: background knowledge and China's international strategy', *The Chinese Journal of International Politics*, 7(3): 309.

[88] Shambaugh, D. (2013) *China Goes Global: The Partial Power*, Oxford: Oxford University Press, p 153.

[89] Lin, J.Y. (2011) 'China and the global economy', *China Economic Journal*, 4(1): 1–14.

[90] Lai, H.H. (2001) 'Behind China's World Trade Organization agreement with the USA', *Third World Quarterly*, 22(2): 237–55.

[91] Leverett, F. and Wu, B. (2017) 'The New Silk Road and China's evolving grand strategy', *The China Journal*, 77: 115.

[92] Beeson (2018).

[93] Beeson, M. and Xu, S. (2019) 'China's evolving role in global governance: the AIIB and the limits of an alternative international order', in K. Zeng (ed), *Handbook of the International Political Economy of China*, Cheltenham: Edward Elgar, pp 345–60.

[94] Friedberg, A.L. (2018) 'Globalisation and Chinese grand strategy', *Survival*: 60(1): 26.

[95] Pillsbury, M. (2015) *The Hundred-year Marathon: China's Secret Strategy to Replace America as the Global Superpower*, New York: Henry Holt; Mosher, S.W. (2000) *Hegemon: China's Plan to Dominate Asia and the World*, San Francisco: Encounter Books.

[96] Organski, A.F.K. (1968) *World Politics*, New York: Knopf; Chan, S. (2008) *China, the US, and the Power-Transition Theory*, London: Routledge; Beeson, M. (2009) 'Hegemonic transition in East Asia? The dynamics of Chinese and American power', *Review of International Studies*, 35(01): 95–112.

[97] Chan, G., Lee, P.K. and Chan, L.-H. (2012) *China Engages Global Governance: A New World Order in the Making?* London: Routledge, p 32.

[98] Fontaine, R. (2020) 'Virus competition is wrecking China–U.S. cooperation hopes', *Foreign Policy*, 20 March.

[99] Zhang, F. (2013) 'The rise of Chinese exceptionalism in international relations', *European Journal of International Relations*, 19(2): 305–28.

[100] Wolf, M. (2018) 'Donald Trump's war on the liberal world order', *Financial Times*, 3 July.

[101] Steinfeld, E.S. (2010) *Playing Our Game: Why China's Rise Doesn't Threaten the West*, New York: Oxford University Press.

[102] Yang, H. and Zhao, D. (2015) 'Performance legitimacy, state autonomy and China's economic miracle', *Journal of Contemporary China*, 24(91): 64–82.

[103] Shambaugh (2013), p 7.

[104] Zhou, L. and Wang, O. (2019) 'How "Made in China 2025" became a lightning rod in "war over China's national destiny"', *South China Morning Post*, 18 January; Stephens, P. (2019) 'Trade is just an opening shot in a wider US–China conflict', *Financial Times*, 16 May.

[105] Simpson, K. (2019) 'Just how green is the Belt and Road?', *The Interpreter*, 23 January; Sims, K. and Pinto, C. (2019) 'Can the land of a million elephants survive the Belt and Road?', *The Diplomat*, 3 January.

106 Myers, S.L. (2020) 'China's pledge to be carbon neutral by 2060: what it means', *New York Times*, 23 September.

107 Feigenbaum, E.A. (2017) 'China and the world', *Foreign Affairs* (Jan–Feb): 33–40.

108 Jacques, M. (2009) *When China Rules the World: The Rise of the Middle Kingdom and the End of the Western World*, London: Allen Lane.

109 Beeson, M. (2020) 'China's charmless offensive', *The Interpreter*, 29 June; Lungu, A. (2020) 'Are we witnessing the end of the golden age of Chinese diplomacy?', *South China Morning Post*, 15 May.

110 Beeson, M. and Wilson, J.D. (2015) 'Coming to terms with China: managing complications in the Sino-Australian economic relationship', *Security Challenges*, 11(2): 21–37.

111 Phillips, A. (2016) *From Hollywood to Bollywood: Recasting Australia's Indo/Pacific Strategic Geography*, Canberra: ASPI; Beeson (2018).

112 Walt, S.M. (1987) *The Origins of Alliances*, Ithaca: Cornell University Press, p 263.

113 Beeson, M. (2020) 'Donald Trump and post-Pivot Asia: the implications of a "transactional" approach to foreign policy', *Asian Studies Review*, 44(1): 10–27.

114 Jennings, P. (2019) 'Risk and reward for Australia as US flexes its muscles in Asia', *The Australian*, 22 June.

115 Berman, T. (2017) 'Canada's most shameful environmental secret must not remain hidden', *The Guardian*, 14 November.

116 Taulbee, J., Kelleher, A. and Grosvenor, P. (2014) *Norway's Peace Policy: Soft Power in a Turbulent World*, Basingstoke: Palgrave Macmillan.

Chapter 6

1 Goodhand, J. (2003) 'Enduring disorder and persistent poverty: a review of the linkages between war and chronic poverty', *World Development*, 31(3): 629–46.

2 Skocpol, T. (1979) *States and Social Revolutions: A Comparative Analysis of France, Russia and China*, Cambridge: Cambridge University Press.

3 Arrow, K., Bolin, B., Costanza, R., Dasgupta, P., Folke, C. and Mäler, K.-G. (1996) 'Economic growth, carrying capacity, and the environment', *Environment and Development Economics*, 1(1): 104–10; Goldstone, J.A. (2001) 'Demography, environment, and security', in P.F. Diehl and N.P. Gleditsch *Environmental Conflict*, Boulder: Westview Press, pp 84–108.

4 Collier, P. (2007) *The Bottom Billion: Why the Poorest Countries Are Failing and What Can Be Done about It*, Oxford: Oxford University Press.

5 Spoor, M. (ed) (2005) *Globalisation, Poverty and Conflict*, Berlin: Springer.

6 Moyn, S. (2018) *Not Enough: Human Rights in an Unequal World*, Cambridge, MA: Harvard University Press, p 218.

7 Kharas, H. and Hamel, K. (2020) 'Turning back the poverty clock: how will COVID-19 impact the world's poorest people?', *Brookings*, 6 May.

8 Beeson, M. (2014) 'Security in Asia: what's different, what's not?', *Journal of Asian Security and International Affairs*, 1(1): 1–23.

9 Pyle, K.B. (2007) *Japan Rising: The Resurgence of Japanese Power and Purpose*, New York: Public Affairs.

10 Rosecrance, R. (1986) *The Rise of the Trading State: Commerce and Conquest in the Modern World*, New York: Basic Books.

11 Dauvergne, P. (2010) *The Shadows of Consumption: Consequences for the Global Environment*, Cambridge, MA: MIT Press, p 215.

12 Brooks, S.G. (2005) *Producing Security: Multinational Corporations, Globalization, and the Changing Calculus of Conflict*, Princeton: Princeton University Press, p 7.

13 King, A.D. (2015) *Global Cities: Post-Imperialism and the Internationalization of London*, London: Routledge.

14 Peel, M., Warrell, H. and Chazan, G. (2020) 'US warns Europe against embracing China's 5G technology', *Financial Times*, 15 February.

15 Farrell, H. and Newman, A.L. (2019) 'Weaponized interdependence: how global economic networks shape state coercion', *International Security*, 44(1): 45.

16 Beeson, M. (2020) 'The revenge of Gaia?', *The Strategist*, 28 March.

17 Polanyi, K. (1957) *The Great Transformation: The Political and Economic Origins of Our Time*, Boston: Beacon Press, p 73.

18 Davis, M. (2004) 'Planet of the slums', *New Left Review*, 26(March): 5–34.

19 Milanovic, B. (2011) *Worlds Apart: Measuring International and Global Inequality*, Princeton: Princeton University Press.

20 Vos, R., Martin, W. and Laborde, D. (2020) 'How much will global poverty increase because of COVID-19?', *International Food Policy Research Institute*, 20 March. Available at: https://www.ifpri.org/blog/how-much-will-global-poverty-increase-because-covid-19

21 Economy, E.C. (2007) 'The great leap backwards: the costs of China's environmental crisis', *Foreign Affairs*, 86(5): 38–59.

22 Homer-Dixon, T. (1991) 'On the threshold: environmental changes as causes of conflict', *International Security*, 16(2): 76–116; Parenti, C. (2011) *Tropic of Chaos: Climate Change and the New Geography of Violence*, New York: Nation Books.

23 Weinstein, D. (2019) 'Herbert Spencer', *The Stanford Encyclopedia of Philosophy*, Edward N. Zalta (ed), available at: https://plato.stanford.edu/archives/fall2019/entries/spencer/

24 Arrighi, G. (1994) *The Long Twentieth Century: Money, Power, and the Origins of Our Times*, London: Verso.

25 Smith, N. (2008) *Uneven Development: Nature, Capital, and the Production of Space* (3rd edn), London: Verso.

26 Wallerstein, I. (1979) *The Capitalist World-Economy*, vol. 2, Cambridge: Cambridge University Press; Fröbel, F., Heinrichs, J. and Kreye, O.(1980) *The New International Division of Labour: Structural Unemployment inIndustrialised Countries and Industrialisation in Developing Countries*, Cambridge: Cambridge University Press.

27 Smith (2008), pp 134–35.

28 Silver, B.J. and Arrighi, G. (2003) 'Polanyi's "double movement": the belle époques of British and US hegemony compared', *Politics & Society*, 31(2): 325–55.

29 Reinert, E.S. (2007) *How Rich Countries Got Rich … and Why Poor Countries Stay Poor*, New York: Carrol & Graf, p 119.

30 Chang, H.-J. (2002) *Kicking Away the Ladder: Development Strategy in Historical Perspective*, London: Anthem Books.

31 Brett, E.A. (1973) *Colonialism and Underdevelopment in East Africa: The Politics of Economic Change, 1919–1939*, London: Heinemann; Abernathy, D.B. (2000) *Global Dominance: European Overseas Empires, 1415–1980*, New Haven: Yale University Press.

32 Dosman, E. (2008) *The Life and Times of Raúl Prebisch, 1901–1986*, Toronto: McGill-Queen's Press.

33 Rostow, W.W. (1990) *The Stages of Economic Growth: A Non-Communist Manifesto*, Cambridge: Cambridge University Press.

34 Ross, M. (2006) 'Is democracy good for the poor?', *American Journal of Political Science*, 50(4): 860–74; Ravalliona, M. (2008) 'Are there lessons for Africa from China's success against poverty?', *World Development*, 37(2): 303–13.

35 Huntington, S.P. (1968) *Political Order in Changing Societies*, New Haven: Yale University Press, p 34.

36 Leffler, M.P. (1992) *A Preponderance of Power: National Security, the Truman Administration, and the Cold War*, Stanford: Stanford University Press.

37 Lin, J.Y. (2011) 'China and the global economy', *China Economic Journal*, 4(1): 1–14.

38 Beeson, M. (2014) *Regionalism and Globalization in East Asia: Politics, Security and Economic Development* (2nd edn), Basingstoke: Palgrave Macmillan; Terry, E. (2002) *How Asia Got Rich: Japan, China, and the Asian Miracle*, Armonk: M.E. Sharpe.

39 Beeson, M. and Islam, I. (2005) 'Neo-liberalism and East Asia: resisting the Washington consensus', *Journal of Development Studies*, 41(2): 197–219.

40 Studwell, J. (2013) *How Asia Works: Success and Failure in the World's Most Dynamic Region*, London: Profile Books, p 87.

41 World Bank (1997) *World Development Report 1997: The State in a Changing World*, New York: Oxford University Press; Wade, R. (2001) 'Showdown at the World Bank', *New Left Review* (7): 124–37.

42 Stubbs, R. (2005) *Rethinking Asia's Economic Miracle*, Basingstoke: Palgrave Macmillan.

43 Haggard, S. (1990) *Pathways From the Periphery: The Politics of Growth in the Newly Industrialising Countries*, Ithaca: Cornell University Press.

44 Quoted in Hersh, S.M. (1982) 'The price of power: Kissinger, Nixon, and Chile', *The Atlantic*, December.

45 Brzezinski, Z. (1997) *The Grand Chess Board: American Primacy and Its Geostrategic Imperatives*, New York: Basic Books, p 40.

46 Johnson, C.A. (2000) *Blowback: The Costs and Consequences of American Empire*, London: Little, Brown & Co.

47 Wohlforth, W.C. (1999) 'The stability of a unipolar world', *International Security*, 24(1): 5–41.

48 Krauthammer, C. (1990–1991) 'The unipolar moment', *Foreign Affairs*, 70(1): 23–33.

49 Mastanduno, M. (1998) 'Economics and security in statecraft and scholarship', *International Organization*, 52(4): 843.

50 Woods, N. (1995) 'Economic ideas and international relations: beyond rational neglect', *International Studies Quarterly*, 39(2): 161–80.

51 Hall, P.A. (1993) 'Policy paradigms, social learning, and the state: the case of economic policymaking in Britain', *Comparative Politics*, 25(3): 275–96.

52 Cockett, R. (1994) *Thinking the Unthinkable: Think-Tanks and the Economic Counter-Revolution 1931–1983*, New York: Harper Collins.

53 Wade, R.H. (2004) 'Is globalization reducing poverty and inequality?', *World Development*, 32(4): 567–89.

54 Carroll, T. (2012) 'Working on, through and around the state: the deep marketisation of development in the Asia-Pacific', *Journal of Contemporary Asia*, 42(3): 378–404.

55 Babb, S. (2012) 'The Washington consensus as transnational policy paradigm: its origins, trajectory and likely successor', *Review of International Political Economy*, 20(2): 268–97.

[56] Ruggie, J.G. (1982) 'International regimes, transactions and change: embedded liberalism in the postwar economic order', *International Organization*, 36(2): 379–415.

[57] Arrighi, G. (2005) 'Hegemony unravelling-1', *New Left Review*, 32: 23–80.

[58] Block, F. (1977) *The Origins of the International Economic Disorder*, Berkeley: University of California Press.

[59] Gowa, J. (1983) *Closing the Gold Window: Domestic Politics and the End of Bretton Woods*, Ithaca: Cornell University Press.

[60] Helleiner, E. (1994) *States and the Reemergence of Global Finance*, Ithaca: Cornell University Press; Panitch, L. and Gindin, S. (2004) 'Finance and American empire', in L. Panitch and C. Leys (eds), *The Socialist Register: The Empire Reloaded*, London: Merlin Press, pp 46–80; Strange, S. (1986) *Casino Capitalism*, Oxford: Basil Blackwell.

[61] Mann, M. (2004) 'The first failed empire of the 21st century', *Review of International Studies*, 30: 609–30; Pape, R.A. (2009) 'Empire falls', *National Interest*, 99: 21–34.

[62] Gray, J. (1998) *False Dawn: The Delusions of Global Capitalism*, London: Granada; Pieterse, J.N. (2004) *Globalization or Empire?* London: Routledge; Wade, R.H. (2004) 'Is globalization reducing poverty and inequality?', *World Development*, 32(4): 567–89.

[63] Harvey, D. (2007) *A Brief History of Neoliberalism*, Oxford: Oxford University Press, p 119.

[64] World Bank (1991) *Managing Development: The Governance Dimension*, Washington: World Bank; Smith, B.C. (2007) *Good Governance and Development*, Basingstoke: Palgrave Macmillan.

[65] Leftwich, A. (1994) 'Governance, the state and the politics of development', *Development and Change*, 25: 363–86.

[66] Polidano defines effective state capacity as 'the ability to structure the decision-making process, coordinate it throughout government, and feed informed analysis into it, and implementation authority (the ability to carry out decisions and enforce rules), within the public sector itself and the wider society'. Polidano, C. (2000) 'Measuring public sector capacity', *World Development*, 28(5): 810.

[67] Gandhi, J. and Przeworski, A. (2007) 'Authoritarian institutions and the survival of autocrats', *Comparative Political Studies*, 40(11): 1280.

[68] Ross, M.L. (1999) 'The political economy of the resource curse', *World Politics*, 51(2): 297–322; Rudra, N. and Jensen, N.M. (2011) 'Globalization and the politics of natural resources', *Comparative Political Studies*, 44(6): 639–61.

[69] Sala-i-Martin, X. and Subramanian, A. (2013) 'Addressing the natural resource curse: an illustration from Nigeria', *Journal of African Economies*, 22(4): 570–615.

[70] Varese, F. (1997) 'The transition to the market and corruption in post-Socialist Russia', *Political Studies*, 45(3): 579–96; Klare, M.T. (2004) *Blood and Oil: How America's Thirst for Petrol Is Killing Us*, London: Penguin.

[71] Shue, H. (1980) *Basic Rights: Subsistence, Affluence, and US Foreign Policy*, Princeton: Princeton University Press, p 23.

[72] Spaaij, R. (2011) *Understanding Lone Wolf Terrorism: Global Patterns, Motivations and Prevention*, Berlin: Springer Science & Business Media.

[73] Sheppard, E. and Leitner, H. (2010) 'Quo vadis neoliberalism? The remaking of global capitalist governance after the Washington Consensus', *Geoforum*, 41(2): 185–94.

[74] The Millennium Development Goals are: to eradicate extreme poverty and hunger; to achieve universal primary education; to promote gender equality and empower women; to reduce child mortality; to improve maternal health; to combat HIV/

AIDS, malaria and other diseases; to ensure environmental sustainability; and to develop a global partnership for development. World Health Organization, available at: https://www.who.int/topics/millennium_development_goals/about/en/

75   Clemens, M.A., Kenny, C.J. and Moss, T.J. (2007) 'The trouble with the MDGs: confronting expectations of aid and development success', *World Development*, 35(5): 735–51.

76   Kwon, H. and Kim, E. (2014) 'Poverty reduction and good governance: examining the rationale of the millennium development goals', *Development and Change*, 45(2): 353–75.

77   Duffield, M. (2002) *Global Governance and the New Wars*, London: Zed Books, p 42.

78   Fukuyama, F. (1992) *The End of History and the Last Man*, New York: Free Press.

79   Gartzke, E. (2007) 'The capitalist peace', *American Journal of Political Science*, 51(1): 166–91.

80   Levitsky, S. and Way, L.A. (2002) 'The rise of competitive authoritarianism', *Journal of Democracy*, 13(2): 51–65; Mounk, Y. and Foa, R.S. (2018) 'The end of the democratic century: autocracy's global ascendance', *Foreign Affairs*, 97(3): 29–36.

81   Barber, B.R. (2001) *Jihad vs. McWorld*, New York: Ballantine Books.

82   Milanovic, B. (2019) *Capitalism, Alone: The Future of the System that Rules the World*, Cambridge, MA: Harvard University Press, p 78.

83   Bremmer, I. (2009) 'State capitalism comes of age: the end of the free market?', *Foreign Affairs*, 88(3): 40–55.

84   Beeson, M., Hang, D.T. and Taylor, J. (forthcoming) 'Comradely comparisons: China, Vietnam and the limits of learning', *Journal of International Relations and Development*.

85   Wyne, A. and Mazarr, M.J. (2020) 'The real US–China competition: competing theories of influence', *The Interpreter*, 29 January.

86   Wallerstein, I. (1994) 'Development: lodestar or illusion?', in L. Sklair (ed), *Capitalism and Development*, London: Routledge, pp 17–34.

87   Rist, G. (1999) *The History of Development: From Western Origins to Global Faith*, London: Zed Books, p 236.

88   Moore, J.W. (2015) *Capitalism in the Web of Life: Ecology and the Accumulation of Capital*, London: Verso Books, p 2.

89   Watts, J. (2018) 'Earth's resources consumed in ever greater destructive volumes', *The Guardian*, 23 July.

90   Brand, U. and Wissen, M. (2012) 'Global environmental politics and the imperial mode of living: articulations of state–capital relations in the multiple crisis', *Globalizations*, 9(4): 704.

91   Sim, D. (2019) 'Why can't Southeast Asia snuff out its haze problem for good?', *South China Morning Post*, 20 September.

92   Vidal, J. (2020) 'Destroyed habitat creates the perfect conditions for coronavirus to emerge: COVID-19 may be just the beginning of mass pandemics', *Scientific American*, 18 March.

93   Stalley, P. (2003) 'Environmental scarcity and international conflict', *Conflict Management and Peace Science*, 20(2): 33–58; Ostby, G., Urdal, H., Tadjoeddin, M.Z., Murshed, S.M. and Strand, H. (2011) 'Population pressure, horizontal inequality and political violence: a disaggregated study of Indonesian provinces, 1990–2003', *Journal of Development Studies*, 47(3): 377–98.

94   Collier, P. and Hoeffler, A. (2004) 'Greed and grievance in civil war', *Oxford Economic Papers*, 56(4): 563–95; Kahl, Colin H. (2006) *States, Scarcity, and Civil Strife in the Developing World*, Princeton: Princeton University Press.

95 Singer, A. and Wildavsky, M. (1993) *The Real World Order: Zones of Peace/Zones of Turmoil*, New Jersey: Chatham House Publishers.

96 Homer-Dixon, T.F. (1999) *Environment, Scarcity, and Violence*, Princeton: Princeton University Press, p 27.

97 Lynas, M. (2008) *Six Degrees: Our Future on a Hotter Planet*, London: Harper.

98 Milman, O. (2020) 'Pandemic side-effects offer glimpse of alternative future on Earth Day 2020', *The Guardian*, 22 April.

99 Maza, C. (2020) 'Authoritarian leaders are using the coronavirus pandemic as an excuse to lock up dissenters and grab power, human rights experts warn', *Business Insider*, 10 April; Acemoglu, D. (2020) 'The coronavirus exposed America's authoritarian turn', *Foreign Affairs*, 23 March.

100 McTernan, J. (2020) 'The Left must decide which Green New Deal they want', *Financial Times*, 16 February.

101 Monbiot, G. (2020) 'How did Michael Moore become a hero to climate deniers and the far right?', *The Guardian*, 7 May.

102 Yoshihara, T. (2012) 'The setting of the sun? Strategic implications of Japan's demographic transition', in S. Yoshihara and D.A. Sylva (eds), *Population Decline and the Remaking of Great Power Politics*, Washington: Potomac Books, pp 137–57.

Conclusion

1 Crosby, Alfred W. (2004) *Ecological Imperialism: The Biological Expansion of Europe, 900–1900*, Cambridge: Cambridge University Press.

2 Gordon, R.J. (2016) *The Rise and Fall of American Growth: The US Standard of Living Since the Civil War*, Princeton: Princeton University Press.

3 Fukuyama, F. (2019) '"Getting to Denmark": how societies build capable, democratic and law-bound states', *CDE Insight*, August. Available at: https://media.africaportal.org/documents/Getting-to-Denmark-Final.pdf

4 Solomon, E. (2020) 'Migration: tales of brutality along Europe's borders', *Financial Times*, 29 March.

5 Milne, R. (2020) 'Coronavirus: Sweden starts to debate its public health experiment', *Financial Times*, 22 June.

6 Frum, D. (2020) 'This is Trump's fault', *The Atlantic*, 7 April.

7 Wheeler, N.J. (2000) *Saving Strangers: Humanitarian Intervention in International Society*, Oxford: Oxford University Press.

8 Berlin argued that 'liberty in the negative sense involves an answer to the question: "What is the area within which the subject – a person or group of persons – is or should be left to do or be what he is able to do or be, without interference by other persons".' Berlin, I. (1969 [1958]) 'Two concepts of liberty', in *Four Essays on Liberty*, Oxford: Oxford University Press.

9 Puddington, A. (2018) 'China: the global leader in political prisoners', Freedom House, 26 July. Available at: https://freedomhouse.org/article/china-global-leader-political-prisoners

10 Mettler, K. (2019) 'States imprison black people at five times the rate of whites – a sign of a narrowing yet still-wide gap', *Washington Post*, 4 December.

11 Kan, K. (2019) 'Mainland Chinese lack sympathy for Hong Kong protesters', *Nikkei Asian Review*, 30 July.

12 Croissant, A., Kuehn, D., Lorenz, P. and Chambers, P. (2013) *Democratization and Civilian Control in Asia*, Berlin: Springer.

13 Ramzy, A. and Buckley, C. (2019) '"Absolutely no mercy": leaked files expose how China organized mass detentions of Muslims', *New York Times*, 16 November.

14 Mozur, P. and Krolik, A. (2019) 'A surveillance net blankets China's cities, giving police vast powers', *New York Times*, 17 December.

15 Walt, S.M. (2020) 'Everyone misunderstands the reason for the U.S.–China cold war', *Foreign Policy*, 30 June.

16 Beeson, M. (2010) 'The coming of environmental authoritarianism', *Environmental Politics*, 19(2): 276–94.

17 Burkett, P. (2006) *Marxism and Ecological Economics: Toward a Red and Green Political Economy*, Chicago: Haymarket Books.

18 There have been an alarming large number of close calls when nuclear war has narrowly been avoided. See Raby, J. (2019) 'My turn: a long history of nuclear near misses', *Concord Monitor*, 29 July. Available at: https://www.concordmonitor.com/Nuclear-weapons-close-calls-26835611

19 Abbott, K.W. (1993) 'Trust but verify: the production of information in arms control treaties and other international agreements', *Cornell International Law Journal*, 26: 1–58.

20 Reiter, D. (1996) *Crucible of Beliefs: Learning, Alliances, and World Wars*, Ithaca: Cornell University Press.

21 Beeson, M. (2020) 'Avoiding a cold war and a hot planet', *The Strategist*, 10 September.

22 *The Economist* (2020) 'Joe Biden wants to re-enter the nuclear deal with Iran', 5 December.

23 Krugman, P. (2020) 'How America lost the war on Covid-19', *New York Times*, 6 July.

24 Sevastopulo, D. (2020) 'Trump's niece calls president a lying narcissist', *Financial Times*, 8 July.

25 Carrington, D. (2020) 'Sixth mass extinction of wildlife accelerating, scientists warn', *The Guardian*, 2 June.

26 Cohen, N. (2019) 'Nigeria falls short of reaping reward from its population bulge', *Financial Times*, 22 November.

27 Urdal, H. (2006) 'A clash of generations? Youth bulges and political violence', *International Studies Quarterly*, 50(3): 607–29.

28 Collier, P. (2013) *Exodus: How Migration Is Changing Our World*, Oxford: Oxford University Press.

29 Dalby, S. (2014) 'Rethinking geopolitics: climate security in the Anthropocene', *Global Policy*, 5(1): 1–9; Parenti, C. (2011) *Tropic of Chaos: Climate Change and the New Geography of Violence*, New York: Nation Books; Spratt, D. and Dunlop, I. (2019) *Existential Climate-Related Security Risk: A Scenario Approach*, Canberra: National Centre for Climate Restoration.

30 Campbell, K.M., Gulledge, J., McNeill, J.R., Podesta, J., Ogden, P. (2007) *The Age of Consequences: The Foreign Policy and National Security Implications of Global Climate Change*, Washington: Centre for Strategic & International Studies; Dale, C. (2014) *The 2014 Quadrennial Defense Review (QDR) and Defense Strategy: Issues for Congress*, Washington: Congressional Research Service.

31 Batchelor, T. (2019) 'Climate change could make frozen Siberia habitable within decades, scientists reveal', *The Independent*, 7 June.

32 Albrecht, G.A. (2019) *Earth Emotions: New Words for a New World*, Ithaca: Cornell University Press, p 38.

33 Bellamy, A.J. (2019) *World Peace and How We Can Achieve It*, Oxford: Oxford University Press; Bleiker, R. (2000) *Popular Dissent, Human Agency and Global Politics*, Cambridge: Cambridge University Press; Burke, A. (2007) *Beyond Security, Ethics and Violence*, London: Routledge; Cabrera, L. (2006) *Political Theory of Global Justice: A Cosmopolitan Case for the World State*, London: Routledge; Dryzek, J.S. and Pickering, J. (2019) *The Politics of the Anthropocene*, Oxford: Oxford University Press; Eckersley, R. (2004) *The Green State: Rethinking Democracy and Sovereignty*, Cambridge, MA: MIT Press; McDonald, M. (2011) *Security, the Environment and Emancipation: Contestation over Environmental Change*, London: Routledge; Shapcott, R. (2001) *Justice, Community and Dialogue in International Relations*. Cambridge: Cambridge University Press.

34 Dryzek, J.S. and Stevenson, H. (2011) 'Global democracy and earth system governance', *Ecological Economics*, 70(11): 1865–74; Bohman, J. (1998) 'Survey article: the coming of age of deliberative democracy', *Journal of Political Philosophy*, 6(4): 400–25.

35 Schweller, R.L. (2014) *Maxwell's Demon and the Golden Apple: Global Discord in the New Millennium*, Baltimore: Johns Hopkins University Press; Rudd, K. (2020) 'The coming post-COVID anarchy', *Foreign Affairs*, 6 May; Cooley, A. and Nexon, D. (2020) *Exit from Hegemony: The Unraveling of the American Global Order*, Oxford: Oxford University Press.

36 Smyth, J. (2019) 'Australia calls emergency meetings as climate crisis intensifies', *Financial Times*, 9 February.

37 Beeson, M. (2019) *Environmental Populism: The Politics of Survival in the Anthropocene*, Basingstoke: Palgrave Macmillan.

38 DeWeerdt, S. (2019) 'Tracing the US opioid crisis to its roots', *Nature*, 11 September.

39 Hickel, J. (2019) 'Is it possible to achieve a good life for all within planetary boundaries?', *Third World Quarterly*, 40(1): 31.

40 Watts, G. (2019) 'Global warming "threatens human civilization"', *Asia Times*, 5 June.

41 Lenton, T.M., Rockström, J., Gaffney, O., Rahmstorf, S., Richardson, K., Steffen, W. and Schellnhuber, H.J. (2019) 'Climate tipping points – too risky to bet against', *Nature*, 592: 575.

42 Geall, S. (2020) 'China still needs to curb King Coal', *Financial Times*, 6 July.

43 Riordan, P. and Smyth, J. (2020) 'Australian mining lobby's power endures despite wildfire crisis', *Financial Times*, 17 February; Blundell-Wignal, A. (2020) 'Myopic Australia looks at the wrong climate number', *Australian Financial Review*, 25 February.

44 Der Derian, J. and Wendt, A. (2020) '"Quantizing international relations": The case for quantum approaches to international theory and security practice', *Security Dialogue*, 51(5): 399–413; Höne, K.E. (2017) *Quantum Social Science*, Oxford: Oxford University Press; Allan, B.B. (2018) 'Social action in quantum social science', *Millennium*, 47(1): 87–98.

45 Beeson, M. (2000) 'Debating defence: time for a paradigm shift?', *Australian Journal of International Affairs*, 54(3): 255–9.

46 Lieven, A. (2020) *Climate Change and the Nation State: The Case for Nationalism in a Warming World*, Oxford: Oxford University Press, p 12.

47 Wendt, A. (2015) *Quantum Mind and Social Science: Unifying Physical and Social Ontology*, Cambridge: Cambridge University Press, p 149.

48 Bohm, D. and Hiley, B.J. (1993) *The Undivided Universe: An Ontological Interpretation of Quantum Theory*, London: Routledge, p 325.

Index

www.ingramcontent.com/pod-product-compliance
Lightning Source LLC
Chambersburg PA
CBHW070923030426
42336CB00014BA/2506